IMPERFECT LOVE

~~~~~~~~~

IMPERFECT JUSTICE

By: Bill Davis
The police detective who investigated the crime

Copyright © 2016

Coastal Winds Publishing House

Publisher@coastalwindspublishinghouse.co

Coastal Winds Publishing House
3167 63rd Street
Port Arthur, Texas 77640

Copyright © 2016 by Bill Davis

All rights reserved, including the right to reproduce this book, or portions thereof, in any form whatsoever. For information contact: Coastal Winds Publishing House
Email: publisher@coastalwindspublishinghouse.co

ISBN: 978-0-9850403-7-6
Library of Congress Control Number: 2016903649

Cover design and layout by:
Pamela Joy Licatino of SeaShore Creations by Design.

Printing and Distribution: Ingram (Lightning Source)

TABLE OF CONTENTS

Acknowledgements.		vi.
Dear Reader.		viii.
A Victim's Prayer.		xi.
Chapter One	Caught.	1
Chapter Two	Thinking Back.	10
Chapter Three	A New Day.	16
Chapter Four	Reporting The Outcry.	22
Chapter Five	Beginning The Investigation.	25
Chapter Six	June's Story.	36
Chapter Seven	Arrested.	38
Chapter Eight	Amelia's Place.	42
Chapter Nine	Preparations.	55
Chapter Ten	Tori's Story.	59
Chapter Eleven	Not Again.	85
Chapter Twelve	Martha's Story.	90
Chapter Thirteen	Happy Birthday Bill.	99
Chapter Fourteen	Road Trip.	112
Chapter Fifteen	Stalking.	127
Chapter Sixteen	Jail.	134
Chapter Seventeen	Post Arrest.	153
Chapter Eighteen	Luke's Story.	163
Chapter Nineteen	Court.	175
Epilogue.		229
Mother's Advice to Her Daughter.		233
Mother's Message To Victims / Survivors.		234
Sgt. Bill Davis Biography.		235

Acknowledgements

There are so many wonderful people to thank involving a project of this magnitude. My first acknowledgement must be to God. I worked on this book for many years. There were time periods, ranging from months to years, when I did not type one letter. Yet, He would bring me back to it time and again. God knew this story needed to be told, not only for a precious eleven year-old girl, but for the millions of other victims/survivors in the world whose story is the same or similar, with only a different name, face, and place. I pray that He receives the honor and glory for this endeavor.

This book would not be possible had a precious young lady not gone through the tortures of abuse at the hand of her father, a person who was supposed to love, cherish, and protect her. This child's mother, brothers, and other relatives also experienced torment because of a perverted person. He is not a man. A real man would not repeatedly commit such horrible deeds against his child and family. I thank this young lady and her family for allowing me the privilege of telling how she went from being a victim, to being a survivor. Their hope is for Tori's story to help other children come forward if they are the victim of sexual abuse, and for other women who were sexually abused as a child to realize they are not alone. She and her family are Christians. They acknowledge that with God's help, they overcame this dark time in their lives.

Pamela Joy Licatino, is my friend and Publisher/Illustrator with Coastal Winds Publishing House. Pam was passionate and committed to telling Tori's story. She knew that in doing so, we were telling the story of millions of other victims. The Lord laid it upon Pam's heart to draw the cover for the book. When I first saw it, tears welled in my eyes as I envisioned Tori being forced down one of the trails in the forest so her father could commit another crime against his daughter.

Megan Anderson was a God-send. As a neighbor (recently moved), she was such a pleasure to visit with over the backyard fence. She helped make this book flow and keep one's interest through her ability to proofread my manuscript and make corrections and amendments where they were needed. Thank you, Megan, for your time and effort.

Another precious friend is my editor, Cheryl Martin. She read my manuscript multiple times and made notes with her red pen. She understood my 'detective' mind and method of presentation, and she applied good grammatical form to the words, phrases and sentences. Cheryl made sure Tori's story was told in a caring, thoughtful, and professional manner.

Many thanks go to my beautiful and wonderful wife, Mary. Her encouragement and help allowed my speaking engagements to expand throughout the country. Since our marriage in 2003, my programs and audiences multiplied in a very short time. She is truly my soul mate, help mate, and best friend.

Bill Davis

Dear Reader,

Everything in this book, from cover to cover, is factual. I investigated the story you are about to read in the mid-1990's, while employed by the Beaumont, Texas Police Department. I was the senior investigator in the department's Sex Crimes Unit at the time. Unlike my first true-crime novel, *So Innocent, Yet So Dead*, where the victim of that tragic story was killed, the victim in this story is alive and well. This book was written with the approval of the victim and with the participation and assistance of her family to ensure all facts are reflected correctly and in chronological order. The final manuscript was approved by the child's mother prior to putting it to print. In order to protect the identity of this child and her innocent family members, all names, except mine, and most locations from the original case file have been changed.

I worked on this book for over twelve years. There were many times when I did not work on the manuscript for over a year due to work or speaking engagements, or raising grandchildren. Suddenly, I would get busy and work on it for a few days or weeks. On many occasions at a speaking engagement, I would give a brief summary of this book and tell my audience that someday I would finish it. Many people have approached me saying this book was telling their story of molestation, only with different names and places. If I am telling Your story, then I hope I have done so with compassion and professionalism. I hope I have enlightened the world that You are out there coping with a difficult past. I hope you understand and realize that You did nothing wrong. I also hope this book lets you know that You are not alone. And, I hope I have been successful in speaking for you and letting the world know that in spite of your victimization, You survived! My ultimate goal, and the goal of the family in this story, is that You go from being a victim, to being a Survivor, and Overcomer.

My hope and prayer is for the story in this book to help change lives. I hope the words in this story will give others courage to come forward and make an outcry regarding their abuse. I hope and pray that this mother's courage helps another mother protect her child, no matter what the future looks like at that moment. I hope that other mother will realize she also is a 'mama bear' and can protect her children. My fervent hope is for whomever a child cries out to, that the person listening will believe the child, no matter who the alleged perpetrator may be. Approximately 94% of the stories told by children about their sexual molestation are true stories. And, approximately 93% of all child molesters are family members, relatives, or people trusted by a family – not a stranger. These molesters are people the child knows, loves, and trusts, and they usually live in the same house.

Remember, children deserve the right to be heard. And, children deserve the right to be believed.

IMPORTANT NOTE – Due to the highly sensitive nature of the subject matter of this book, please be aware that the story includes detailed information and descriptive language from investigative interviews with the victim and other important persons involved.

A Victim's Prayer

Now I lay me down to sleep.
Please Lord, God, watch over me;
And, if Daddy comes in my room tonight,
Pull my soul up to you and hold me tight.
When he's done, please don't let me remember the pain,
As you put me back in my bed again,
Give me strength to wake up tomorrow and say,
"I'll be able to tell someone, anyone, today."
And, if tomorrow I can't find the courage to tell,
When he comes in at night, please allow me to yell…
Yell really loud so Mommy can hear.
Help her to see the reality of her worst fear.
And, if I can't yell really loud at night,
Please help my Daddy to see the light.
Help him to see what he's doing to me.
Let him love me enough to let me be!

~Anonymous

Chapter One

Caught

Martha's car headlights lit up the driveway to her home. It had been an exhausting day. She helped her husband, Steve Carpenter, sanding wood all day and was quite dirty. Martha usually stayed in town while her fourteen year-old son was at church for youth Bible study, but tonight she decided to go back home, put up her groceries, and take a quick shower before going back to town to get Luke. Martha grabbed a sack of groceries from the back seat of her truck and walked to the front door. She and her family lived in the country and rarely locked the doors to their home. She turned the door knob and walked in. The stairway to the second floor of their home was only a few feet away from the front door. Martha had been listening to the radio as she drove home and the DJ announced a couple of minutes earlier that it was 8:00 p.m. Suddenly, an urge hit her as she realized she had gone for hours without going to the bathroom. She set the bag of groceries on the floor beside the stairs and began the climb to the bathroom at the top of the stairway. Her husband, Steve, had completed enough construction on their new house so they could now live in it while he finished its construction. It surely beat the cramped thirty-three foot travel trailer parked a few feet away from the new home's front door. She and her family had lived in the trailer for the past several months while Steve got the house 'dried in' and livable. The light was on upstairs where the bathroom was located. Thank goodness Steve finally got the bathroom air conditioned; however, there was still no bathroom door. For the time being, their 'door' was a black plastic curtain, and it served as the only mode of privacy while in the bathroom. Martha began to ascend the stairs when Steve suddenly appeared through the black curtain. He began descending the stairs while Martha continued her ascent. They met in the middle of the stairway, both continuing their respective stairway journey. Steve muttered to Martha in an almost inaudible tone, "Back so soon. Where's Luke?" "Still at Bible study," Martha replied. "I have to put the perishables in the fridge." Martha was barely able to understand Steve's words. Her response was purely a semi-conscious statement. Steve was clad only in a pair of boxer shorts and was displaying a very noticeable erection. The expression on his face looked like the cat that had just gotten caught eating the canary.

Martha approached the black plastic curtain and mechanically called out, "Next!" It was a habit the family adopted due to the limited privacy the black plastic curtain provided with no bathroom door yet in place.

"I'm almost dressed, I'm hurrying," was the response from the soft voice Martha immediately recognized as that of her eleven year-old daughter, Tori. Why was Steve coming from a place that everyone, especially a budding eleven year-old, deserved their privacy? Martha's eyes rested on her daughter, clad only in a white bra and a pair of cotton panties, sitting on the commode seat. Fear gripped Martha as she saw her little girl staring at the floor, refusing to meet her mother's gaze. Martha's throat had a huge lump in it as her voice quivered, "What's going on here, Victoria?" Martha only used her daughter's full name when Tori was in trouble or the situation was serious and Martha was trying to emphasize a major point. "Why was your daddy in here while you were naked?" Martha continued, "What's going on?" "Why is daddy in here with you naked?" Even without an answer, Martha kept thinking in her mind, 'Oh God, not again!' The silence was deafening as Tori continued to stare at the tile floor. Martha repeated the question, her voice still quivering but now slightly louder. "I asked you a question, Victoria!" Martha declared as tears began to swell in her eyes. She was fighting the realization that Tori's silence was becoming the answer she did not want to hear.

Martha's mind was racing. She was hyperventilating and yet she couldn't breathe. She'd been married to Steve for twenty years and had two beautiful children. They were building a home. She was a full-time homemaker and mother. Steve was a successful building contractor. Martha did all of Steve's office work for his business. He had just finished remodeling an office for Smith, Smith & Lange Law Firm in Beaumont, the metropolitan area in the county just south of their residence. They were a Christian family. But she was not stupid. She knew what she had just seen.

With a shaking voice, Tori muttered, "I don't know." She also mentioned something about Steve needing to get something over there, pointing to one of the cabinets. Martha knew better. Everyone's actions spoke volumes. "Tori, why is your daddy in here with you naked?" Martha asked again. The child continued her silence but her body language was giving way. Tears were starting to slide down her soft cheeks. She drew her knees up to her chest and wrapped her arms around them. She had pulled herself into a fetal position. "He's been touching me here and here," Tori said in a voice that was almost a whisper as she pointed with her hand to her breasts and crotch. There it was! – The secret! – It was finally out!

Martha's maternal instincts were in high gear. She saw that her baby was hurting; not from any physical pain – but from a pain much deeper – a pain that came from her very soul. Martha knelt beside Tori. Her arms wrapped around her baby – her daughter. "It's okay," Martha said. "You've done nothing wrong."

Tori laid her head on her mother's shoulder and wept. At last it was out. No more secrets. "How long has it been going on?" Martha quietly asked. Tori shrugged her shoulders. "Just tonight?" Martha asked. Tori slowly shook her head, no. Martha's own tears began to slide down her cheeks as a knot swelled in her throat. "How many times?" Martha asked. Again the child remained silent and shrugged her shoulders. "Tori, how long," Martha continued, "A week, a month, two months, a year, two years?" With tears flowing Tori cried out, "I DON'T KNOW! So long I don't remember!" Martha gave Tori another hug, kissed her on the forehead and said, "It's not your fault. I love you." To Martha, it felt like hours had passed as she asked questions and Tori answered them, but in reality, it had been only minutes. "Now, get dressed while I find your father," she instructed Tori.

Tori stood and began dressing. Martha also stood and looked at her daughter and told her again, "This is not your fault. I love you very much." Martha knew that many times mothers don't do this simple task. When mothers suddenly realize they are about to lose their home, security, income, and status in the community, and no matter how great the evidence might be that their child has been molested by the male figure in the home, many often side with him rather than doing the right thing and standing up for their child, no matter what the odds may be. Martha did the right thing when she made that statement, and as Tori looked at her mother, she saw the reassuring look on Martha's face that everything, somehow, some way, was going to be okay. Martha turned away from Tori, parted the plastic curtain, and started down the stairs. The wrath of a 'mama bear' was about to be unleashed. Martha was a good mother and felt she had always protected her children well. She doctored their wounds and nursed them back to health when they were sick. She taught them to be leery of strangers and watch for cars when crossing the street. Never in her wildest dreams did she ever think she would have to protect one of her children from their own father. Yet there was no doubt, no debate, and no negotiation. Martha had to protect her child, and Martha would protect her child.

Martha had dealt with a similar situation years earlier when her son from a previous marriage, Ronnie, molested Tori as an infant and Luke as a toddler. He was placed in a mental institution to not only protect Tori and her brothers, but to protect other little children from his deviant mind. Martha had heard stories of how some mothers take their child in front of the accused male and have the child confront the father, step-father, or boyfriend with the accusation. But that would not happen in her house. Martha believed her daughter's story and that was that. She had to get her baby to safety and then rationally think of her next move.

Confronting Steve was taking all of the strength Martha could muster. He was a big man, about five-foot-eleven-inches, with a stocky build. She was only five-foot-three-inches. She had been a good Christian wife and submissive as she read in the Bible that wives should be. She had confronted him only one time in their marriage. Steve had thrown a silly temper tantrum while playing a game with the family. He lost and was accusing Tori of helping Luke win the game. He refused to talk to the children for over a week and he hid all of the Bibles in the house from everyone. Tori left him notes on the dinner table saying she was sorry and that it was her fault. She told him that Jesus loved him and she did too. Martha finally got the courage to confront him. She told him that if he didn't straighten up she would divorce him. But today's confrontation was different – much, much different.

Martha was on the prowl as she reached the bottom of the stairs. She called Steve's name as she roamed the first floor of the house. As she passed a window she spotted him. He was rummaging through the cab of the truck Martha had just driven home. Martha knew there was an envelope in the glove box of the truck containing approximately $5,000.00. She needed that money for her and the children to live on. She quickly approached the truck, yelling "Come here, I want to talk to you." Steve quickly stepped out of the truck. He saw a look on his wife's face that he had never seen before. He was physically bigger and stronger than her, but that look made him decide to walk in the opposite direction down the driveway. Martha's short legs had no trouble catching up to him and she demanded to know what he thought he was doing. "It's not what you think. It hasn't been going on very long. You don't realize how many other people do this," Steve meekly proclaimed. Martha retaliated by telling Steve that Tori had said the molestation had been going on for a very long time. "She's lying," he protested, and then he really went into a tailspin. "You know that I've been fasting and praying and having others lay hands on me and I've really been trying, and this is why I wanted to move to West Texas," Steve declared. "I just wanted to get moved to West Texas and read the Bible a lot and be alone and then send for ya'll when I get my head straight. I even tried to get a snake to bite me and kill me because of this," Steve said. "I'll go away, I'll give you everything, just don't ruin me," Steve pled in sick desperation. He told Martha he was overworked and stressed and this caused him to do what he had done to their daughter. These statements from her husband left Martha with no doubt that he had just confessed to the unthinkable, the sexual molestation of their precious daughter.

Tori came out of the house clutching a pillow to her stomach. It was as if she needed to place some form of insulation between her and him. "We need to go get Luke," Tori said meekly, but obviously wanting to get away. "I didn't mean to hurt you. I'm sorry," Steve pleaded with his daughter. He took a step toward her and Martha stepped in his path. He would have to go through her to ever touch her daughter in any way, ever again. Martha had stood her ground only once before with Steve. She was taught that Biblically, the man is the head of the house, the leader of the family, and ultimately the maker of family decisions. Steve mistreated her and the children on a prior occasion over the outcome of a game. But tonight wasn't a game. This was the most serious moment of her life. "Get in the truck, Tori," Martha said quietly but firmly. Tori quietly and quickly obeyed her mother. Steve didn't say a word. He was desperate, but he wasn't stupid. He'd been married to this woman for twenty years and he was seeing a side of her he had never seen. He knew the woman in front of him was not one to be messed with, at least not right now.

Martha realized that Steve had at least said, "I'm sorry" to Tori. That was so much more than most children hear when their parents are wrong. The words tonight were too little, too late. He wouldn't get off easily by offering a hollow apology. Martha knew the apology was only being offered because he had been caught. Yet, they were words that Tori needed to hear.

As Steve continued to plead with Martha, she realized she needed to leave a little light at the end of the tunnel. They lived on the dead-end of a road. Steve had their gun safe just inside the front door of the house. He could easily reach one of his rifles and shoot them before her truck was out of sight. "I'll be right back and we can talk," Martha told Steve, giving him some hope that everything would be all right. But it was a ploy. Martha had no intention of ever coming back. She only wanted to get Tori and herself safely out of sight. She got into the driver's seat and drove off their property. She drove down their road – not too fast – not too slow. She breathed a sigh of relief as she arrived at the stop sign and turned left to head toward town. She looked in the glove box as she drove. The envelope of money was gone.

As Martha drove toward town to get Luke, she looked over at her daughter. Tori was again sitting in a fetal position with the pillow pulled tightly to her chest and stomach and her knees were drawn up behind the pillow. "It's okay," Martha assured her daughter. "He won't hurt you again." But Martha knew there was more. As she continued driving, she asked her daughter what else her daddy had done to her.

Obviously very embarrassed, but wanting to finally get everything out in the open, Tori told her mother how her daddy would put his mouth on her 'down there.' Martha realized that Tori was giving her more and more information every time she asked her daughter more questions. She was realizing that her husband had been sexually molesting their daughter for a very long time. This man who was supposed to be her daughter's protector had actually been her daughter's tormentor. Tori went on, describing for her mom detail after detail of what her father had done to her. The weight was being lifted off her little chest.

Martha knew she was not thinking straight and needed some help. As she entered Lumberton's city limits, she stopped at the first pay phone she saw and called her son, Greg. Martha had previously been married to a man named Ben Swain. They had two sons, Greg and Ronnie. David died in 1975, and Martha met Steve a year later. Greg was at home and answered the phone. He recognized his mother's voice and could sense something was wrong as she asked him to meet her and Tori at the Wal-Mart on Hwy. 69. Martha ended the conversation with Greg by instructing him to not call or talk to his step-father prior to meeting her.

While waiting for Greg, Martha drove to the church to get Luke. He got into the truck, looked at his little sister curled up on the seat and wondered what was wrong. Martha began telling Luke what happened and how their father had been sexually molesting his little sister for a very long time. "I knew something was going on but I couldn't catch them," Luke stated as his mother finished her summary of Tori's abuse. "I tried all the time. I'm sorry. I tried, Tori!" Luke exclaimed. "You were this close," Tori told her brother, holding up her thumb and forefinger with them almost touching. They hugged, and their tears blended together.

Greg jumped in his truck and was at the Wal-Mart in a matter of minutes. Martha, Tori, and Luke climbed into the cab of Greg's truck. He looked at his mother and younger half-sister, and knew something was terribly wrong. As Martha told her son of the evening's events and of Tori's declaration that the molestation had been ongoing for many years, Greg became enraged. He began screaming how he was going to kill Steve. His rage and his statements made Tori's tears flow again. She wished she had kept her mouth shut. Inside, Greg felt that he let his little sister down, that he failed to protect her from a predator, even if that predator was her own father. But Greg's rage was a very typical response from many innocent dads, or step-dads, or older brothers upon hearing stories like Tori's. They fly into a rant in front of the child, saying how they are going to kill the molester, not realizing the additional damage they are inflicting upon the child at that moment. If Greg carried out his threats, he would surely go to prison. Tori erroneously felt that if Greg went to jail for hurting or killing her father, it would be her fault. She loved her big half-brother, but his ranting and raving was causing her to pull her knees up to her chest in a fetal position again as she sat next to him in the truck. As a family, they had already lost Steve. As a family, they didn't need to lose Greg too.

Martha gave Greg a look that he recognized instantly. He had seen that look from his mother many times in the past. It was a look that meant he needed to immediately calm down. He then realized his rage was not helping the situation. After all, he was not the victim here, Tori was. He sat beside his little sister and put his arms around her and held her close. He whispered to her that everything would be okay. She began to calm and her tears stopped a few minutes later. Tori knew Greg would make sure nothing bad would happen to her or her mom and brother. She cuddled next to her big brother. She felt good and safe in his arms.

Martha knew she needed a safe place for them to spend the night. She couldn't go back to her home. It wasn't a home anymore. It was Steve's house and nothing more. It seemed terribly wrong that she and her children should be displaced from their home. Steve was the one who had done wrong. Shouldn't he be the one to find a place to stay? It wasn't fair that she and her daughter and son couldn't sleep in their comfortable beds that night, or the next night, or all the nights after that. Being displaced is typically what happens to abused children and their innocent parent. It seems they are the ones being punished, not the perpetrator.

Martha told Greg of the need for a safe place to stay for the night, and he suggested they go to the beach. Greg's wife and mother-in-law had rented a beach cabin in a small beach community. It would give them a place of safety to rationally think and plan what their next move needed to be.

Luke rode with Greg as he led the way to the beach house with Martha and Tori following. As she drove, Martha encouraged Tori to continue telling her what Steve had done to her through the years. Tori slowly started telling Martha of the thousands of incidents. Then, it was as if she couldn't stop, and she told her mom of incident after incident and location after location. Martha said later on that the one and one-half hour drive to the beach that night was one of the hardest times she experienced in her life. She felt she was going to break the steering wheel at times, yet she kept her voice calm for her daughter. The more Tori talked and told her story, the more Martha could see, hear, and feel the stress inside Tori being relieved. It was a stress that had built up inside her daughter for years. Martha knew a chapter in her life had closed and another chapter was about to open.

Chapter Two

Thinking Back

Greg exited the interstate highway about twenty-five miles later with Martha and Tori right behind him. They drove through Winnie, a community filled with people who grow rice and cattle. In fact, the people of Winnie hold a festival every October that draws thousands of people to celebrate the rice harvest. Winnie also boasts of having a monthly event, 'Old Time Trade Days,' one of the largest flea markets in the nation. As they passed by the flea market, Martha recalled a tragic incident that happened at the flea market several years earlier when it was based in Beaumont. A ten year-old little girl had been kidnapped, raped, and killed. Martha thought of that little girl and how she was so sweet, so innocent, and also dead. Martha looked at her precious daughter and reached out and touched her on the head. Martha knew this loving gesture was something that little ten year-old girl's mother would never be able to do again. She passed the flea market and continued following her son as they drove south. Martha was glad that Greg's wife, Sheila, and her mother, Myra, had rented a beach cabin for the week. This location was an out-of-the-way, safe place for her to protect her children while thinking of what to do next.

As she drove, Martha and Tori talked the entire way to the beach cabin. "I just let it all flow out of her," Martha later told Greg. "It was so hard to stay calm and not cry as Tori told incident upon incident of how Steve molested her," Martha said. With her mother being supportive, Tori talked non-stop.

Martha fought to control her emotions, but she knew it was in Tori's best interest to let her daughter talk. By controlling her own emotions, Tori was allowed to purge more and more stories of her abuse. Tori poured her heart out to her mom. It was such a relief to get this burden off her chest. It was a burden that crushed her for so many years of her young life.

As Martha drove along, she thought about how flat the land was around her. This land was a far cry from the mountains in northern Pennsylvania and southern New York where she was born and raised. Martha was born in a small town in northern Pennsylvania, a place with majestic mountains, gorgeous autumn trees, and long winters. Her father had been a police officer and a preacher and had five children from a previous marriage. He met and married Martha's mother, and they had five more children. Her father died when Martha was eight months old. After her father's death, her mother moved the family to a small community in New York. The family lived on welfare until Martha was in the first grade.

Martha was five years old when her mother met and married a man named Sam Burns. He seemed to be okay for a step-dad but not really great. After their marriage, Sam and Martha's mother had two more children. Sam seemed to have a special attraction to Martha's sister, Stacy, who was three years older than Martha. When Martha was in the sixth grade, Sam suddenly ran off with Stacy and the two youngest children. Her mother got the police involved, and they got the FBI involved. The FBI looked as far away as Mexico for Sam. They finally found Sam, Stacy, and the two little ones in Oregon, living with some of his relatives. According to the FBI agents, Sam and Stacy were living as husband and wife when they were found. Sam was arrested.

As Martha continued driving under the full moon of the night, she thought about the night's events involving Steve and Tori. She also thought of her own incidents with her step-father years earlier. Sam sexually molested Martha on two occasions about two weeks before he absconded to the west coast with Stacy. Several of his nephews also sexually molested Martha. She thought that only step-fathers, and their nephews, fondled their step-daughters, not real fathers. Sam went to prison for two to three years for molesting Stacy. Martha told her mother that Sam also molested her but she didn't tell her about his nephews. It was a real shock when Martha's mother took her little sisters and moved to Oregon to be with Sam while he was on parole.

Martha's mother left her with an older brother, Johnny. That was a pretty good time in her life because she and Johnny got along really well. Martha continued her drive to the beach and managed a slight grin as she thought about her teenage years and when she started dating.

Johnny was a typical big brother and was pretty strict, but he let her date occasionally. Time passed by really quickly.

Her mother showed up a year-and-a-half later with Sam by her side. Sam was still a great manipulator after his stint in prison. He had finished his parole in Oregon and convinced her mother that he received Jesus as his Savior while in prison and no longer lusted after young girls. Stacy was thin with dark hair and Sam convinced Martha's mother that he ran off with Stacy because she reminded him of a girl he'd been in love with while he was stationed in South Korea during the Korean War. Sam brainwashed her mother into believing he was a changed man. Martha remembered her mother forcing her to rejoin the family.

Her mom was a great and very loving mother and a good Christian woman, but she was also very gullible and controlled by Sam. Johnny had been really good to Martha and she did not want to leave his house. Her mother didn't know anything about sexual predators – or that they don't change their ways. Her mother had her way, and very soon they were setting up housekeeping in a small town in Pennsylvania. Sadly, Martha's sister Stacy thought 'sex' meant 'love' because of the molestation their step-father subjected her to. Stacy got on drugs and died at twenty-three years of age. Martha continued following Greg toward the beach road and thought about one of her younger half-sisters who told Martha several years earlier that she believed Sam molested her children when they were little.

Not long after their move to Pennsylvania, Martha began dating a man named David Swain and a wonderful love affair began. Martha remembered her feelings of being pregnant with Greg, their first child. She worked at a factory but lost her job because they felt her pregnancy was a liability. After trying to make things work in Pennsylvania, David and she decided to move to get a fresh start. David was tired of living with his alcoholic parents and wanted to get away. David had an uncle who was a college professor at a university in Texas. Greg was two years old and Martha was pregnant with their second child, Ronnie. It was time for a new beginning for the young couple.

Martha continued following Greg as they turned from one highway onto what is known locally as the beach road. The Gulf of

Mexico was breathtaking under the full moon. Moonbeams bounced off the crests of waves as they rolled toward the beach. The bright moonlight illuminated a couple of late-night fishermen at the end of a fishing pier as Martha passed the popular fishing spot. Seconds turned into minutes as Martha tried to rationalize what to do.

April 1972 didn't seem that long ago as Martha thought of her and David arriving in Beaumont. It was 72 degrees in the heat of the day and they just couldn't understand why everyone wasn't swimming at the beach with it being so warm. Snow was still on the ground in some places in the mountains of Pennsylvania. The summer was rough on Martha, and the heat and humidity in the coastal area took its toll on her. Their little house had no air conditioning, and Martha was in the last months of pregnancy with Ronnie.

Life was tough for the young couple and David had a rough time dealing with making ends meet for his young family. Slowly but surely, he began to change and drown his troubles with a bottle. He was following in his alcoholic parents' footsteps. He reminisced a lot about his twin brother who died when they were nineteen years old. The more David drank the more he thought of how his drunken mother used to tell him that he should have died instead of his brother. Martha thought about the awful things some parents say, belittling their children constantly, and yelling at them about not being like their big brother or sister, and then thinking the child should grow up with a positive and wholesome attitude. As the alcoholism continued to set in on David, Martha began to look more and more like his mother. Then hatred set in and David's fists began leaving their mark on Martha's face and body. The alcohol finally won its battle with David. He died at the young age of twenty-nine, choking to death on his own vomit.

It seemed there was always one trial or tribulation after another for Martha. A few months after David's death, Martha met one of David's cousins who lived close to Beaumont. They dated for a while and had a short affair, but things just didn't work out. Martha was a Christian and knew this was not the Christian thing to do. She knew she needed to get right with God and she started going to church. One of the church deacons, a young man named Steve, started calling Martha, checking to see if everything was okay for her and her two sons. He seemed nice enough. He talked about how rough it was going through a divorce. He was very convincing. As Martha got to know other people in the church, she learned that Steve was lying and trying to manipulate her. He wasn't going through a divorce. He hadn't filed for a divorce at all. His wife was away with a group from the church on a missionary venture and her husband was hustling Martha. She immediately broke off the relationship. Steve was very persistent, and he finally filed for divorce. Martha allowed him to come around on a regular basis, but she broke up with him several times before his divorce was final. Steve and Martha continued to date and were finally married. He seemed so nice while they were dating, but after the marriage Steve started to change. His ex-wife got custody of their two boys but they spent more time with Steve and Martha than at their mother's house. That made four boys in one house. While dating, Martha told Steve she would like to have more children, especially a little girl. After the marriage, Steve became very adamant that he did not want any more children, especially a girl. When Steve's ex-wife moved to Jackson, Texas, his youngest son moved with her. A few weeks later, a car wreck in front of Jackson High School took his life. It was a tragedy that Steve never seemed to get over.

Martha's thoughts were brought back to the present as Greg finally pulled up to one of the many beach cabins at Crystal Beach. Martha looked at her precious daughter.

The moonlight bathed Tori's innocent eleven year-old face with a soft creamy glow. She was so beautiful, Martha thought. Greg and Luke were already out of their truck and inside the cabin. Martha realized that her daughter did not have to worry about being molested for the first night in a very long time.

Tori ran to her sister-in-law, Sheila, as she came down the cabin stairs. Tori opened up to Sheila and they shared events until early hours of the morning. A bond was formed that night. Sheila had her own story to tell as she also was a survivor. Sheila had been molested by her step-father for years. The man she thought was her real father growing up treated her as his wife in all respects. Sheila took care of her half-siblings and cleaned the house. Wifely duties in all respects occurred frequently.

Sheila found out she had a real dad and ran away to find her biological father when she was a young teen. Her mother was in and out of mental health facilities, but she was a good mom when she was at home.

From her own experiences, Martha always thought that only step-fathers, or uncles, or grandfathers, molested little girls that were kin to them. She learned differently tonight. The events of midsummer 1994 changed the lives of every person in Martha's family – forever.

Chapter Three

A New Day

Greg and his wife, Sheila, finally dozed off with her head nestled on his chest. Martha couldn't sleep. Her mind was still racing, and yet she knew she desperately needed to rest. She would require strength and a clear head to carry out her plan of action. Protecting her children and herself against Steve was the first order of business. He was a headstrong man and used to getting his way – he was a control freak. Martha needed to be very careful for the safety of her children and herself. Bringing Steve to justice was next in line. He was very self-centered and there was no way to know what he would do when he realized he may lose both his family and his freedom. But her mind was set. There simply was no alternative, and no turning back. So, with a sense of peace and direction within her soul, she closed her eyes. Her inner peace brought sleep almost immediately.

Sunlight bouncing off the breakers as they roared onto the beach was a glistening and beautiful sight. The sound of the waves crashing onto the shore was peaceful, yet invigorating. Martha stood against the porch railing of the beach cabin and sipped a hot cup of coffee. A few hours of sleep recharged her batteries. Now it was time for action. This Thursday morning was a new day – a new beginning for her and her children. She walked into the cabin with determination in her stride. There was nothing like starting the day on a positive note and with a wholesome breakfast. Bacon was frying, and Martha noticed Tori beginning to stir. Tori's beautiful almond shaped eyes opened. She inhaled the aroma of breakfast but she did not arise from her cozy bed. She knew breakfast was not quite ready. Myra poured herself a cup of coffee, and Martha began helping her with breakfast. Myra could see the steadiness in Martha's demeanor and patted her friend on the shoulder. The smell of breakfast finally got to Greg and he and Sheila got out of bed. He walked over to his mother and wrapped his strong arms around her and rested his head on her shoulder. She smiled and hugged him back. Martha knew she was very fortunate. She thought about women who did not have support within their family to stand up to a situation of family violence or sexual molestation. In many instances a woman faces family scorn for breaking up the family, as if the violence or molestation was somehow her fault and not that of the perpetrator. Martha realized she was very fortunate to have her family's caring support. With Luke and Tori finally out of bed, and breakfast on the table, it was time to eat. Myra prayed the blessing over the food and for the families at the table. Martha quietly thanked God for His many blessings and for His help in protecting her family. When the blessing was finished, Martha smiled as Myra's canned biscuits disappeared from the platter. Luke and Tori pushed themselves away from the table and Martha gently gave instructions in preparation for leaving. It was time to get to the business at hand.

Myra and Sheila began cleaning up the kitchen as Martha dialed the phone for the information operator. "City and state, please," the operator asked. "Silsbee, Texas," Martha stated, "Mr. Tim Landry, attorney-at-law." The operator gave the number to Martha and she immediately dialed the phone number. She had met Mr. Landry a few times. He was a kind man and a very good attorney. He was well thought of throughout Hardin County and neighboring counties in Southeast Texas. Martha also knew Tim because they attended the same church. It was also quite ironic that Steve and Tim Landry worked together in a prison ministry through their church.

Mr. Landry was about to leave his office for the courthouse. It was a trip that involved a fifteen-minute drive from Silsbee to the courthouse parking lot in Kountze. He would have to be present for Judge Perry's docket call in fifteen minutes. He listened intently as Martha summarized the bizarre events of the last twelve hours. He then set an appointment for her to meet him at his office at 1:30 p.m. Mr. Landry also made a very profound statement. He told Martha that the criminal investigation and the judicial process would be much easier on Tori if Steve would turn himself in to the authorities. Martha pondered that possibility as she hung up the phone.

Martha knew she could not go home. The stark reality was that she and her children were now homeless. Everyone helped make the beds and straighten the cabin. Greg pulled his mother to the side. He and Sheila had discussed the problem and decided that Tori, Luke, and Martha would stay at a friend's house for a few days. In a matter of moments, Martha and her children were no longer homeless. Martha was thankful that her son and daughter-in-law had given them a temporary home. But it would not have mattered, thought Martha. As a last resort, she and her children would have lived at the battered women's shelter until criminal charges were filed against Steve and he was in jail. As long as there was a breath of air in her body, she was going to protect her children.

Martha decided to give Steve one last chance – not that she would ever go back to him – not that kind of chance. She felt she should give Steve a chance to do the right thing – to turn himself in to the Hardin County Sheriff's Department and confess his crimes against their daughter.

Martha dialed their number and Steve picked up the phone at their house on the third ring. Martha immediately told him she had a deal for him. "Okay, what?" Steve replied in a tone of voice that sounded arrogant and indignant. Martha told Steve again that what he did was wrong. She continued by telling him that he could make all of this mess much easier on Tori and Luke by turning himself into the authorities. "There has to be another way," Steve said. He told Martha to put Tori and Luke on the phone. "No way," she said. She was not about to let him browbeat her children or try and put them on some kind of guilt trip to keep daddy out of jail. "Our kids don't want to talk to you," Martha said. "Who else have you turned against me?" Steve defiantly asked Martha. Steve always had a way of turning things around and making matters seem like they were Martha's fault and that she was always the one in the wrong. "There is no other way," Martha repeated defiantly. "Turn yourself in to the sheriff's department by noon tomorrow if you love your children," Martha said. "I'm firm on this Steve." Her voice was getting stronger with each and every word. She had been strong when confronting him face-to-face right after she walked in on him and Tori. But several hours had passed. So often in cases like this, women listen to their spouse and are manipulated one more time by their perpetrator. Many women would realize their predicament – no home, no job, no money, and nowhere to turn – and cave in to the demands of a man like Steve. But Martha was no ordinary woman. Steve was discovering a woman inside Martha that he had never known in over twenty years of marriage. Martha was the type of woman that a normal man would be proud to call his wife and the mother of his children. But Steve was not a normal man by any stretch of the imagination. If he thought he had trained her better than this, then he was quickly finding out he was wrong. The conversation ended. Steve was in a self-centered, survival mode. So was Martha. But hers was a protective mode – for her children.

Martha's mind was racing with thoughts and facts as she drove from the beach to Silsbee. This was not a meeting for her children to attend. Tori and Luke stayed with Myra and Sheila. Martha would meet them later that night at Greg and Sheila's home. Martha needed support and she found it in the other man in her life, her grown son, Greg. She sometimes talked to herself during the one-and-one-half hour trip, fully aware of what she was about to do, and sometimes she asked Greg for his advice. She did not have a job, and yet her job had been full-time. She was a homemaker and mother. She thought – not if – but when – Steve goes to jail, how would she pay the bills? Greg was listening to his mom thinking out loud and reminded her of the construction firm's cash flow money at the bank. Lawyers were not cheap. Even though Mr. Landry was a friend, she knew he would still charge her hundreds if not thousands of dollars to represent her in divorcing Steve. As they entered Silsbee, she drove straight to the bank.

Greg was raised to be chivalrous and respectful, and held the door for his mother to enter the bank. They were halfway through the lobby and about to get in line at one of the teller stations, when the man at the front of the line finished his business and turned to exit the bank. It was Steve, and he had a large sum of money in his hand. His eyes showed that he was surprised to see Martha and Greg, but he kept the rest of his emotions totally in control. "Well, well, well, what do we have here?" Steve exclaimed in a very sarcastic manner as he saw his wife and step-son. Martha wasn't backing down. She pointed to the wad of $100.00 bills in Steve's hand and in her own sarcastic tone asked, "Well, does this mean you're running?" Steve wasn't accustomed to Martha's brazenness. He thought he had taught her to be more subservient and not question his actions. He was not in total control, and he did not like it. "Let's go outside and talk," he suggested. People were starting to look in their direction and the bank's security guard had eased a little closer to them. Martha looked at the guard to acknowledge his presence and their eye contact let him know that Martha wanted him to stay nearby. Since his bluff had not worked on Martha, Steve turned to Greg and told him he wanted his tools out of Greg's truck. Greg became furious and it was all he could do to control himself. "I have witnesses that you gave me those tools," Greg stated. Greg's defiance was more than Steve could take. He would have to put this boy down a notch or two, he thought. He had to regain control. Steve stepped toward Greg leaving no doubt he was about to hit the young man, but he noticed others in the bank through his peripheral vision. He suddenly looked around and saw that everyone was watching them. He looked down at the floor and then stepped back. Regaining his composure would help him gain control of the situation, he thought. He looked back at Martha and told her he would give her half of the money if she would give him his tools in the bed of the truck. "Nope," she said, "you need to turn yourself into the authorities." "You're ruining me. You're killing me. You're ruining our children's future," Steve pleaded. But Martha stood firm. She stood strong. "No, Steve, you're killing yourself. You did this," Martha said. Finally Steve told her to wait there by the exit door and he would be right back. He told her he would close out the construction company's account and give her half the money. The line at the teller's window had dwindled and Steve was next in line. Martha watched intently as Steve stepped to the window and began his transaction. He suddenly turned and began walking toward the exit at the far side of the lobby. Martha couldn't believe her eyes. Steve had another wad of money in his hand and was almost running out the door at the far side of the lobby. Martha and Greg ran out of the bank door just in time to see Steve climbing into the cab of a brand new gray Dodge pickup. The paper license plates showed the truck was purchased that morning. Martha was now yelling at Steve as he backed the truck from the parking slot. "Does this mean you're running?" Martha yelled over and over. Steve just looked at her with defiance as he finished backing the truck and started driving away. He never lowered the window. He never gave her a penny of the money he had withdrawn. It was Thursday, July 18, 1994 – a new day. He was back in control. Everything would work out all right, Steve surmised. It would just take a little time.

As Martha stood in the parking lot of the bank watching Steve turn the corner and disappear, she began to cry. "Where do my children and I go?" she asked aloud. Greg put his arm around his mom and told her they could stay at his house. Her mind was whirling. Martha knew that Greg's house would be one of the first places Steve would look for her and the children. She thought of several families from her church that would give her and her children refuge. But Steve was such a manipulator, he would convince them he had done nothing wrong and that she was making a mountain out of a molehill.

Chapter Four

Reporting The Outcry

Tim Landry listened as Martha told him the story of walking in on Steve molesting Tori and of Tori's outcry that her dad had been molesting her for years. He knew that two legal procedures needed to be initiated. He was aware of the seriousness of the allegations Tori made against her father. He also was aware that lawyers are not exempt from reporting incidents of child abuse, and this was certainly one of those incidents. He knew that Steve had committed a very serious felony crime against Tori. He also knew that child protective services did not need to be called. That was a civil agency and Steve had committed a crime. As Martha and Greg sat across from Mr. Landry in his office, the attorney advised his new clients that he had taken the liberty of contacting Major Ben Moore with the Hardin County Sheriff's Department and briefly explained the situation. An appointment with Major Moore was set for Friday, July 18, at 9:00 a.m. He also reassured Martha that his fee could wait. He knew she would pay it when she could. Right now, there were more important matters at hand. He knew Steve was becoming a desperate and dangerous man with each passing moment. Mr. Landry began filling out necessary paperwork to begin divorce procedures against Steve. He also began prepared paperwork for a protective order to be issued against Steve. Mr. Landry knew that a sheet of paper alone was not going to stop Steve from hurting Martha or the children, but he also knew that if Steve was caught by law enforcement officers anywhere near Martha and the kids, he would go to jail immediately just for being in their proximity. He had to do his part to protect Martha, Tori, and Luke from a very threatening situation.

Martha and Tori arrived at the Hardin County Sheriff's Department promptly at 9:00 a.m. on Friday morning. The receptionist notified Major Moore of their arrival. As Ben Moore entered the waiting area, Tori noticed that the veteran investigator talked with a Texas drawl and had a nice smile. He seemed like a kind man, Tori thought, as the major introduced himself to her and her mother. He then escorted them to his office for Tori's criminal investigation to begin.

Ben had been in law enforcement for quite a number of years. He always dreaded child abuse cases. They always made him uncomfortable. He surmised he didn't work on such cases enough to feel comfortable. And most of all, he didn't want to work enough of them to ever feel comfortable. He would rather leave such cases to the sex crimes and child abuse detectives at Beaumont P.D.

Ben told Tori he needed to ask her only a few questions. He also asked her if it was okay for him to call her Tori, and she told him that was fine. She began telling him about the incident that had happened only a few nights ago. She left out a lot of details because it was embarrassing for her to talk about the details with this man who was a complete stranger. But he needed some of the sexual details so he could do his job. Being a parent, it was upsetting to sit behind his desk and listen to this pretty eleven year old girl tell the sordid details of her father molesting her. Tori told Major Moore enough detail for him to complete his offense report. Tori told the officer how her father would have her hold his private part in her hands. She told him how her father would touch her breasts and private part with his hands and mouth. She ended by telling the major that her daddy would also take his private part and rub it on her private part until some 'gunk' would come out and he would catch the liquid in a rag or a paper.

Major Moore had heard enough. He called Amelia's Place in Beaumont. Amelia's Place is a children's advocacy center that works with law enforcement agencies and child protective service offices in Southeast Texas. Major Moore talked with Lucy Carrier, an Amelia's Place child forensic interviewer, and he made an appointment for her to interview Tori at 10:30 a.m. on Tuesday, July 23. He also called Barbara Harrison, a sexual assault nurse examiner with Southeast Texas Forensic Services in Beaumont, and made an appointment for a forensic examination to be conducted on Tori at 1:30 p.m., following the Amelia's Place interview.

As Martha left the Hardin County Courthouse, she scanned the parking lot thoroughly before exiting the courthouse doors. Her heart was in her throat. Fear saturated her body. She looked at every vehicle wondering if Steve was hiding, lying in wait for them to venture into the parking lot. She thought about going back to Major Moore's office and asking him to escort them to their vehicle, but then she thought he would think she was just being foolish. Besides, if Steve was in the parking lot, and if he did grab her, she would create a scene and deputy sheriffs, who were all over the courthouse, would be there in a matter of seconds. With a deep breath, she opened the courthouse door and they briskly walked to her truck.

Chapter Five

Beginning the Investigation

Child sexual abuse investigations are no longer a one person or one agency investigation. With modern technology, these investigations have become multi disciplinary, with a variety of agencies working together on behalf of the child. Major Moore was glad he had some other experts at his disposal to help with this complex investigation.

Tori thought the beige brick one-story business complex looked like any other set of businesses in Beaumont. She and her mother walked inside to Suite A150. There was a sign on the door that simply said, 'Amelia's Place.' Ms. Margaret answered the door and greeted the pretty young lady and her mother with a sweet smile. Ms. Margaret had worked as a part-time employee of Amelia's Place for several years. She escorted Tori and Martha into the reception area of the children's advocacy center. She handed Martha a clipboard with several papers that were needed for the interview. As Martha filled out the papers, Tori occupied her time walking casually through the reception area of the pretty office complex. She looked at the pictures hanging on the walls. She enjoyed reading two framed poems hanging on the wall. They were both written by someone named Chelsea. It was obvious from the poems that Chelsea had also been sexually molested by her father. Reading those poems helped Tori with the task at hand. The poems let her know she was not alone and there were others like her in the world, even in Beaumont. She drew strength from the poems and silently thanked this unknown lady named Chelsea for helping her.

At the time, a children's advocacy center was a relatively new tool in investigating child abuse crimes. The concept began in Huntsville, Alabama, several years earlier. When our forefathers penned the Constitution of the United States and wrote the part about the accused being faced by his accusers in an open court of law, they probably had no idea that years later little children would be given rights. Moreover, they probably could not conceive the thought of a small child having to testify against a father or some other relative concerning such things as incest. Until recently, small children were not considered credible witnesses in a court of law. If children had the courage to make an outcry in years past, many of them were whipped or punished in some manner for telling 'horrible lies' against such good and kind men as dad, step dad, or grandpa. Most of the men accused were upstanding citizens of a community. Many members of a community couldn't fathom the thought of upstanding leaders of society committing such atrocities against little children. Prior to advocacy centers, a child who mustered the courage to come forward with such an allegation was required to tell their story of molestation ten, fifteen, or more times to different people. The system was re victimizing the victims. Advocacy centers gave children the opportunity to tell their sensitive story of molestation while maintaining a sense of dignity. Children are interviewed by a skilled forensic interviewer in a special interview room at the advocacy center, and the interview is usually recorded. This way, if someone wants to know what the child said about their molestation, the inquiring person can watch the videoed interview of the child rather than interviewing the child repeatedly in person.

Southeast Texas was fortunate to have a group of eight people who saw the need for an advocacy center. These people ranged from child protective services directors, to law enforcement detectives who worked child abuse investigations, prosecutors, and psychologists. They knew something had to be better than the method that was being used. They knew that having 'just anyone' instead of someone highly trained to interview children in their investigations was not working. Then, along came advocacy centers. One of the group of eight, a detective with the Beaumont Police Department, Sgt. Bill Davis, called on one of his realtor friends. His friend donated a large suite at his largest and newest commercial property. Sgt. Davis thought the middle name of his granddaughter was the perfect name for the advocacy center of Southeast Texas. Thus, Amelia's Place was born. Grants and community support for Amelia's Place had already helped thousands of children before Tori walked through the door.

Lucy Carrier entered the reception area of Amelia's Place. She was a pretty young woman and Tori immediately noticed her smile. As

Lucy said hello to Tori and Martha, Tori noticed her deep Texas drawl. Lucy's grammar was very articulate, yet soft-spoken. After talking with Martha a few minutes and looking over the paperwork, Lucy turned to Tori and asked if she was ready. With a deep breath, she nodded yes. She and Lucy walked to a closed door. Lucy opened it and she and Tori entered into the part of Amelia's Place where the interviews were conducted. Lucy closed the door and they sat on a cushioned bench that was fastened to the far wall of the room. Tori noticed a large mirror on the opposite wall from where they were sitting. She later learned that another lady employed by Amelia's Place, Lori East, was working a video camera on the other side of the mirror while she and Lucy talked.

"What is your full name?" Lucy asked Tori, as the interview began. "Victoria, but you can call me Tori," the child proclaimed. Lucy continued with normal questions about Tori's address, who lived with her at her house, what school she attended, what grade she was in, her favorite school subjects, and so forth, to establish rapport with the pretty eleven year-old child. These questions also showed Tori's level of intelligence. Matters like this had to be covered not only for the sake of rapport, but also because everything being recorded would be scrutinized by many people – law enforcement investigators involved with the investigation, prosecutors with the district attorney's office, defense attorneys, judges, juries, and possibly even appellate court justices.

"Do you know why you're here?" Lucy asked Tori. "Yes ma'am," was the young girl's reply. "Do you want to tell me what happened?" Lucy asked. "Mama walked in right after daddy had done some things to me," Tori replied. Things like this were so hard for children to talk about. But Lucy's soft and reassuring voice made everything so much easier. "What things?" Lucy asked. "He put his mouth down there and put his finger inside me down there," Tori stated. "What room of the house were you in?" Lucy continued with her questions. "We were in the bathroom," Tori said. "He took all of my clothes off and laid me on the vanity counter top." Tori continued her story as she told how her father made her hold his private part while he put his finger inside her private part and his mouth was on her breasts. Tori told Lucy this was not the first time. Her daddy had been doing this to her many times for many years. Tori said she was approximately two-and-one-half to three years old the first time she could remember him doing sexual things to her. Lucy asked where these first incidents happened and Tori told Lucy it began at their house in Beaumont. Several incidents also happened in some warehouses her daddy owned. She continued by saying that her daddy had also done lots of sexual things to her where they now lived in Hardin County. Lucy realized that this beautiful eleven year-old girl had literally been through a lifetime of sexual abuse. She knew that much more information would be needed for the complete story to be brought forward. But for now, Lucy had enough information for Major Moore to get a warrant for Steve's arrest on the latest incident. It would then be up to an investigator to piece together the complete story for Tori.

As Lucy was interviewing Tori, Martha was nervously sitting in the Amelia's Place reception area. Ms. Margaret was at her desk, which was a few feet away from Martha, busily answering another phone call. The call ended and Ms. Margaret walked over to Martha and sat beside her on the couch. She told Martha that her last phone call was from a lady named June, asking if she and Tori were there. Ms. Margaret explained it was the policy of Amelia's Place to not divulge information concerning someone at the advocacy center to anyone over the telephone. Martha knew that June was June Green, Steve's sister. Martha immediately called June at her office and explained that she and Tori were at Amelia's Place and Tori was being interviewed as they were talking. June explained that she had just received a phone call from an attorney friend in Hardin County. Her friend advised her that her brother, Steve, had just been arrested about an hour earlier and was in the Hardin County Jail. June explained that she called Major Ben Moore with the Hardin County Sheriff's Department. He advised her that he had arrested her brother for sexually assaulting her niece. He also advised June that he had set up an appointment for Tori to be interviewed at Amelia's Place, and she and her mother should be there now. June told Martha that this was how she knew to call Amelia's Place looking for them. Martha advised June that they would be at

Barbara Harrison's office for an examination shortly and asked her sister-in-law if she could meet them there. June knew the location and advised Martha she would meet them at Southeast Texas Forensic Services as soon as she could finalize some legal issues at her office.

Tori's interview ended with Lucy asking her if she knew the difference between telling the truth and telling a lie. The child explained that telling a lie was telling about something that was not true. Telling the truth was accurately telling an exact accounting of something. Lucy asked Tori if she had told the complete truth since entering the interview room. "Yes ma'am," Tori answered.

Tori was hungry. She and Martha left Amelia's Place and drove to the nearest McDonald's restaurant. After a Big Mac and some scrumptious French fries, it was time to make the 1:30 p.m. appointment with Barbara Harrison.

Martha and Tori drove to the three-story professional building on College Street. It was next door to a hospital, and Tori did not know what to expect. She saw the building marquis as they were about to enter the building and saw a lot of doctors' names. As they walked down the main hallway, they came to Suite #105. As they opened the door to the office, to Tori's surprise, the lobby to this office looked like the living room in someone's home . It did not look like an office at all. There were comfortable chairs to sit in and a faux fireplace against the wall. The sliding glass window to the receptionist's area was made of lead crystal depicting beautiful pink flowers.

Hearing the doorbell, Barbara Harrison's daughter, Selena, entered the lobby and introduced herself to Martha and Tori. Her sweet smile and soft eyes made the two visitors feel at ease. Major Moore had visited the office earlier in the day and provided all of the information needed for Tori's exam. Selena handed a clipboard to Martha with several papers that needed to be completed for medical and forensic purposes. Tori and Martha took seats in the lobby and Selena assured them that Barbara would be with them shortly.

Using sexual assault nurses for forensic sexual examinations was also a relatively new tool in sexual assault investigations. For years rape victims and child molestation victims could only go to their family doctor or to an emergency room physician for an examination as a criminal investigation began. Many doctors were reluctant to conduct the examinations because of their very limited knowledge of forensic genital examinations, and possible collection of evidence for a criminal trial, especially if the patient was a child. Many doctors were also reluctant to become involved because of problems concerning their availability for court testimony. For some doctors, time was money, and sitting on a bench outside a courtroom waiting to be called to testify was not the way they wanted to spend their day. This may explain why so many doctors concluded their paperwork after conducting a sexual assault examination with a finding of 'inconclusive.'

In the mid-1980's, an emergency room supervising nurse named Janie Foreman in Amarillo, Texas, realized the need for better care for these patients. She saw that nurses assigned to a sex crime patient were doing the majority of the work in conducting the examinations. She saw how nurses at her hospital were taking sensitive care of the patients. Then a doctor would enter the patient's room and usually spend less than five minutes conducting the forensic examination. He would quickly do swabs of the violated area, make a quick diagnosis, and go on to the next patient. The manner of care in a hospital emergency facility was largely dictated by the number of patients in the emergency facility. With many of these facilities having motor vehicle accident victims, shooting victims, heart attack victims, and many more issues, sex crime victims were usually a low priority. This fact was no one's fault. It was, quite literally, a fact of life because a hospital emergency department is always dictated by life and death situations.

Janie Foreman developed a program for registered nurses and nurse practitioners. These specially trained nurses conducted the specialized sexual assault forensic examinations on rape victims and sexual assault victims with the program overseen by a doctor labeled as their medical director. These nurses became known as sexual assault nurse examiners, or S.A.N.E. nurses.

Janie came to Beaumont in 1993 at the invitation of one of the local hospitals to train twelve nurses to be S.A.N.E. nurses. Barbara Harrison was one of those dozen nurses who sat through Janie's weekend training sessions. Barbara's regular assignment was in the hospital nursery. She enjoyed taking care of the precious newborn babies, but she wanted to do more. She studied hard and completed her clinical examination faster than any of the other nurses. As the nurses completed their training, they began a schedule of being on-call during their off-duty hours. At other times, they may have just gotten home and been at the dining table ready to enjoy a meal and quality time with their family and the phone would ring, or their pager would go off, and they would have to immediately return the hospital. Their services were needed. Another victim awaited their care and forensic examination.

Barbara Harrison's mother succumbed to cancer in 1996. It was an emotionally draining experience for her. With the loss of her mother, she felt a terrible void in her life. She enjoyed working with the beautiful newborn babies every day, but her schedule working twelve hours at the hospital and then being on-call the next twelve hours during her off duty time was beginning to take its toll. Something would have to give. Barbara felt a calling, and she resigned from the hospital. With the help of the director of another hospital, Barbara was provided a suite in the hospital's professional building. She received money from grants, and a couple of affluent local citizens bought a state of the art colposcope. Barbara opened the door to Southeast Texas Forensic Services, specializing in forensic examinations for child molestation and rape victims.

With pertinent information obtained from the forms Martha completed, Barbara entered the lobby and introduced herself to Martha and Tori. They talked for a few minutes and then Barbara and Tori walked to the exam room, leaving Martha in the lobby.

Barbara had learned through her training that parents and guardians do not need to be in the exam room with children. When children or rape victims seemed apprehensive, Barbara would always call the rape crisis office or the crime victim's assistance office and have a trained counselor on hand for the child or rape victim. Children tend to be less talkative and more apprehensive with parents or guardians in the exam room, especially when incest cases are involved.

Barbara began her examination by gathering a history from

Tori establishing why she was at Southeast Texas Forensic Services. "My daddy has been doing things to me," Tori stated. "What things?" Barbara replied. "He puts his finger inside of me and puts his mouth on my breasts and down there," Tori said. "He rubs his thing between my legs and some "gunk" comes out of his thing and he lets it come in a tissue or a towel," Tori continued to explain. "Has he ever put his thing inside of you?" Barbara asked. Tori lowered her head and nodded, yes. Tori stated that on one occasion Steve started putting his penis inside her vagina, but she said it hurt really badly so he pulled it out. All the other times he rubbed his penis back and forth next to her vagina. She explained that she could feel the lips of her vagina being separated by his penis. This action constituted legal penetration.

    Barbara was ever so gentle with her questions and demeanor. She continued her questioning and learned that Tori's first remembrance of her father sexually molesting her was when she was three years old. He had continued his incidents of sexually touching and penetrating her until the night Martha had caught him. Sometimes there would be numerous incidents per week. Barbara quickly realized that Tori's investigation had just begun.

    Barbara began the second part of her exam, a head-to-toe examination of Tori. Barbara knew that most people thought that if there was an allegation of sexual abuse to a child, no other type of abuse would usually be imagined. Realizing there are four types of child abuse – physical abuse, physical neglect, emotional maltreatment, and sexual abuse – Barbara knew her examination must be thorough. Her experience through thousands of examinations taught her that many children reveal only one type of abuse, and then her head-to-toe exam reveals that one or more types of abuse were inflicted upon the child. She knew her examination would ultimately lead to a thorough examination of Tori's genitalia. But she was trained to let that most sensitive area be the last area to examine. This also helped her develop rapport with her patient. Many times, Barbara's sensitivity and taking her time with her patients led them to reveal even more information. Barbara always began with the head. She checked Tori's hair, scalp, face, and neck. Everything looked normal. Barbara let Tori slowly undress herself with a sheet held up between her and Tori. As Tori completed undressing, she lay on the examination table and Barbara covered Tori to her shoulders with the sheet. Barbara then began examining Tori from her shoulders to her toes, exposing and examining only one body part at a time. This method made the examination much easier for Tori. Barbara's examination revealed that Tori was a healthy eleven year-old white female that was developmentally in "Tanner Stage IV." With "Tanner Stage I" being an infant child and "Tanner Stage V" being a mature adult, this meant Tori was well into puberty.

As she talked with Tori, Barbara thought for a brief moment about how exams were formerly conducted. Many emergency room physicians that did forensic examinations would automatically break open a rape kit just because a sexual incident was involved. The nurse in charge of that patient would take head and pubic hair combings and pluckings just because the rape kit examination paperwork said to do it, even if such parts of the examination were totally inapplicable. The doctor would then take the swabs of the mouth, anus, and inside the vagina just because the rape kit paperwork said to do it, and then immediately place the cotton swabs back into their tube containers. Not realizing the basics of forensic examination, these swabs were not dried prior to being placed back in their tubes, thereby causing the now damp cotton swabs to mildew and render them useless for analysis. Many people do not understand that doctors are trained in medical school to do medical exams, not forensic exams. It was not until 1996 that medical schools began training doctors in forensic exams and preservation of evidence for possible criminal prosecution. Sexual assault nurse examiner programs had already started growing throughout the United States by this time. Many doctors were more than willing to let registered nurses or nurse practitioners do the job. To prosecutors, it was also obvious that the nurses made better witnesses in the prosecution of a case than did doctors.

Barbara's soothing voice and mannerisms were comforting to Tori. With the rapport they built during the exam, Tori felt comfortable as Barbara asked her to place her feet in the examination table stirrups. The sheet was gently raised and Barbara moved her colposcope into position. This was an instrument that gynecologists use to look inside the female genitalia for abnormalities. Barbara's colposcope also had a 35mm camera mounted to the instrument so photographs of the outside and inside of the genitalia could be taken. Her photographs became evidence, for her part of an investigation may ultimately be used as evidence in court if needed. With the aid of the colposcope and her vast training and experience, Barbara could tell that Tori's genitalia had been sexually abused for a long time. She found scar tissue on one side of Tori's vaginal canal. As Barbara shared this information with Tori, she told Barbara that many times when her dad had his finger inside her vagina, it would hurt and she would sometimes bleed. Both of them felt that Steve's fingernail could have easily torn the lining of her vaginal canal, causing the scarring that Barbara documented. This was indicative of possible penetration of Tori's vaginal canal, corroborating her story of abuse.

After completing her photographs with the colposcope and taking swabs of the vaginal canal in case there was a need to do sexually transmitted disease testing, Barbara's examination was complete. However, one thing worried Tori. She asked Barbara if she could be pregnant from what her daddy had done. Barbara asked Tori to excuse her a moment and exited the exam room.

Martha was in Barbara's waiting room along with another woman. Martha introduced the woman as her sister-in-law, Steve's sister, June. Barbara said hello to June and then turned to Martha.

Barbara explained Tori's concern of being pregnant by her father's actions. Barbara asked Martha for permission to discuss this matter with her daughter. Of course, Martha gave Barbara permission. Barbara returned to the exam room and began talking to Tori about her abuse and that the possibility of not being pregnant was much greater than the possibility of being pregnant. Tori told Barbara that she didn't believe in abortion. Her father's sexual abuse had her very worried about being pregnant with his child. Barbara was able to calm Tori's fear of being pregnant with facts and evidence that pointed to her not being pregnant.

As Tori exited the exam room and walked to the lobby where her mom waited, she was pleasantly surprised to see her Aunt June there also. Tori hugged her favorite aunt and June hugged her favorite niece. June's hug gave Tori even more assurance that everything was going to be all right. The examination was over and had been painless for Tori. Thanks to Barbara Harrison's training as a S.A.N.E. nurse, her method of examination was not traumatic and left the child with a sense of worthiness. Tori thanked her new medical friend as she, her mom, and her aunt left the office.

As Barbara watched them exit her office, she thought of the hundreds of times she had heard child molestation victims and rape victims tell her of their fear of being pregnant by the molester. It was a fear that gripped victims for days and even weeks until they found out they were or were not pregnant from their rape or sexual abuse.

Chapter Six

June's Story

After Barbara Harrison visited with Martha and got permission to talk to Tori about pregnancy and returned to the exam room, June explained to Martha that she learned through an attorney friend that Steve had been arrested. June knew that it was very possible that Steve might bond out of jail. She was worried for the safety of Martha and her children. She and her husband, Frank, had no children and there was plenty of room in her spacious home. She invited Martha, Tori and Luke to stay with her temporarily for their safety. Martha knew even though June was Steve's sister, she and her husband would be a safe refuge. June and Frank were both successful attorneys and their home was in Beaumont. This meant Martha and her children would be in a bigger town with a larger police department that could better protect her and the children. Martha also knew that June did not like Steve. She didn't know why, but June had no use for Steve. Martha could only surmise that something had happened between June and Steve while they were growing up that caused her to not be close to her brother.

Martha began telling June about the events of the last few days. June listened as Martha described how Steve molested Tori for many years. June had hoped she would never hear the story she was now being told. The facts of the incidents being told to her were all too familiar, just the name of the victim was different. Thirty-eight years previously, June was in Tori's place and she was the one to endure Steve's perverted actions. She could not tell Martha, not yet. But, June knew that before this investigation was finalized she would be able to tell the secret she had kept inside herself for almost four decades.

June was abused at the hands of her brother from three to six years old. Finally, June could stand no more of the sexual abuse and went to her parents and told them what her older brother had been doing to her for a long time. Her parents did not believe her. Steve was the eldest child, and could do no wrong. To make matters worse and to gain control of the situation, Steve put a gun to his chest and pulled the trigger. This caused serious injury, but not death. Steve and June's parents put both children in the back seat of their car and rushed to the hospital. Their parents made sure to tell June that she should not have told such horrible lies about her brother to the point that he shot himself. They even made June hold Steve in her lap while they raced to the hospital. Her dress was soaked with Steve's blood, a picture that is forever etched in her mind. Their parents were very involved in their church. After getting Steve to the hospital, the parents decided they needed to pray for June to not tell such lies. After prayer, June received a vicious spanking for telling the horrible lies on her sweet brother.

As Steve recovered, it was June who suffered the consequences. She was the one that was blamed for Steve's attempted suicide. She was told time and time again that Steve would not have tried to take his life if she had not told the horrible lies on her beloved brother. She had to endure hearing how her wretched lies had forced her loving brother to the brink of death. June endured the family scorn. But she also swore to herself that she would never allow anyone to have control over her body and well-being ever again.

The story was all too familiar as June listened to Martha. So many child victims are not believed, and they are punished for telling such a story on the alleged perpetrator. As their conversation ended, June remembered a saying, Children deserve the right to be heard, and, children deserve the right to be believed. She wished more people believed it. With Tori telling her story, June knew she could finally tell her story when the time was right during this investigation.

Chapter Seven

Arrested

While Tori and Martha were getting ready for their visit to Amelia's Place, Major Moore and Lt. Fred Reynolds were getting ready for their own meeting with a man named Steve Carpenter. Martha spent the weekend writing out an affidavit that covered several pages. It covered the incident of the past Thursday night as well as background information going back to before the time when she and Steve met. Major Moore took this information as well as other facts of the case and submitted a 'probable cause affidavit' to Hardin County Precinct #6 Justice of the Peace Laura Williams. She issued a warrant for Steve's arrest for the charge of Aggravated Sexual Assault of a Child. This charge is a first degree felony in Texas and carries a punishment of probation up to life in prison. A short drive from Kountze and the lawmen were eastbound on Hwy. 418. A few miles later and they turned onto Summers Road. Steve's home was located in the middle of a wooded area at the end of the street. As the lawmen got out of their unmarked sheriff's car, they noticed the sprawling two-story home under construction. Reynolds stood to the right of the front door as Major Moore took the left side and knocked loudly. A few seconds later and the door swung open. The large white male that stood in the doorway was cordial but his voice shook as he noticed the badges over the heart of each man. "Yes, can I help you?" Steve asked. "Are you Steve Carpenter?" Major Moore asked as he looked over this large man dressed in Levi jeans, work shirt, work boots, and a baseball cap advertising the name of a local hardware store. "I am," Steve replied as his voice began to quiver. "I have a warrant for your arrest," Major Moore proclaimed. He and Reynolds had worked together enough to know things to be on the lookout for when it was time to affect an arrest. Steve displayed the usual signs of nervousness any individual would display that was about to lose their freedom. But, he was old enough that he did not display the usual tendencies to run. Moore and Reynolds had both decided years ago that they were through with foot chases. They would leave those arrests to younger officers.

Their greatest worry was that Steve would suddenly slam the door to get a gun or try to fight the officers. Steve looked at the warrant and it looked legal. He asked if he could get a bank bag from his truck that had some money in it, and Major Moore agreed to this request. He told Steve they would have to accompany him to wherever the money bag was located. As the officers escorted Steve back into his home, they observed the stairway that Martha described in her affidavit that led to the bathroom. They saw the piece of black plastic draped over a piece of wire at the top of the stairway just as Martha had described. They continued to follow Steve into a large room where he retrieved a bank bag from a coffee table in front of the couch. "I'm ready," he proclaimed to Moore. Reynolds reached and took the bank bag from Steve and had him turn around and lock his fingers together on top of his head. Steve did as he was told and stood in silence as the deputy frisked him. Reynolds removed a pocket knife from Steve's right front jeans pocket and placed it on the coffee table. He then proceeded to handcuff Steve behind his back. Being a large man, this position was very uncomfortable. But, this man was accused of committing a despicable crime and handcuffs were not designed for comfort or to be worn as a piece of jewelry. As the three men exited the front door, Major Moore checked to make sure Steve had his house keys. They were in his left front jeans pocket. Steve was placed in the backseat of Major Moore's police car. The ride to the jail in Kountze took about fifteen minutes. The three men stopped off at Justice of the Peace Benson's office. Steve was given his Miranda Warning and Steve stated he understood his rights. Judge Benson then placed Steve under a $50,000.00 bond for his perverted charge. A few minutes later, Steve was safely behind bars. As with any prisoner, Steve was allowed a phone call. He made it to Quick Bonding Company whose office was just across the side street from the county courthouse and jail. With a smirkish grin, Steve sat in a holding cell knowing his time behind bars would be short-lived.

    Tony Lopez quickly walked from his bonding company office to the jail. He filled out the customary papers to make bond for a prisoner. A few minutes later Steve walked out of the Hardin County jail with his bondsman. A bonding fee is usually twenty percent of the bond. But because Steve had never been arrested and had been a 'model' citizen, his fee from the bonding company was only ten percent. Steve reached into his bank bag and handed Lopez his fee. Lopez thought $5,000.00 wasn't bad work for the few minutes he put forth to free this man accused of a terribly perverted crime. But Steve was still innocent until proven guilty in a court of law. That's the way the law works. In Steve's estimation, this mess had gone way too far. It was time to get things under control. Lopez gave Steve a ride to his house. He got into his new pickup truck and headed to Beaumont. It was time to start scurrying the bushes and find Martha, Luke, and Tori and get them back under his thumb.

Martha drove out of the parking lot at Southeast Texas Forensic Services. She and Tori stopped at a restaurant just before reaching Interstate 10. She had to use the phone. The Hardin County Sheriff's Department receptionist answered and Martha asked for Major Moore. When the call was transferred to him, Martha told of their day's events at Amelia's Place and Southeast Texas Forensic Services. She was anxious to get through this criminal process and get home. She was ready to unwind from all of this stress and sleep in her own bed. As Martha completed her report to Major Moore, he told her he had good news and bad news. The good news was that a judge had issued a warrant for Steve. He continued by telling her that he and a fellow officer arrested Steve at their home earlier that morning. He also told Martha that a justice of the peace placed Steve under a $50,000.00 bond. The bad news was that Steve had evidently used the money he removed from their bank account, and a bonding company had already bonded Steve out of jail. Martha couldn't believe her ears. She thought she and her children would be safe. Now they were in more danger than ever. "Can you provide us with police protection?" Martha asked in a terrified state of desperation. Moore knew her predicament, but there was nothing he could do. "Police protection is only in the movies and the federal witness protection program," he told Martha. She fought back the fear that was gripping her. She knew Steve would be more desperate than ever, and more dangerous than ever. She thought that once Steve was arrested and placed behind bars everything would be okay. She never thought about him making bond. She was homeless, penniless, and desperate. But she would not go back. He would not hurt her daughter ever again, no matter what.

Chapter Eight

Amelia's Place

After Friday's interview with Tori and Martha, Major Moore realized this investigation would reach far beyond the incidents that happened in Hardin County. Because of the length of time the Carpenter family lived and worked in the Beaumont area, Major Moore's investigative intuition told him that most of Tori's victimization had probably happened in that city. As he was setting up appointments for Tori at Amelia's Place and Southeast Texas Forensic Services, he made one additional telephone call – to the Beaumont Police Department's Sex Crimes Unit.

Sgt. Bill Davis was at his desk completing the paperwork on an investigation he had been working on for the past week. It was regarding the sexual molestation of a six year old girl. He received a warrant for the perpetrator, arrested him, and also obtained a written confession from the suspect, the little girl's step-father. Bill smiled as he finished his supplementary report for the district attorney's case file for prosecution. It was a smile of satisfaction. There were many people who had doubted the story of this little girl, but Bill believed her. His vast experience and expertise in such investigations told him that this precious little girl had told the truth and nothing but the truth against her step-father. Family members, especially the child's mother, had badgered the child, trying to get her to say she lied against her step-father. The little girl's story never changed. Now Bill had a confession to corroborate her story. This seasoned investigator had worked on thousands of child abuse and sex crimes investigations for over eighteen years. After all those years, he still felt a tremendous satisfaction from investigating these crimes and helping abused children and rape victims put their lives back together.

As his telephone rang, Bill picked up the phone and welcomed a rest from pounding on the computer keyboard. He listened as his friend, Ben Moore, told him about Tori's investigation. There was no doubt in Bill's mind that Tori's father didn't just start molesting her because the family had moved to Hardin County. His knowledge of child sex offenders told him Tori's molestation probably began when she was a small child, possibly as an infant. The two investigators talked a few more minutes with Bill being made aware of the interview and forensic examination that was to take place the next day. He and Moore finished their conversation and made an appointment for a couple of days later to see where this investigation would lead them.

Wednesday morning, July 23, the work day began with Bill entering his office and having a usual cup or two of black coffee. He reviewed his calendar and made sure it was clear for the rest of the week. His gut feeling from the phone conversation with Moore told him he was going be busy for a while. Finishing a second cup of coffee, Bill grabbed his briefcase, closed his office door and exited the back door of the police station. He would be in the Hardin County Sheriff's Department in less than thirty minutes. Little did this experienced detective realize that Tori's investigation was about to leave a lasting effect on the rest of his life.

Bill entered the reception area of the Hardin County Sheriff's Department and saw an old friend, Nell Lopez, one of the department's receptionists. He got a big hug from his long-time friend and they spent a few minutes catching up on each other's news. Ben Moore was in his office and heard the commotion in the reception area. He smiled as he heard Bill's familiar voice laughing and joking with everyone in the outer offices. Everyone in Southeast Texas seemed to know Bill. He was on the television often, promoting child abuse prevention and child safety public service announcements. Ben entered the lobby and shook hands with his Beaumont colleague. After pleasantries were exchanged, the two investigators walked back to Ben's office. It was time to get busy.

Ben filled Bill in with a summary of what had been learned through Tori's Amelia's Place interview. He also told Bill of Tori's abnormal examination, and that Barbara Harrison had found evidence consistent with chronic sexual abuse. Ben also showed Bill thirty hand-written pages of information that Martha had written on a 'yellow notepad.' Ben informed Bill that Martha's hand-written pages were being reduced to an affidavit that Martha would swear to and sign for their investigation, and he would provide Bill with a copy when the document was completed. Ben also provided Bill with a VHS taped copy of Tori's interview at Amelia's Place. Bill had plenty of information to get him up-to-speed on Tori's outcry.

With a handshake, Bill and Ben ended their conversation. On the drive back to Beaumont, Bill was realizing this case was going to be extensive. When he arrived at his office, he put the VHS tape in the television in his office. With a 'yellow pad' in hand, Bill began to take notes as he watched Lucy Carrier conduct her Amelia's Place interview with Tori.

The interview began at 10:31 a.m. Lucy began by asking simple questions, building rapport with the eleven year-old child. She asked Tori her name, age, address, school, favorite subjects, things she liked to do, etc. Lucy then began her questioning gently, but in earnest.

> Lucy: Do you know why you came here to talk to me today?
> Tori: (Nods yes)
> Lucy: Start at the beginning and tell me what you came here for.
> Tori: Because my daddy's been touching me. You know, touching me here (points to her breasts and groin area). You could say having sex with me but not exactly having sex with me.
> Lucy: What's your dad's name?
> Tori: Steve Carpenter
> Lucy: When did this start?
> Tori: Uh, me and my mom figured it out, probably when I was four or five years old.
> Lucy: Do you live with your dad, or, did you live with your dad?
> Tori: Uh-huh.
> Lucy: Who all lives there?
> Tori: My brother, Luke, and he's fourteen, and then my mom, my dad, and me.
> Lucy: Would he do that with your clothes on, or off?

Tori: Sometimes, like when, like if my mom had just walked out of the room and how he wanted to do it, he would just rub me there (pointed to her breasts and groin area) outside real fast. And then other times when we were alone he would do it with my clothes off.

Bill stopped the tape for a moment and pondered. He couldn't remember the number of times he heard mothers and other relatives say to him that there was no way a perpetrator had molested their child because they had not left the child alone with the suspect. Bill shook his head at how naive people were when it came to child molesters. Tori's statement had just shown how her father would fondle her with her mother in the next room. Bill thought, if only people would realize how easily child molesters victimized children with innocent family members just a few feet away. Then, if the child made an outcry, the suspect would deny the incident and say the child was lying and there was no possible way he could have done what the child said with mom a few feet away. Bill began to see as he watched Tori's interview that Tori's father was a 'classic' child molester, apparently obsessed with molesting her at every opportunity. He pressed 'forward' and the interview continued.

Lucy: What kinds of things would he say to you?
Tori: Uh, he would ask me if it felt good. Uh, uh, asked me if I liked it.
Lucy: Okay, where would these things happen at?
Tori: Uh, well, when we used to live over on Rosewood over here.
Lucy: Is that in Beaumont?
Tori: Uh-huh, 8890 Rosewood, we used to live there, and sometimes it would be in the house, and other times it would be two places he has on Martin Street. Now, one of them is bought, and one of them is being rented out now.
Lucy: On Martin Street, here in Beaumont?

Tori: Yes, downtown. And, uh, we would go there and 'do it,' and when we moved here (Hardin County), we 'did it' once in the camper, and sometimes it was in the woods.
Lucy: Is that where you live now?
Tori: Yes.
Lucy: Where was the camper at?
Tori: It was in the front yard
Lucy: Of your house there?
Tori: Yes.
Lucy: So, he would rub you with his hand, sometimes with your clothes on, and when mom was gone, with your clothes off?
Tori: Uh-huh, sometimes we would 'do it' with her there, like sometimes she would be working, or, taking her bath. She was there and he would just take me upstairs.

Bill stopped the tape again. Tori was again describing how perverts take advantage of every opportunity to molest children. Bill wished that the mothers of molested children could hear Tori's tape. But then he thought, those mothers would just call her a liar, too. He pushed 'forward' again.

Lucy: At the house where you've been living?
Tori: Uh-huh.
Lucy: What about his clothes, were they on, or off?
Tori: When we were alone they were off, and the times when he would tell me to touch him, it would be with his clothes off.
Lucy: How would he tell you to touch him? What would he want you to do?
Tori: My mom told me the word, 'caress.'

Lucy knew Tori's last statement would give a defense attorney ammunition. She knew a defense attorney would jump up in a courtroom and argue that Tori had been coached. He would insist the whole thing had been fabricated and ask a judge for a mistrial. But Lucy was an experienced interviewer. She was one of the best in the nation, and Southeast Texas was very fortunate to have her.

> Lucy: I know your mom said ya'll talked quite a bit about this. What's important today is to remember to use your own words. It's okay that ya'll have talked about it. But, try to think about it in what happened.
> Tori: (Nod yes)
> Lucy: Would that be with his clothes on or off like on his skin when you would rub him?
> Tori: Off.
> Lucy: Which part of his body would he have you rub?
> Tori: His private.
> Lucy: Would this happen when you were standing or sitting or laying down?
> Tori: All.
> Lucy: Tell me about the very last time – what happened?
> Tori: My mom had left. We had to sand paper a few more pieces of molding.
> Lucy: Molding?
> Tori: Yes, we were working on the house.
> Lucy: Out there, or here in Beaumont?

Tori began telling how her dad had planned their evening. She said that after lunch that day, her mom told her to clean off the table and she would do the dishes. While cleaning off the table, Steve came to Tori and told her not to go to church that evening. He told her to stay with him and they would 'have some fun.' Tori said that was her dad's way of telling her that they were going to have sex later that evening. Tori told her dad that she wanted to go to church and see her friends. He told her that she could see her friends later. Tori reminded her dad that he was planning on moving all of them to West Texas, and she would not get to see her friends when they moved. Tori then went into the kitchen and began putting things away from lunch.

Tori continued her interview telling how later that afternoon, he very smart and always got his way. A short time later, Tori said that her mom came to her and asked her to stay and help her dad instead of going to church because he really needed her help.

Bill stopped the tape. He was learning more and more about Steve. As with most sexual predators, Steve was no different. He was a very good manipulator. He had manipulated Martha in just the right way so that he could get his way. Bill thought of the many other cases he investigated where the mom in an incest home had been manipulated by the perpetrator so he could have his way sexually with the children. With Martha, it was happening once again. Bill noticed something else while watching the tape. Tori had gotten comfortable with Lucy. She was now talking non-stop. It was as if a dam had burst. Tori was overflowing. The words kept coming and coming. She was getting this horrible burden off her chest. Tori could feel the weight of the burden she carried for years being lifted from her body with each word. Bill pressed the 'play' button once more.

Tori continued, saying that Martha later told her daughter that she thought she had seen tears in her eyes. Tori said that Martha thought the tears were because she was not going to go and see her friends at church. But, Tori told Lucy her tears were because she was going to have to stay home and have sex with her dad and she didn't like it. She said there were a few times when she liked it, but her mom told her that it was normal to like those feelings. Lucy immediately stopped Tori and told her something that was so very important.

    Lucy: You're not in any trouble, okay?
    Tori: She already told me that it was okay, that it wasn't my fault.

Bill stopped the tape again. Several things had just occurred. Many times people make the mistake of asking a child, "Did he hurt you?" From his training and experience Bill knew that many times there was no physical pain when a child was sexually molested. The question the parents or caretakers should have asked their child was, "How did make you feel?" Most of the time, sexual molesters were very easy and gentle with children. Most molesters would take their time and the molestation would take place over a period of months, even years, with Steve waited until he was with Martha, Luke, and Tori. He told Martha that he needed Tori to help him with the work on the house instead of going to church. He needed to finish his project that day. Tori said she knew the project did not need to be completed that day. Steve was just manipulating everyone so that he could have sex with her while everyone was gone from the house. Tori explained that her dad was countless numbers of sexual incidents taking place with the child. Many times there was no physical pain with these sexual incidents because of the molester's gentleness. But as Bill was witnessing, the psychological pain was always there, as Tori described her tears. It was also very important that Tori be reassured by Lucy that she had done nothing wrong. It was also reassuring to hear Tori say that her mom had told her it was not her fault, too. So often, Bill thought, many moms blame the child for their outcry of the abuse and put the child on a guilt trip for breaking up the home with their selfishness and lies.

Tori told how her mom and Luke left for church while she and her dad finished working with the molding. Finally, her dad said he was going to go upstairs and take his bath. Tori's half-brother, Greg was supposed to bring a truck to Steve and he gave Tori instructions on where to tell Greg to park the truck and then he could leave. Steve finished his bath and came back downstairs. He told Tori to go and get her bath and not to get dressed when she finished. He told her that he would wait for Greg in the swing out in the yard. Tori said she did as he told her and went upstairs and took her bath. As she finished, she wrapped herself in a towel and looked outside to see that Greg had just driven up to drop off Steve's truck, with Sheila in the second vehicle. They left and Steve came back into the house and came upstairs. Tori said her dad told her to 'take that off,' and she obediently dropped the towel to the floor. She was now standing naked before her father. She described for Lucy how Steve placed two towels on top of the vanity and then had her lie down on the towels. Tori described how her dad began to fondle her breasts and genital area with his hands. She said she was wearing a pair of underwear and some shorts. She said he then physically positioned her so that he could have better access. Tori described how he put his mouth on her genital area. Tori then said that her dad stood up and he had pulled down his underwear and his 'private part' was showing.

>
> Tori: He said "somebody's looking at you."
> Lucy: He calls his private area "somebody" or "he?"
> Tori: Yea, he says, "Somebody's looking at you," or, He's looking at you." And he usually calls my area my "magic spot" or something like that. Then he said, "Kiss it" and I said no, I don't want to. He said that he washed it downstairs after they left. I said, "I don't want to." First he rubbed it past my cheek and then he put it on my mouth for about two seconds and I turned my head. And then when I turned my head again he put it in my mouth and it tasted rubbery.
> Lucy: You call it his private. Was it sticking out, or was it hanging down?
> Tori: I never saw it hanging down. It was always sticking out.
> Lucy: And it was in your mouth?
> Tori: I just touched it with my tongue. And then my mom came in downstairs.

Tori told how her dad quickly pulled up his underwear and put on a pair of shorts. He turned out the light in the bathroom and told her to quickly get dressed. He then left the bathroom area and began walking downstairs to obviously stop Martha from coming upstairs where Tori was still naked. Tori said that her mom saw his 'hard-on' which meant that she could see his penis sticking straight out. Tori said she turned on the bathroom light and a few seconds later, and her mom walked into the bathroom. Tori described how she had just pulled on her panties and put on her bra as her mom entered the bathroom. She demanded to know what was going on and Tori told her, "Nothing." Tori said that Martha shook her finger at her and said, "Tell me now, I want to know what's going on." Tori told her mom that he had been touching her. She said that Martha began to cry and said "It's a mother's worst nightmare." Tori told Lucy that her mom told her to get dressed, and she did. They both went downstairs and her mom was looking for her dad because he was probably hiding because he knew that he'd been caught. Tori said that she and her mom looked outside and found Steve by their truck. Tori told Lucy how her mom told her to stay put and then her mom went outside to confront her dad. Tori said that she ran and grabbed the phone because her dad would sometimes get mad and she was afraid he would hurt her mother. Tori said that she could hear her dad telling her mom that it was "not like you think." Tori told Lucy she could see them arguing and both Steve and Martha saw her looking out the window. Her mom told her to come outside and she did. Tori said she was crying and her dad told her he didn't mean to hurt her in any way. Tori told Lucy, "Yea, right, because he had already hurt me."

Lucy: Has he just put his private in your mouth one time, or more times?
Tori: More times.
Lucy: Has he put your hand on his private one time, or more times?
Tori: More times.
Lucy: Has he ever put his private on you anywhere else on your body?
Tori: He puts his private area between my legs and one time I felt a hurt. And he had also stuck his finger up inside me.
Lucy: How did that feel?
Tori: It hurt. I felt a pain.

Tori then described for Lucy how her dad would perform digital penetration on her. She finished the description by saying that her dad told her "One day, we'll really do it." Tori and even her dad did not know what Texas laws had to say about sexual penetration. Steve's statement to Tori showed that his definition of sexual penetration was complete penile/vaginal penetration. Little did he know that he had already committed the Texas definition of sexual penetration many times over a period of many years.

>Lucy: Do you ever see anything ever come out of his private?
>Tori: (Nods, yes.) Some white stuff.
>Lucy: Would it get on your body?
>Tori: Yes.
>Lucy: Where would it get on you?
>Tori: On my private area and one time he caught it in his hand. Sometimes it goes on a towel.

Lucy asked if Steve had ever showed Tori any pornographic films or photos, and Tori told her, no. Other than the sexual incidents, Lucy asked how Tori and her dad got along, and Tori described that they got along great. Lucy then asked how Steve treated Luke, and Tori described how Steve was really mean to her brother.

Lucy asked Tori if she knew that she had done the right thing by telling, and Tori nodded, yes.

>Lucy: What would he say to you about telling?
>Tori: He told me twice not to tell, and I figured it was wrong. My mom asked me sometimes if he had ever touched me and I told her, no. I guess she asked me this because of what had happened to her sister and earlier to me. I told dad one time that I thought this wasn't right, and he told me that this would be the last time, but it wasn't. He kept doing it to me time and time again.
>Lucy: Is your mom protecting you?
>Tori: Yes.
>Lucy: Does your mom believe you?
>Tori: Yes.
>Lucy: Did anyone talk to you and tell you what to say today?
>Tori: No.
>Lucy: Did anyone ask you to keep any secrets today?
>Tori: No.

Lucy: Telling the truth, what does that mean to you?
Tori: Telling everything that happened.
Lucy: And when you tell a lie, what does that mean?
Tori: Telling something that is not true.
Lucy: Have you told me the whole truth today?
Tori: (Nods, yes.) Uh-huh.
Lucy: I know there were some things you said you don't remember, and that's okay. If you talk to someone one else and they ask you something that you don't know, or don't remember, it's okay to say you don't know, or, you don't remember. Do you have any questions that you'd like to ask me?
Tori: No.
Lucy: Thanks for coming. Let's go back to the reception area.

The timer on the video-tape showed 11:06 a.m. Tori's video-taped interview was over. Bill stopped the video tape and ejected it from his television. Lucy had ended the interview in her usual manner. It was imperative for Lucy to establish that Tori knew the difference between telling the truth and telling a lie. It was just as important that she establish that Tori had told the whole truth, and Lucy had also done that. Lucy had also allowed Tori the opportunity to ask questions, because many children have lots of questions about what will happen next. The interview had answered a lot of questions for the investigator. The interview had also created a lot of new questions. Tori had shared a lifetime of molestation with Lucy in thirty-five short minutes.

Bill was now more convinced that this case was going to be quite extensive. Tori mentioned that there had been lots of sexual incidents in Beaumont. She mentioned three separate locations inside Bill's jurisdiction. Another interview with Tori was needed. But Bill had to make a decision. Did he want to go back to Amelia's Place for another interview involving incidents that happened in Beaumont? Or, did he want her to come to his office, conduct the interview himself and take a sworn affidavit from Tori? Many detectives would have immediately picked up the telephone and called the advocacy center. Many detectives would have let Lucy do the work for them. That would be the easy way out. It wasn't that Lucy wouldn't do a great job conducting the interview. She was the best interviewer Bill had ever known. But, Tori was different. She wasn't a small child. She was a very intelligent eleven year-old adolescent that had seven to eight years of information concerning her molestation that needed to be told. That information could not be told in a twenty, thirty, or forty minute interview. It could only be done with meticulous questions and answers. Bill knew that taking Tori's 'sworn affidavit' would take hours. But, it was the right thing to do. And, she was worth it.

Chapter Nine

Preparations

Bill picked up the telephone to call Martha. He needed to set up an interview with her and Tori. He was about to call the Carpenter residence when he remembered that Steve had posted bond. He realized that Steve would be at the residence. Steve was the one who had to be in control, and he was not about to be kicked out of his 'castle.'

Bill picked up the telephone again and called Ben Moore. The Hardin County Investigator remembered that Martha had mentioned possibly staying with Steve's sister, an attorney in Beaumont. Bill thought this was strange. Usually the old saying, 'blood is thicker than water,' holds true. Something must have happened in the past, Bill thought, to cause this sister to go against her brother. Ben gave Bill the name of the sister, June Green, and the name of her law firm.

Bill found the listing in the phone directory, Green & Green, L.L.P. He dialed the number and a receptionist answered, "Green & Green, how may I help you?" Bill asked for June Green and was told to hold. A moment later, a secretary answered, "June Green's office, may I help you?" Bill identified himself and asked for Ms. Green. He was told to hold on again. A moment later a woman identified herself as June Green. Bill identified himself and told Ms. Green that he was trying to locate Martha and Tori. He explained that he was handling the investigation for all of the incidents that happened to Tori in Beaumont. He also explained that in order to file additional charges against Steve for the crimes he committed against Tori, it would be necessary for him to conduct an additional interview with the eleven year-old girl. Bill explained that the Amelia's Place video covered the last incident that occurred in Hardin County, but only touched on incidents happening in Beaumont. Even though June was a civil attorney and not a criminal attorney, her limited criminal law training told her that additional facts and information would be needed. She gave Bill the private telephone number to her residence. A telephone call later and Bill had an appointment with Martha to bring Tori to the Beaumont Police

Department's Special Crimes Bureau for 8:30 a.m. the next day.

Before leaving the office, Bill made another very important telephone call. He called the Jefferson County Crime Victim's Assistance office. This office worked under the umbrella of the Jefferson County District Attorney's office. Judge Ted Ballanger, a former assistant district attorney and county court-at-law judge, was now the county's district attorney. Judge Ballanger had created this office as a support mechanism for victims and their immediate family members. Members of this office played a vital role in helping victims, especially of violent crimes, to continue their lives by getting them help through professional counseling and to prepare these victims and witnesses for courtroom testimony. Without the help of the personnel from this office, many cases would not have been successfully prosecuted. Mrs. Crystal Roosevelt talked with Bill from the victim's assistance office and advised she would be at his office the next morning.

Bill arrived for work at about 8:00 a.m. Thursday morning, July 25. He followed his normal routine of filling his cup with black coffee. He sat at his desk and scanned papers in the file he started with Tori's name attached. At 8:15 a.m., Ms. Frankie Burns, the special crimes bureau secretary, phoned Bill saying that Crystal Roosevelt had arrived. Bill walked to the lobby and introduced himself to the victim's advocate. They walked back to his office and he offered her a cup of coffee.

At 8:25 a.m., Ms. Burns phoned Bill to let him know his appointment had arrived. Bill and Crystal walked to the lobby. Martha and June recognized Bill as the detective that worked on a horrible case several years earlier involving the kidnapping, rape, and murder of a ten year-old girl from a flea market that was located in Beaumont at the time. Bill immediately recognized the beautiful and innocent face of Tori from her interview video tape. Bill was surprised when Martha, Tori, and Luke began hugging Crystal and saying how good it was to see her. Obviously Crystal Roosevelt and the Carpenters knew each other. Bill introduced himself to June, Martha, Tori, and Luke. Crystal explained that she and her husband purchased the Carpenters' residence in Beaumont a couple of years earlier. The families became friends as the real estate transaction took its course. This bit of information was too good to be true. This was the same residence where the Carpenters lived for years and the same residence where Steve molested Tori. What were the odds of this happening? Beaumont was a city of approximately 120,000 people. In the investigation with the ten year-old girl that was kidnapped from the flea market, Bill had felt that Divine intervention put people, places, and facts in the hands and path of the investigators and those details had allowed him to handcuff the perpetrator within forty hours of the child's disappearance. Similar events were starting to occur in this investigation. Bill didn't believe in circumstance and coincidence. He did believe in God's intervention to put things in place to help investigators stop perverts from further committing their horrible deeds.

    Crystal and Bill sat with the others in the lobby and explained the importance of Tori's statement regarding the incidents in Beaumont. Bill advised them that her statement would need to be very explicit and very detailed; this was so that Tori would not have to be questioned and tell her story repeatedly. Bill knew from the thousands of cases he had investigated, that private citizens are not aware of what goes on with a real investigation. Most citizens only know about investigations and trials from what they see on television, which are usually very inaccurate. Bill did not yet know all of the details of Tori's molestation in Beaumont, but his experience told him that if Tori's molestation started when she was about four years old, and most of this time was spent living in Beaumont, then the incidents of molestation could be quite numerous and her statement could be quite lengthy. Bill advised them that taking Tori's sworn statement may take a while. June had legal matters to attend to at her law firm, and she said she would take Luke and he could spend the day with her. Martha would stay at the police station with her daughter. As June was leaving, Bill told her that he would need to take a sworn statement from her one day soon concerning background on her family, any incidents involving her and her brother, and her involvement in Tori's case. June knew what was needed. To save time, June told Bill that she would dictate a 'sworn affidavit' to her secretary and have it to him within a couple of days.

Bill spoke with Martha and explained that she would not be allowed in his office while Tori was interviewed and her statement taken. He would brief her periodically as to their progress and she would have the opportunity to her read her daughter's statement prior to Tori signing it. Bill further explained that it was not to keep anything from her, it was to make the giving of the statement easier for Tori. The reason for having Crystal Roosevelt present while Tori's statement was being taken was to have someone with Tori, to hold her hand if needed, and to be an advocate for her now and as the investigative and judicial process continued through the weeks and months ahead. Bill also wanted someone else in the room with him and this female child as they would be spending hours together. Bill explained that it is often very difficult for children to talk about such delicate and embarrassing matters in front of their parents. The reason is because they love their parents and don't want to see the hurt in their parents' eyes as they tell about their molestation. Another reason Bill did not allow parents to be present while taking a child's statement is because parents become emotional while listening to their child voice the details of their molestation. Parents often cry, become angry, make outbursts with statements such as, 'I can't believe you're doing this to our family,' or 'I can't believe you're lying on your sweet grandpa like this,' or 'I'm going to kill him for what he did to you.' This only upsets the child even more than they already are. Bill's vast experience told him it was best for parents and caretakers to wait outside his office while the interview takes place. Martha stated that she understood. She hugged Tori and told her to tell the truth about everything. She assured Tori that she would be right there in the lobby waiting for her. Tori hugged her mom and told her she would be okay. Bill took Tori by the hand and they walked to his office with Crystal following. It was time to find out what really happened in Beaumont.

Chapter Ten

Tori's Story

Tori sat comfortably in the padded chair in front of Bill's desk and Crystal Rosevelt sat in a chair next to Tori holding her hand. Bill began Tori's affidavit with the preliminary paragraph requesting her name, address, age, etc. He then stopped, sat back in his chair, and asked Tori to tell him everything about what her father had done to her, from the very first time that she could remember, to the last incident. Tori began to describe her first recollections of her dad sexually molesting her. She was four years old. As Tori continued to talk, Bill thought for a moment, "Who in the world would get sexually aroused by an innocent four year-old child?" Of course, he already knew the answer – pedophiles – people who like to have sex with children. As Tori kept talking, Bill again thought, "How sick, how perverted, but so prevalent this is in all of our communities." As Tori continued her summary, Bill realized that Steve had molested her at three locations in Beaumont, one location in Jasper County, at a ranch in West Texas, and at their current residence in Hardin County. Tori also mentioned a vacation the family took in the summer of 1991, where they traveled to the states of Arizona, Utah, Colorado, New Mexico, and California. Steve had also molested Tori in all five states. Tori continued her summary, telling Bill of the numerous times her dad had molested her on their property in Hardin County and leading up to the last time when her mom walked in unexpectedly and caught him.

Tori's summary lasted approximately twenty minutes. Bill knew that to take an affidavit covering Tori's seven to eight year ordeal would take hours and hours. He had to make a choice – to do what was easiest for himself or what was best for this eleven year-old girl. He knew it would be easy to take Tori's statement dealing just with the incidents that happened within the city limits of Beaumont. But he also knew that if criminal charges were to be filed against Steve for molesting Tori in these other jurisdictions, she would have to travel to those additional jurisdictions and give separate statements to other investigators. Bill had seen other investigators take the easy way out. He had seen other investigators worry only about clearing out cases as quickly as possible so they could move on. He had seen victims like Tori become exhausted and so tired of telling their story over and over, until finally they refused to tell their story one more time, even if it meant the perpetrator would walk free. Bill was not that type of investigator. Throughout his entire career, he had always put the victim first. He explained the choices to Tori and Crystal. He also told Tori that if she could bear with him, taking her statement covering her molestation from beginning to end and all of the places where the incidents occurred would be far easier on her in the long run. She understood. She liked this detective. She didn't understand all of the investigative and judicial procedures, but she understood that this kind man with a pleasant smile had her best interests at heart, and she trusted him.

Bill excused himself and walked to the lobby to update Martha. He found her sitting patiently. He explained his strategy and his reasoning behind it. Martha agreed that this was the right thing to do for Tori. Bill returned to his office and sat down to the keyboard of his computer. It was time to begin.

Tori's beginning sentence to her statement was a bombshell. "My dad began sexually molesting me when I was a little girl." One of Bill's favorite sayings is 'being a child should be fun.' Tori began her life story like so many other children Bill had been in contact with – a life filled with perversion instead of peace. Tori's next two sentences were just as profound. "To me, my dad has rubbed and touched me on my breasts and vagina as far back as I can remember." "Wow," Bill thought, Tori was using medical terms for body parts. This was quite unusual for a child. As Bill's interview with Tori continued, he discovered that she was no ordinary child. She was quite intelligent for her age. "The first time that I remember my dad touching me was when I was four years old." Tori continued by saying that her first recollection of Steve molesting her was at their home on Rosewood Street. Again, Bill had another quick thought as Tori paused in her statement while he typed her words and they appeared on the computer screen. Steve was molesting Tori in their home, the place that should be a safe haven for a child. Bill wished Americans would wake up and realize that the most violent places in America are not schools; it is the home, the place that should be the safest haven for women and children. He realized that for so many women and children the home is not their safe haven, but rather, the home is a place of torment, molestation, fear, and domestic violence. Tori continued by saying that many times when her dad molested her, he would 'do it' while they were in the upstairs part of their house and her brother and mom would be in the downstairs part of the house.

As Bill continued typing Tori's statement, he was amazed at her intelligence and ability to formulate her thoughts and sentences. No one had put words in her mouth. She had obviously thought about these perverted events that had happened to her most of her life and was glad to finally be able to tell someone who would listen and understand. Tori continued by saying that a couple of years later, when she was six years old, her dad acquired a warehouse on Martin Street. She said that one day she went with her dad to the warehouse and it was really hot. She was wearing a t-shirt and shorts. Tori said, "He told me to come and go with him and we walked together to the back storeroom. Lots of times when he and I went to the storeroom, dad would take off my clothes and on other occasions, he told me to undress myself. I remember that my t-shirt was up, my shorts were off of me and my panties were around my ankle only on one leg. Dad had me sit on the couch and he began rubbing his hand on my nipples and he would rub my nipples until they got hard. He also put his mouth on them. He took his fingers and also rubbed my vagina. He pulled his pants down. He was wearing jeans and he doesn't wear underwear with his jeans. I saw his penis and it was sticking straight out. He then had me stand up and he sat on the couch and leaned back. He then had me climb up on his lap facing him. He had me scoot up on his lap to where my vagina was touching the underside of his penis, pressing it toward his abdomen. He put his hands around my waist and began rocking me back and forth which made my vagina slide up and down on the underside of his penis. He did this until some white stuff came out the end of his penis. The white stuff got on his stomach and his penis and on my vagina. He had gotten some baby wipes from a box that he kept in the bathroom. He then wiped the white stuff off himself and off of me. He then told me to get dressed. We got what he came to get from the warehouse and we left. Dad would do the things to me I have just described at the warehouse at least twice a week and sometimes three times a week if he got the chance."

Tori needed to get a drink of water and stepped out of Bill's office to the water fountain down the hallway. The break gave her and Crystal a chance to stretch their legs and gave Bill a chance to rest his fingers.

As Bill sat at his desk resting for a few minutes while Tori and Crystal were out of his office, his mind recalled a trip he had made a year earlier to Fort Worth, Texas, to the Texas Counseling Association's annual conference. He received the Texas Exemplary Layperson of the Year award from this very prestigious organization through a nomination by one of the local high school counselors. He had gone to the evening awards banquet and during the conference he received the award. The next day, he strolled to an outlet mall a block from the hotel that was hosting the conference, just as the mall's stores were opening. He entered a small shop and the friendly clerk struck up a conversation. She asked if she could help him, and he merely replied that he was just looking around. She asked him where he was from and he replied, Beaumont, Texas. She asked what brought him to Fort Worth and he told her that he was a police officer, a sex crimes detective, and about the award he received the night before. Her eyes lit up and said, "I have always wanted to ask someone like you a question. Why do these little five, six, and eight year-old girls want to lie on their dads and step dads like they do, because, you know, it's impossible for a grown man to have sex with a little child?" Bill was dumbfounded by her question. His first thought was, "How could she be so naïve?" At the same time, he realized this woman's thoughts and reasoning concerning child sexual abuse was no different than what over ninety-five percent of our population believes concerning sexual abuse and sexual penetration of a child. Bill decided to give this lady a quick education on the sexual abuse of children by beginning with a question. "Ma'am, how do you think grown men have sex with little girls?" he asked the store clerk. Now, quite embarrassed, she said, "Well, you know." Bill grinned as he saw the clerk's face flush, "No ma'am, tell me," he replied. Her voice was now shaking and obviously she was wishing she had not broached the subject, she answered, "Well, you know, the regular way." Bill decided to let the poor woman off the hook. "Oh, you mean penile/vaginal penetration," he said. "Yes," the clerk replied. Bill now began the clerk's education. "Ma'am that is the least used form of penetration on a child," he explained. "The most often used form of sexual penetration on a child is digital penetration - with the fingers," he told her. Her eyes opened wide and she suddenly comprehended what he had just said. "Oh my God!" she exclaimed. "I never thought about that." Bill continued her education. "Ma'am, the second most used type of penetration on a child is oral penetration, whether the oral sexual penetration is on the child, or, having the child perform oral sex on the perpetrator." "Oh my God! I never thought about that!" she exclaimed again. "The third most often used form of penetration is placing inanimate objects inside the vagina or anus of the child," he stated. "Oh no, I never thought about that either," she whispered, trying to comprehend what this detective was telling her. He concluded by stating, "Ma'am, the least used form of sexual penetration used on a child is penile/vaginal penetration." Her education was over for the moment. Bill gave her a moment to absorb all she had just heard. Finally, she looked at Bill and asked, "Most people don't know this, do they?" "No, ma'am," he replied. "Many people believe the child is lying against the perpetrator, who is usually daddy, step-daddy, mom's boyfriend, mother, uncle, grandfather, or brother. The child is chastised, even subjected to whipping, for lying against such a wonderful person," Bill told her. Other customers were walking into the store, and he knew the clerk needed to attend to them. He ended their conversation by offering one final thought. "Ma'am, children deserve the right to be heard. And, children deserve the right to be believed!" Bill stated to the clerk as he exited the store and continued his stroll through the mall.

  As Bill walked on through the mall, he hoped the clerk comprehended and understood what he tried to teach her. Tori was a classic example. Her father had penetrated her sexually and there had been no pain, there had been no bleeding, and there had been no bruising. Yet, there had been sexual intercourse as defined by law, with a child under thirteen years of age – a crime as serious, by punishment, as the crime of murder. Most people do not realize there is sometimes a difference between the medical definition of sexual penetration and the legal definition of sexual penetration.

Tori and Crystal entered Bill's office and sat down. They were ready to continue. Tori told Bill of several more incidents that she remembered at the warehouse and each incident's explicit details. Most of the events were similar in that Steve would take his daughter to the storeroom with the yellow couch and have sexual intercourse with her. Tori then told of another time when Steve drove his blue truck inside the warehouse instead of leaving it outside the building. He then had her undress and stay seated in the truck. He dropped his jeans to his ankles and then began his usual thing of fondling and kissing her breasts and digitally penetrating her vagina. Tori said that this time, he brought a jar of Vaseline. He had her stand on the passenger's running board of the truck and he rubbed some Vaseline on her vaginal area. He placed his penis, that Tori described as always sticking straight out, between her legs. Tori said her dad then began moving back and forth until the white stuff came out of his penis and onto a towel that he'd placed on the running board between her feet. She said they cleaned up, got dressed, and then left the warehouse.

As Bill typed, Tori continued telling her story and describing sexual encounters with her dad at their house on Rosewood Street. She said that most of the time, Luke and Mom were gone and he would do it in places all over the house. "In the hot tub room we would both be naked," she said. He would pick me up from the floor and put his hands under my butt. He would place my vagina on his penis and slide me back and forth on his penis. After a few minutes, he quit rubbing my vagina on his penis and put me back on the floor. I could then see the white stuff coming out of his penis and dripping onto a towel that he had placed on the floor."

Tori described other locations in the house where her dad sexually molested her. It had happened in the garage, hot tub room, hot tub bathroom, Luke's bedroom before it was remodeled, but not after the remodeling, in Luke's bathroom, and in Mom and Dad's bathroom after it had been remodeled, but not before the remodeling. Tori also said the house on Rosewood Street had an office with a bathroom. She described how her dad took her into the office bathroom, had her get naked, and then had her stand on the commode. Tori said that by her standing on the commode, this put her hips at about the same height as her dad's hips. She then described how he placed his penis between her legs, separating the labia of her vagina, and moved his penis back and forth until the white stuff came out of his penis and dropped into the water of the commode.

Tori described so many sexual episodes. Bill thought he would throw a "trick" question at her to see if she was exaggerating. "So, he had sex with you in every room of the house?" he asked. "No," she corrected him. "We didn't have sex in the kitchen, the dining room, the front door entry, my bedroom, nor the video room." A child's home is supposed to be their safe haven, Bill thought, not a place to be sexually exploited in almost every room of the house.

Bill felt that he covered the sexual incidents on Rosewood and the warehouse as thoroughly as possible. He asked Tori if her dad had molested her in any other locations. Not hesitating at all, Tori said, yes, at their old place in Jasper, Texas, and on a vacation trip the family took in 1994. It was time for another break. In fact, it was close to lunch. Bill decided that everyone should meet back at his office at 1:30 p.m. to continue Tori's statement.

Rejuvenated from a break and a good lunch, Bill and Tori continued her affidavit with Crystal quietly sitting by Tori's side. Tori began her recall of events at their place in Jasper. She remembered that the incident probably occurred around July 4th because it was very hot and the family shot some fireworks. Martha didn't want Tori fooling with the fireworks because she was only six or seven years old. Tori's story made the timeframe for this incident in 1988 or 1989. Tori said the house had silver metal sides on it and a metal roof. She said this was the house they lived in before they moved to 8890 Rosewood. Mom and Luke went to the store, leaving her and her dad at the house. Tori said the incident took place in the workshop area of the house. After they were in the workshop, Tori remembered that her jeans and panties were around her knees and her shirt was pulled up exposing her breasts. Her dad had also lowered his jeans, exposing his already erect penis to his daughter. His method appeared to be the same in the late 80's as it was now. He began by fondling her breasts for several minutes then concentrated his perverted behavior to her genital area. As he rubbed his six to seven year-old daughter's vagina, he took her hand and placed it on his erect penis. He placed his hand over hers and began moving it back and forth on his penis. After several minutes of this activity, Steve got a five gallon paint bucket from the storeroom and had Tori stand on it. This extra height made Tori's waist almost equal in height to her dad's waist. Steve then placed his penis between his little daughter's legs and began moving back and forth. Tori told the detective that she could feel her dad's penis sliding back and forth next to her vagina. Her dad pushed down on her waist with his hands which caused her to be an inch or so lower. This downward movement ever so slightly now caused her dad's penis to not only touch her vagina, but actually separated the right side from the left side of her vagina. Tori said that her dad continued to move back and forth until the white stuff started coming out of his penis. He reached into the pocket of his jeans and removed a tissue and let the white stuff go onto the tissue so that it wouldn't get on their clothes. She said that they got dressed and then continued with whatever they had been doing.

    Bill realized that every incident of 'penetration' Tori described was under punishment, as serious as the crime of murder. The incidents Tori described, and Bill reduced to typing in her affidavit, incriminated Steve with the Texas crime of Aggravated Sexual Assault of a Child, a first degree felony, a crime punishable by five to ninety-nine years or life in prison. Steve had not committed Aggravated Sexual Assault because he had not threatened his daughter with death if she did not do as he told her to do. He had not committed this first degree felony because he had not displayed a deadly weapon in her presence or placed her in fear of serious bodily injury or death.

    The crime of Aggravated Sexual Assault has seven ways a person can be convicted of this crime. Steve had not committed part one of this law, by using or displaying a deadly weapon against Tori. He had not committed part two of this law by threatening Tori with serious bodily injury or death if she didn't have sex with him. Steve had not committed part three of this law against Tori by threatening to seriously injure or kill another person if she didn't have sex with him. He had not committed part four of this law, by seriously injuring Tori in connection with forcing her to have sex with him. Steve had not committed part five of this law by giving Tori a 'date rape' drug and then having sex with her. Steve had not committed part seven of this law, which deals with sexually assaulting an elderly or disabled individual. But, he violated part six of the Aggravated Sexual Assault crime. He had sex with a child who was thirteen years of age, or younger.

Bill knew that when Steve fondled or kissed Tori's breasts, even as a little child, he had committed a serious crime – Indecency With A Child – a second degree felony with punishment of two to twenty years in prison. When this perverted father separated his little daughter's labia with his penis, he committed a much more serious crime, penetration of the female sex organ of a child. And Bill was going to do his best to make sure Steve got what he deserved. Bill knew that Steve had committed the same 'First Degree Felony' crime in Beaumont. His thoughts were to get Steve indicted and convicted in as many jurisdictions as possible, with the most serious crimes possible.

Bill asked Tori if she needed a break. "No, I'm okay for now," she said. Bill excused himself and stepped outside his office to the coffee pot in the hallway. He poured the cold coffee in his cup into the wastebasket and then re-filled the cup with fresh, hot coffee. He re-entered his office and settled in his chair. After a good sip of coffee, Bill looked into the eyes of the sweet eleven year-old girl and said two words – "What's next?"

"Three years ago, in the early 90's, we took a vacation to the four-corners and California. We went to Arizona, Utah, Colorado, and New Mexico, and also to California." Tori continued her story telling Bill that "One night in a hotel in Albuquerque, New Mexico, Luke and Mom slept in one bed and Dad and I slept in another bed." Tori said that this was the only night during the entire vacation that she slept in the same bed with her dad. Tori remembered this night quite vividly and told Bill that she had worn a big t-shirt and shorts and panties under the shirt. Tori said that the lights were out in the hotel room and she was lying on her left side away from her dad and facing her mom's bed. She suddenly felt her dad's hand go under her t-shirt and around to the front of her body. He fondled her nipples for several minutes. She didn't move, hoping that he would think she was asleep and leave her alone. He slid his hand away from her breasts and then she felt him rubbing her butt. Tori said the shorts she was wearing had an elastic waistband. He slid his hand inside her shorts and panties. He rubbed her butt for a few seconds and then moved on to her vagina. "He rubbed his finger separating the labia of my genital area." This was a big medical word for an eleven year-old child. Bill asked her if she knew what that word meant. She said, "The lips down there." She was correct, and Bill instructed her to continue. Tori said she felt him remove his hand from her clothes and he then gently put his hand on her right wrist. He moved her hand backward until she was touching his erect penis. He placed her little hand on his penis, and with his hand wrapped around hers, he moved her hand back and forth. He finally let go of her hand and she took it off his penis. She then felt his hand back inside her panties and shorts. He rubbed his finger inside and outside of her vagina for several minutes. He finally removed his hand from her clothes. A few minutes later, Tori said she could tell he had gone to sleep by his breathing.

    Bill stopped typing for a minute to let his fingers rest. He drank several sips of coffee as his mind pondered. Martha and Luke had been asleep during this incident in Albuquerque. But, they were right there – right there in the same room, within a few feet of Tori and her dad. Bill again thought of how so many moms defended their husband or boyfriend in past investigations by stating their husband or boyfriend could not have molested their daughter because they were right there with their daughter in the same room of the same house. Tori had proven once again that such perverts will molest children some way, some how. Martha had been only a few feet away as Steve had, once again, violated their little girl. Her presence did not deter Steve at all. Her presence had only heightened his pleasure of being able to commit his perversion literally in the presence of others and not get caught.

Tori continued the chronology of the interview, moving from the vacation incident to their home in Hardin County. She looked at Crystal sitting next to her and told Bill that her mom and dad sold their home to Crystal and her husband in 1992. They bought one hundred twenty-five acres of land at the dead-end of a dirt road off Hwy. 647. With no home on the property, and Steve being a contractor, he decided that he would build their new house. However, this new house would not be quick to construct. Steve was going to pay cash and build as the money became available. To have a place to live, Steve bought a thirty-three foot travel trailer for his family of four to live in and call 'home' for several months, or possibly longer. Tori said that her dad bought another warehouse a block away at 546 Martin Street. He started moving all of the things he had at the warehouse at 649 Martin Street to the new warehouse. The family also began boxing up almost all of their belongings and putting them in the new warehouse. Each family member could have only a few things to move into the travel trailer while the new house was being constructed. Tori told Bill that her dad immediately began doing sexual things to her at the new warehouse. She said he particularly liked to do things in his new upstairs office. It had a black patent leather couch in it and he liked to do sexual things to her on the couch. Tori described her dad's foreplay to Bill, which was much the same as always. He would start with undressing his daughter, or having her undress herself for him, which added to his perverted pleasure. He would then fondle her breasts or orally stimulate them. Next, he would fondle her genital area. Tori said that her dad kept a jar of Vaseline in the office. On one occasion, she stated that after he undressed her and fondled her breasts and vagina, he put some Vaseline on her vagina. He dropped his jeans to below his knees and lay on the office floor. His penis was erect and sticking straight up from his body. Steve then told his daughter to straddle him and she did as she was told. Tori said that she sat on his penis but it did not go inside her vagina. Instead, she sat on his penis and the tip of it pointed at his feet. Tori said the pressure of her dad's penis shaft separated the lips of her vagina and she could feel his shaft inside the lips of her vagina. As Bill typed Tori's description of this incident, he was aware once again of the legal significance of what she was saying. Texas law describes sexual penetration of the female genitalia as any form of penetration to the 'female sex organ.' Texas law also describes the labia majora and labia minora (the outer and inner lips of the vagina) as a part of the female sex organ. Tori's description of her father's actions had once again described him committing the crime of Aggravated Sexual Assault again with her. Tori continued detailing the episode by telling Bill that after she was 'seated' on his penis, that he told her to rock back and forth. She said that she did as her dad told her to do. After a while, he told her to get off of him. She said that she did and as she got off her father, she noticed that nothing was coming out of his penis. Then suddenly, the white stuff started coming out of his penis and went all over his penis and stomach. He had some paper towels in his office and he used some of them to clean the white stuff off of himself.

Tori told Bill of another episode that happened at the office at the warehouse. She said it was not too long after the incident she had just described. She said it happened in 1992 and she was in the fifth grade. The incident again happened on the couch in the office. He had already removed the bottom half of her clothes and pulled up the top half of her clothes. Tori described how her dad fondled and kissed her breasts, and this time, he put his finger inside her vagina and rubbed his finger back and forth. Bill made a note that Tori had again described how her father had committed Aggravated Sexual Assault against his daughter. But, the episode wasn't over. Tori said that this time, her father had her lie on the couch with her head in the corner and her legs toward her father. She said her father then put her legs on either side of his head. She then described how her father performed oral sex on her for the first time. But she was still not through with this episode. Steve then had his daughter get off the couch and stand in front of him. He then bent down in front of Tori, placed his penis between her legs, and moved his penis back and forth until he achieved an ejaculation. She said that the white stuff got on the carpet and her dad had to get some paper towels and get the white stuff off the carpet really quick. Tori described two more occasions at the warehouse office where her dad performed oral sex on her and had her 'sit' on his penis.

She told Bill that the couch was later moved from the office at the warehouse to the gazebo in their backyard. He made a note of this so that photos of the couch could be taken when he visited their property in a few days.

Many times there was evidently too much activity going on around the construction of the new house and within the confines of the camper for Steve to continue with his perverted activities with his daughter. But, he was like most pedophiles. He needed, he wanted and had to have sex with his daughter. Steve's perversion with his daughter had gone from perversion to obsession. Bill began to realize more and more that this man, this pervert, was one of the most skilled and manipulative pedophiles he'd dealt with in a long time. Tori continued her interview by telling Bill that her dad bought two four-wheelers for them to ride on their property. She said that on many occasions, he would tell her to take off from the camper riding one of the ATVs. He would then follow her, riding the remaining four-wheeler. This way, both four-wheelers were in use and no one could follow them. Tori said that many times her brother, Luke, wanted to ride the four-wheelers with them, but his presence would have foiled her dad's plans. So, her dad would send her ahead to ride the trails and he would follow, leaving Luke behind. Many times Luke would jump on his bike and to try and keep up. But he would tire and return home. Her dad would lead them to a secluded part of the property and make sure that Luke was not following. "We would park the four-wheelers and he would pull my bottom clothes to my knees or tell me to do it and I would do as I was told." Tori said he raised her upper clothes and rubbed and kissed her nipples until they were hard. Next, she said, "He would put his finger between my legs and rub in between the lips of my vagina. At the same time, Dad would put my hand on his penis have me move my hand back and forth. Sometimes when I did this", she said, "the white stuff would come out of his penis and he would let it fall on the ground." Other times, Tori said "He would have me rub his penis for a while, and then he would bend down and put his penis between my legs." She continued, saying "He would move back and forth and I could feel his penis separating the lips of my vagina and then the white stuff would come out and he would let it drip on the ground." Tori said that one time her dad had a tissue in his pocket and he put the tissue in his hand and let the white stuff come on the tissue. He then took the heel of his shoe and kicked a hole in the dirt. He buried the tissue in the dirt so no one could find it. Tori told Bill that the tissue might still be buried on the property and she might be able to find it. Bill thought how nice it would be if they could find Steve's souvenir for evidence. He made another note for his visit to Steve's property.

Tori explained that from the fall of 1992 to the present time, her dad would molest her on an almost daily basis. Sometimes he would molest her on more than one occasion in one day. He would molest her in the woods, at his office, in the car, or wherever he could manipulate an occasion for them to be alone, even if it was for just a few minutes. He also had little phrases or words that he would use to let her know he wanted to be alone with her. He would tell her "Let's go have some fun," or "Let's have some funzies," and she always knew this was his cue that he wanted to do something sexual with her. Tori said that when they would be alone and his penis would get hard, he also liked to use little phrases like "He's looking at you," or "Somebody's looking at you."

Tori said that as the days and weeks passed, her dad began building their combination house and workshop for his construction business. The first part of the structure he built was not their home. It was a section of the structure that he called his paint room. Bill thought it was interesting to see where Steve had his priorities. Tori said the family moved from the camper to the paint room in August 1993. She and Luke were home schooled but their studies were delayed for about two weeks so their moving could be completed. Tori said she and Luke began home schooling on Monday, August 27, 1993. About a week later, her mom and Luke went to the store, which left her and Steve alone at the house. Not to pass up an opportunity of them being alone and having sex, Steve had Tori help him move some more items from the camper to the paint room. Being inside the camper also allowed Steve to see Martha and Luke returning from the store through the windows of the camper, but did not allow Martha and Luke to see what was going on inside the camper. Tori said she was wearing a t-shirt, shorts, panties, and bra, and she and dad were in his and mom's bedroom of the camper. Her dad pulled her shorts and panties to her knees and his jeans to his knees. She said that he pulled up her t-shirt and bra and began kissing her breasts and putting his finger between the lips of her vagina and rubbing back and forth. "By not removing our clothing completely, Dad knew it allowed us to dress quickly if Mom and Luke returned quicker than expected. Dad put my hand on his penis and made me move my hand back and forth for a while. He got a jar of Vaseline that was in one of the drawers in the bedroom and put some Vaseline on his penis. I was now tall enough that dad didn't have to bend down very much to put his penis between my legs. He then moved his penis back and forth until the white stuff came out of his penis." Tori told Bill she didn't remember what her dad did with the white stuff. As soon as their clothes were in order, they returned to the task of moving items from the camper to the paint room.

As Tori continued to tell her story, Bill was amazed at her detailed recollection of dates and times. Bill knew that when cases were submitted to the district attorney's office, that the attorneys always wanted to know information by specific time. Formal complaints against a defendant from the district attorney and an indictment against a defendant from a grand jury always including wording such as "On or about _____ (date) at _____ (time) ..." and the document would continue with the alleged crime being described.

While her dad was building their house and while they were living in the camper, Tori said her dad built a kitchen/bathroom separate from all other structures. After moving into the paint room, he molested her twice in this outdoor bathroom. She said the first incident occurred in October 1993. She remembered that the incident was during this month because school had begun and this incident was right after she had cut her hair. Tori said that her mom and Luke had gone to church, so it had to be a Wednesday night. She had taken a shower and had gotten dressed in a t-shirt and shorts. She was combing her hair and her dad came into the bathroom. Tori said she wasn't paying attention to him, but suddenly she realized that he had undressed and gotten into the shower. Bill thought about other dads and their daughters. Most dads have enough respect for their daughters to give them privacy when they are in the bathroom, especially at ten or eleven years old. But not Steve – he saw this as another opportunity to play while Luke and Martha were away. Tori explained that her dad told her to get undressed and get in the shower with him and scrub his back. She did as she was told. Bill could just imagine how Tori's heart sank as she had to obey her father, and slowly undressed. She entered the shower and washed her dad's back as she had been told to do. He then turned around and she saw that his penis was sticking straight out. But, she was not surprised. She was not in shock. She knew what was going to happen as it had so many, many times before. The water continued to run as Steve bent over and began kissing his daughter's breasts. He fondled her vagina while he had Tori masturbate him. He then bent his knees so that he could put his penis between her legs. Tori remarked that her dad had a big belly and so he had to lean back in order to put his penis between her legs. He then moved back and forth until the 'gunk' came out. Tori said that some of the 'gunk' got on her vagina, but the water was still running and immediately washed it off her body. Bill asked her about the second incident. Tori said the same thing had happened, but just on a different day. Bill thought of how many thousands of times the incidents of Steve molesting his little daughter had been the same thing – just a different day and time.

    Martha got tired of fixing the blinds in the outbuilding. It seemed like every day the blinds were in disarray, and anyone outside the outbuilding could look inside. Having the blinds messed up would not allow someone in the bathroom part of the outbuilding to have privacy. As the investigation began to unfold, Tori told her mom that the blinds were always messed up so that her dad could watch her as she went into the bathroom to pee. Martha realized now that it all made sense. So many naïve mothers and other family members erroneously think that just because they are at home, that a pervert cannot molest a victim. To a pervert, this only adds to their perverted challenge and heightens their sexual pleasure when they accomplish their deviant goal.

Tori began the next paragraph in her affidavit discussing her new house. She said, "In our new house, Dad has molested me in the bathroom upstairs, his office, in the humidity free room, in the attic which is on the third floor, the downstairs tool room which currently has Mom's and Dad's bed in it, the hardware room (he molested me there twice), and the downstairs bathroom that is currently working, and the downstairs bathroom that is by the kitchen but is not currently working. He molested me lots of times in the tool room where their bed is located." Many people would wonder how all of this molestation could be possible with mom and older brother living there. Bill knew the answers before Tori said them. Tori said her mom was usually at the store and Luke went with her, or, her dad would make Luke go for a long walk. She said that her dad would have her come into the tool room, but he would not molest her while she was standing. He would usually be naked and lying on his back on the bed. After he told her to get undressed and she had done as she was told, he would have her straddle him and sit on his penis. He would make sure that there was no penetration as one would think of medically speaking (inserting his penis inside her vaginal canal). But there would be penetration legally speaking, as she could feel the shaft of his penis separating the lips of her vagina. Tori said her dad would place his hands on her hips and rock her back and forth until the white stuff came out of his penis. She said that if his penis was pointed between his legs, he would put a shop towel between his legs so the white stuff would go on the towel. She said that if his penis was pointed toward his stomach, he would let the white stuff go on his stomach and her vagina and then he would use some baby wipes for them to clean themselves when he was finished.

June 1, 1994, was a profound day in Tori's life. She told Bill that this was the day she began her first period. Her mom had been telling her that this was going to happen, and it was finally here. Her dad had done some work for a man named Buck Sturlock from Buna, Texas. Mr. Sturlock had been very impressed with her dad's work and wanted him to do some projects at his ranch. The ranch was not close. It was in West Texas, several hundred miles away. In fact, Mr. Sturlock had his own airplane and her dad and Luke had flown with Mr. Sturlock to his ranch that was located in the Davis Mountains near Marfa, Texas.

Tori stated, "Dad and Luke came home the next morning after I had begun my period and Mom told Dad that I had become a woman. That evening, I had to go to the bathroom and I went to the one downstairs. Mom was in the house part of the structure paying bills for Dad's construction business. Luke was doing something on the computer. Dad met me as I was coming out of the bathroom and told me to meet him upstairs. I went to the game room in the upstairs part of the structure. Dad came to the room a few minutes later wearing his boxer shorts and a t-shirt. I could tell that his penis was already hard because the front of his boxer shorts was sticking out. He took my hand and led me to the attic which is the third floor of the structure. He pulled my pants and panties down to my ankles. I was wearing a sanitary pad for my period and it was pretty dark in the attic. Dad evidently could not see the sanitary pad in my panties that were around my ankles because he asked me if I was wearing one of those things that you put up inside yourself when on your period, and I told him, no. There was a little bit of light coming from a hole in the attic floor from a light that was on in the second floor room. As our eyes adjusted to the darkness we could see each other. I never wanted to do anything sexual with Dad, but now that I had begun my period, I was really scared because I didn't know what might happen. Dad began fondling my vagina with his finger between my legs. He asked me if I knew how to use the thing for my period that goes inside of me, and I told him, no. While he was asking me about that thing, he was pulling his boxer shorts down. He put his penis between my legs and began moving back and forth. I could feel his penis separating the lips of my vagina. The white stuff started coming out of his penis. Daddy was slow about moving his penis away from me while the white stuff was coming and I was suddenly horrified that my dad had just gotten me pregnant. My mom had told me when she and I had had mother/daughter talks in the past, that once I started my period, if the stuff that comes out of a man's penis got on my vagina, even on the outside of my vagina, that I could get pregnant. I was so scared that my dad had just gotten me pregnant, that I visibly started shaking. All I could think of was that I had started my period less than twenty-four hours ago, I was only eleven years old, and my father had just gotten me pregnant. I'd had a couple of cramps with the starting of my period. But after my dad had sex with me, I had a lot of cramps. All I could think about was that I had these cramps were because my dad had gotten me pregnant." Tori told Bill that she was very thankful that Barbara Harrison talked to her about pregnancy when she was at Barbara's office for her forensic examination. Barbara's conversation was able to relieve her fears of being pregnant.

"Mr. Sturlock wanted Dad to move to his ranch in West Texas and construct a lodge on one of his ranches. He said the ranch was very remote and Luke and me being home schooled made us a perfect family for living on the ranch and Dad constructing the lodge. Luke had seen the ranch but Mom and I had not. So, on July 3, 1994, we drove to Mr. Sturlock's Davis Mountain Ranch. Mr. Sturlock let us stay at his ranch house which was way back in the mountains. He has this building he calls a 'lodge' that is partially completed and he wanted Dad to complete it. The lodge only has a round concrete base, a metal frame, and a partial roof. Mr. Sturlock let us use one of his Jeeps and we got to ride around on his huge ranch. On July 4th, right after lunch, Dad told me to go with him because he was going to teach me how to drive a standard shift vehicle. Mom and Luke were reading a book and stayed at the ranch house, and Jesus, Mr. Sturlock's worker on the ranch, was doing some mechanical work on a construction crane. We got into Mr. Sturlock's jeep and began driving one of the rustic roads on the ranch. Dad was driving and we drove to the lodge, which is about two miles from the ranch house. It seemed as though we were in the middle of nowhere – miles and miles from anyone. We got out of the Jeep and dad got a denim coat and a roll of toilet paper that was behind the seats of the Jeep. We walked inside the lodge and there were some dark brown colored benches sitting on the concrete. Dad placed the coat over the dark brown plastic covering on one of the benches and then told me to take off my bottom clothes. I did as he told me to do. He told me to sit on the coat and I did. He raised my blouse and bra and kissed and fondled my breasts as he always did. He rubbed my vagina with his finger for a few minutes and then he had me stand up. He dropped his jeans to his knees and I could see his penis was hard. Dad sat on the bench on top of the coat and had me sit on top of him, like we had done before back home. He was in a sitting position and my arms were at my side but his arms were around my waist. Dad's big belly was preventing his penis from having contact with my vagina. So, he layed back on the bench and now his penis had contact with my vagina. It was pointed toward his stomach and his hands were still on my waist, moving me back and forth on his penis. He kept doing this until the 'gunk' came out of his penis and it got all over his stomach and my vagina. He gave me some of the toilet paper to get the white stuff off of me. I wiped all of the white stuff that I could see off my vagina." Tori said she knew some of the 'gunk' got on the lips of her vagina, but she couldn't tell if some of it got in between the lips. She said she wiped extra good in that area in case some of the 'gunk' got there. But, she told Bill, she wasn't too worried about her dad getting her pregnant this time, because she had just finished her second period before the trip to the ranch and her mom had told her she could only get pregnant if she had sex while she was on her period. Tori concluded the ranch story by saying that they drove back to the ranch house after they got dressed. They left Mr. Sturlock's ranch and drove back to their home the next day.

It was time for a break in taking Tori's statement. Bill's fingers and mind were tired. It was getting close to the end of the second day of Tori's statement. Bill was also disturbed by Tori's last comments about not worrying about being pregnant from the sexual episode with her dad at the ranch. She'd mentioned to Bill that the conversation she had a few months ago with her mom about pregnancy and periods was that she could only get pregnant if she had sex while on her menstrual period. But, Tori had misunderstood the part in her mom's conversation that the most likely time to get pregnant was the seventh to fourteenth day after her period. Bill's training as a sex crimes investigator, and especially from working with sexual assault nurse examiners and gynecologists, had taught him that 'getting pregnant only occurs while on your period' was nothing more than an erroneous myth. He knew that a woman could conceivably get pregnant at any time; however, the most likely time for pregnancy was during a woman's ovulation period, which usually occurs from the eleventh to the twenty-first day after the first day of her menstrual period. Bill knew that this ovulation period was when a woman's ovaries released a mature egg into her fallopian tubes, which then travels and adheres to the thickened wall of her uterus, awaiting fertilization by a single sperm. He also knew that the least likely time for a woman to get pregnant was during her menstrual period, the time when a woman's body is shedding unused eggs and the thickened lining of the uterus through the blood of the menstrual period.

As Tori and Crystal returned from their break and sat in their chairs, Bill looked at Tori and began to explain ovulation and the most likely time to get pregnant. Bill then calculated Tori's time from the beginning of her second period to the incident at the ranch. The incident had happened on the eleventh day of Tori's cycle. As Tori absorbed the realization that the ranch incident was possibly at the beginning of her ovulation period and that her father could have easily gotten her pregnant, she became visibly disturbed. Everyone in the room breathed a united sigh of relief that this beautiful eleven year-old innocent girl had not conceived that day and was not sitting in Bill's office pregnant by her perverted father. It was sad that Tori could describe her body parts using medical terms that were very advanced for her age, and yet, she did not know about her ovulation cycle. Bill realized that this information was foreign to not only young girls, but to adult women as well.

Bill's efforts to have Tori's affidavit, going from the first sexual incident to the last incident involving her father, was almost complete. Tori had recovered from Bill's educational session about pregnancy, menstrual periods, and ovulation periods. They reached the final incident in her chronology of the events that occurred with her father over almost her entire lifetime.

Right after lunch, Tori began the last incident of her story. Steve told her to stay home from church that night and they would have some fun. Tori told Bill she knew that meant her dad wanted to have sex with her while her mom and Luke were at Wednesday night church services. How sad, Bill thought, this father was keeping his little girl from going to God's house so he could sexually victimize her one more time. Well, at least this was the last time. Tori continued by saying that her dad told her mom that he needed her help doing some carpentry work that evening. Martha affirmed this by turning to Tori and saying she told her to stay home from church that evening to help her dad. After all, Steve made sure everyone knew that he was the "head of his house" not only spiritually, but also physically. Tori said she didn't want to stay at home that night with her dad. She knew what was going to happen. She told Bill that tears swelled up in her eyes and she fought the urge to cry. Tori had to turn her head away from Martha so that her mother would not see that something was wrong.

    A short time later, Tori said her mom and brother left the house for church. She and Steve did some carpentry work for a little while. She figured this work was just for show, so that her mom could see that some work had been done while she was at church. They finished their work and then sat in the swing outside the house waiting for Greg to return her dad's truck, which he'd borrowed earlier that day. When Greg didn't show up right away, her dad left the swing and said he was going to take his shower. He returned about fifteen minutes later. It was obvious to Tori that her dad had cleaned up. As he sat on the swing once again, Tori said she did not move. She hoped that Greg having to come to the house would foil her dad's plans to have sex with her that night. That thought had just entered her mind when her dad told her to go on in the house and get her shower. He told her that he would wait for Greg and that he would be in as soon as Greg left. Tori told Bill that she said nothing, but obediently rose from the swing and walked into the house. She said there was nothing to say. There was no getting away from what was about to happen. Tori told Bill she felt like an abused robot.

    Tori had just gotten out of the shower and heard voices outside the house. She peeked out the bathroom window and saw that her dad was talking to Greg. Her half brother had arrived with the truck. Greg's wife, Sheila, was waiting for him in another vehicle. Tori desperately wanted to open the window and cry out. She knew that her big brother would rescue her, protect her, if only she would, or could, cry out to him. But her father's physical and mental hold on her was too strong. She wrapped herself in a towel, sat on a vanity chair and waited. She heard Greg say goodbye to her dad. A few seconds later, Tori heard the truck door slam as Greg got into the truck with Sheila. She heard the truck engine as they backed out of the driveway. The motor noise grew quieter as Greg and Sheila drove farther and farther down the road away from her house. She knew it wouldn't be long now.

The door closed and Tori heard her father's footsteps as he ascended the stairway. The black plastic curtain opened and he was there. He saw that she was dressed only in a towel and he told her to get rid of it. She did as she was told. She was now standing before her father completely nude. Tori explained to Bill that her dad took two towels from a clothes basket and placed them on the vanity. Steve had her lie on the towels and began fondling her breasts. His hand went between her legs and his finger began rubbing her vagina. Tori said that she could feel his finger force its way inside her vagina. She said it felt like most of his finger was inside of her. Bill needed the information describing Steve's digital penetration of Tori so that he could again show a prosecutor, grand jury, judge, and jury that Steve had committed the crime of aggravated sexual assault against Tori, again. Tori told Bill she was more scared than ever before. Through her mother/daughter talks, she knew that when men and women had sex, the man places his penis inside the woman's vagina. Her dad had become bolder with each episode since she had become a woman and had begun her periods. What if, she thought, this was the day that instead of his finger he would try to put his penis inside her vagina? She told Bill she was horrified, but she didn't let her fear show to her dad. She methodically, robotically did as she was told. Tori said she was laying on the vanity with her head to her dad's right side and her feet were toward his left side. Steve told her to turn the opposite that she was positioned on the vanity. This new position was evidently going to give him a better angle to complete his deeds. Tori sat up, turned around, and lay back down on the vanity. Her dad got another towel, folded it, and put it behind her head for a pillow. He took his hands and scooted her legs and butt close to the edge of the vanity. He put her legs over his shoulders and Tori said that she could feel his tongue licking and penetrating her vagina. A few minutes later, her dad stood up and pulled his boxer shorts to his knees.

Tori said her dad looked at her and said, "He's looking at you." Tori said that he moved close to her head and told her to put his penis in her mouth. This was the first time he'd ever asked her to do something like this and she turned her head away. How sick, she thought. Tori said she could feel his penis next to her cheek and he moved her head toward him and forced his penis into her mouth. She described to Bill that it felt hard and rubbery. Tori told Bill that this new sexual act reinforced her fear that her dad may have decided that it was finally time for him to put his penis way up inside her vagina. Bill noted that this latest detail was another act of aggravated sexual assault against this child.

    A noise suddenly came from downstairs. It was a sound Tori recognized immediately. It was a sound her dad recognized immediately. The front door had opened. A second later they heard it close. Someone was there. Tori told Bill the look on her dad's face was one of horror. He was now the one that was scared. He quickly pulled up his boxers and Tori said he whispered for her to get dressed. He turned off the bathroom light and brushed the black plastic 'baggie' curtain aside and descended the stairs. Tori told Bill that she got off the vanity and turned the light back on so she could see. She grabbed her bra, panties, blouse, and shorts and began dressing. She still had no idea who had come through the door, then suddenly she heard, "Next!" It was their family call word warning that someone was about to go through the plastic curtain to use the bathroom and for them to have privacy. Tori recognized the voice. It was her mom. She told Bill that she was in shock. She was numb. She did not know whether to be scared or relieved. Her mom was about to discover what her dad had been doing to her for so many years. Her thoughts were racing. Would her mom be mad at her? Would she be mad at her dad? Would she blame both of them for what had been going on for so long? Tori said that she instinctively replied, "I'm almost dressed, I'm hurrying," in a voice that was barely audible. Tori said that she tried to have a calm voice but she could hear her voice quivering as she mumbled the words. She had managed to put on her bra and panties, but nothing else. She could see down the stairway. The curtain opened and she could first see her mom's hair, then her face, and the rest of her mom's body with each ascending step. Tori watched her mother's expression turn to shock as she realized her daughter was dressed only in her underwear and that her husband had just left the same room her partially dressed eleven year-old daughter was in. Martha asked Tori why her dad was in the bathroom with her and Tori responded that her dad had been looking for something. Tori said her mom's voice was trembling and she asked again why her dad had been in the bathroom with her. Tori said she stumbled through the same answer again. Tori said her tears suddenly began to stream down her face. She couldn't hold them back any longer. "Tori, why is your daddy in here with you?" Martha asked. Tori said the words wouldn't come out. Her tears continued to fall as she looked at the bathroom floor. Tori said she couldn't look at her mother, and she closed her eyes. Suddenly, she felt it. Her mom's arms wrapped around her and she heard her mom say, "It's okay, you did nothing wrong." Tori looked at Bill and said, "Mom didn't blame me." Tori said she laid her head on her mom's shoulder and cried. They both cried. It was over. It was finally over.

Bill completed Tori's marathon affidavit with an interesting closing paragraph:

"When I was only four or five years old, I did not know what my daddy was doing to me was wrong. I thought that all dads did these things with their daughters. Then, when I was about six years old, Mom began asking me if Dad was touching me on my privates. I don't know why she asked me and I don't know why I told her, no, even though he had been touching me on my breasts and vagina. By her asking these questions, I figured out that what Dad was doing was probably wrong. I do not like what my dad has done to me for many years and in lots of places, and I would like for criminal charges to be filed against him in all of these places. I think he should be locked up for the rest of his life for what he has done to me from the time I was four years old until now. I will not be twelve years old for two more months."

Bill let Tori and Crystal read the document. He went to the lobby where Martha had patiently sat for two separate days. He brought her to his office and let her read the document. After Tori and Martha gave their approval to the document, Tori signed it. Because of the necessity of Bill having to work on other cases, Tori's second day of taking her affidavit was five days after the first day. It was July 30, 1994.

Chapter Eleven

Not Again

Tori's statement was completed and as she, Martha, and Crystal were about to leave at the end of Tori's affidavit interview, Bill had a brainstorm. Tori's innocence was evident to anyone who looked at her. There was an innocent aura about her that words could not express. Bill had already decided that when he finished the investigation, he was going to send copies of Tori's files to the district attorneys in Jefferson County, Hardin County, Jasper County, and Jeff Davis County. Bill wanted to show Steve no quarter. He wanted him prosecuted to the fullest extent of the law. Bill wanted Steve to never breathe another breath of free air once he put him in jail. None of those prosecutors knew what Tori looked like. He knew they would wonder if this eleven year old girl looked eleven or much older, even though under the law, her physical maturity should make no difference. He also wanted these prosecutors to see this young lady as a little girl, not as a maturing eleven, almost twelve year old person. He turned to Martha and told her an affidavit needed to be taken from her. Bill knew Martha's affidavit would also be a lengthy process. He checked his calendar and saw that several other investigations that had already been assigned to him would take most of his time the following week. He scheduled Martha's affidavit to be taken on Monday, August 5, 1994. He also gave Martha a homework assignment. Bill told her that he wanted photos of Tori for every year of her life, beginning at age four. He wanted one or two photos of Tori when she was four years old, five years old, six years old, seven years old, eight years old, nine years old, and ten years old. He wanted to show those other county prosecutors how Tori looked while her father was sexually molesting her through each year of her life since the molestation began. Bill reached for his phone and dialed the department's I.D. unit. One of the civilian technicians, Sharon Pate, answered the phone. Bill asked Sharon to bring her camera to his office. She arrived a few minutes later and Bill asked her to take a full-length photo of Tori, and a second photo from about the waist, up. Tori stood against the cinder block wall of Bill's office. She smiled at the camera as Sharon took the photos that Bill had requested. He now had the photos he wanted of Tori when she was eleven years old.

The photos of Tori were ready the following Monday morning. Bill had been talking to Martha when Sharon took the photos and he did not pay any attention to Tori. When Bill gave the photos his full attention, he was astounded. He couldn't believe what he was seeing. Tori's hands were clasped together in front of her groin area, a kinesics sign of protecting, covering herself. It was as if her hands were in front of her to block out an intrusion. Bill also noticed that Tori's head was pointed downward with her eyes raised to look at the camera. It was a classic sign of submission. She displayed these same signs in the close-up photo.

After analyzing Tori's photos, Bill called Buck Sturlock in Buna. Buck stated that he allowed Steve access to the ranch when his family visited. He allowed Steve to drive a Jeep-type vehicle anywhere he wanted to go on the ranch. Bill asked Buck if there was a coat in that vehicle. Buck said he kept a brown Carhartt-type jacket in the back of the vehicle and explained that the West Texas weather could go from hot to cold in a matter of minutes. Bill told Buck that he or another investigator would contact him in the next few days to take his sworn statement. Buck said he was happy to help in any way.

Bill then called the Hardin County District Attorney's office. The criminal case of Steve molesting Tori at their property in Hardin County had already been filed with the Hardin County District Attorney's Office. Bill knew that Tori's lengthy affidavit contained additional information that may possibly help the Hardin County trial. The secretary answered and Bill asked for Mr. Rick Lucas, the investigator for the district attorney. Rick was quite a legendary law enforcement officer. His mere presence was intimidating at six-feet-ten-inches. He retired the previous year from the Texas Department of Public Safety after serving as a detective for almost thirty years. Rick was assigned to the D.P.S. Intelligence Unit for most of his career. He was also one of the state trooper/agents that led the assault at Huntsville state prison when legendary Mexican mafia leader and two other inmates attempted a prison break in 1972. The mafia leader and several other inmates managed to get their hands on some guns and caused a riot in the prison, taking over one hundred hostages and murdering five people, as the two-week riot began. Finally, the commanders in charge decided an offensive assault had to be made. D.P.S. intelligence officers, Texas Rangers, and the D.P.S. S.W.A.T. team members were to lead the charge. When the smoke settled on that fateful day, July 29, 1972, the mafia leader and his partners in the prison siege were dead. Some say the inmates committed suicide in the final seconds of the assault. Others spread the rumor that Lucas fired the fatal shot that killed the ring leader.

As Rick answered the phone, Bill immediately recognized the articulate baritone voice of his friend. He and Rick worked together on several investigations in the past. Rick had seen Tori's case filed with the D.A.'s office by Major Ben Moore. Bill told Rick of Tori's new affidavit and the chronological detail within it. Rick was very interested in the new information of this case and Bill decided to go to Kountze and meet with Rick.

It was after 11:00 a.m. when Bill entered the Hardin County D.A.'s office. A secretary summoned Rick to the front office and he greeted his old friend. The two investigators sat in Rick's office mulling over the facts and evidence from the Hardin County and the Beaumont P.D. investigations. "Have you had lunch?" Rick asked. Breakfast had been a long time ago and Bill's stomach was starting to growl. "No," he replied, as Rick got up from his desk. "Have you ever eaten at Thibodeaux's?" Rick asked. Bill was familiar with the small restaurant on the north end of Kountze but had never eaten there. They left the courthouse and were parking in front of the homely looking restaurant within five minutes. Rick explained that a black lady ran the restaurant and had 'down-home' cooked meals for lunch every day. As they two men entered the door, Bill could see the place was nothing fancy, but the aromas from the steam table at Thibodeaux's would rival the aromas from a five-star restaurant. That day, Mama Thibodeaux's had fried pork chops, rice and gravy, black-eyed peas, homemade cornbread, peach cobbler, and fresh iced tea. It was a meal fit for a king.

Bill and Rick walked, or rather waddled, out of Thibodeaux's and returned to Rick's office. They continued to review the facts and evidence of the two case files. Rick agreed to take a statement from Tori's brother, Luke. He also said he would get in touch with the West Texas ranch owner, Buck Sturlock, whose permanent residence and businesses were northeast of Kountze in the small community of Buna. Rick had known Buck for a number of years. Bill mentioned that he had talked with Buck earlier in the day. He told Rick that Buck verified he had a coat stored in the back of his Jeep for emergency purposes and that Steve would have had access to the coat when he used the vehicle. Bill agreed to get photos of the two warehouses in Beaumont and to take Martha's affidavit. The two men agreed to stay in touch as their investigations continued to unfold.

Bill's week was going to be quite busy with his commitment to some of his other investigations. Real-life detectives and their investigations are not like the investigations depicted in a Hollywood movie or weekly television show where television detectives are assigned just one case and have it solved before the end of the show. Most detectives work on several investigations at one time, with an exception of the occasional homicide, rape, or kidnapping.

After a weekend of rest and completing some necessary work on several other cases, Bill was anxious to get back to Tori's investigation. He arrived for work a few minutes before 8:00 a.m., poured his cup full of black coffee and sat at his desk, pondering Martha's statement that lay ahead. Major Thibodeaux gave Bill a copy of the affidavit his office took from Martha on July 18. Bill read through the document as he sipped his coffee. The Hardin County affidavit was a bit rambling and mainly dealt with only the incident she knew of at the time the affidavit was taken – the incident the night Steve got caught. Bill noticed on the first page as Martha described coming home that night, she said, "He had his head down and was trying to get down the stairs quickly. I said something and looked up as his body reached my eye-level as I was going up and him coming down and I saw he had an erection. My eyes went back and forth from his eyes to his bulging boxer shorts as I said whatever it was I said. I also heard my daughter in the same breath, the plastic curtain covering the doors saying something to the effect of "I'm almost dressed or I'm hurrying" or something. I was shaking and my heart was pounding so fast I thought it was going to pop out of my chest. My body lost all its strength." Bill read on and another sentence caught his eye. Tori had just finished telling her mother that her father had been molesting her for a long time and Martha responded, "I remember saying this is a mother's worst nightmare and my God, not again." Bill definitely wanted Martha to clarify what she meant by, "not again."

Chapter Twelve

Martha's Story

Martha arrived punctually at the Special Crimes Unit lobby on Monday morning, August 4. She had already told her story to Major Ben Moore as it related to her daughter being molested in Hardin County. But, her daughter's investigation revealed that the molestation in Hardin County was only the 'tip of the iceberg.' Bill's interview with Tori revealed that hundreds, even thousands of sexual incidents involving Steve victimizing Tori had occurred within the city limits of Beaumont. Martha had already observed from spending two days in the Special Crimes Unit's lobby a week earlier that Bill was going to be quite thorough in taking her statement. It was going to be a very long day – or days – depending on the amount of detail that Bill was going to go into with her statement. Bill rounded the corner and walked into the lobby. He was surprised to also see Tori and Luke. Martha explained that she had to protect her children. She brought them because she knew they would be safe at the police station. They were staying at June's house, but June had to work, June's husband had to work, and she had to be at the police station. Steve was not to be trusted. Martha knew that if Steve got his hands on Tori and Luke, he would basically hold them for ransom until she dropped the charges against him. After her brief explanation about her children being there, Bill told the kids to make themselves comfortable. It would be a long day. As he escorted Martha to his office, he thought to himself how he wished more mothers would be this protective over their children.

Martha's affidavit began with Bill asking her questions, and as she answered, he typed her statement into the computer. She began with a brief history of her marriage to her first husband and by that marriage she had two sons. The marriage lasted seven years, until her husband's death. She told Bill that she met Steve in church. Martha said she found out he was still married but he repeatedly begged Martha to go out with him. He said that his wife was away on a missionary journey. Martha said she refused every request Steve made. A short time later, Steve filed for a divorce from his wife. After the divorce was final, Martha and Steve dated for several months and finally married. Bill continued typing as Martha stated that Steve had two sons from his previous marriage and she had two sons from hers. Martha learned that Steve felt four boys were enough and he wanted no more children. One of Steve's sons was killed in an automobile accident in 1978. Martha explained that after the funeral and when his grieving subsided, Steve began telling her that he wanted another child. So, in February 1980, the first child of their marriage, Luke, was born. Martha said she became pregnant again a few months later; however, the pregnancy ended in a miscarriage. After recovering from the miscarriage, Martha said that everything seemed to be going great until the end of 1981, when she became pregnant again. Martha told Bill that Steve began acting very peculiar and making weird statements. She said he became very adamant that this child needed to be a boy also. He became so adamant, she said, that he refused to pick out a girl's name. In September 1982, Martha gave birth to a daughter. Martha told Bill that when she was in high school, she babysat a child that was only a few months old. The grandmother hid the child at Martha's parents' house because the mother was on drugs. She said the baby was so beautiful and precious, and her name was Tori. Since Steve would not pick out a girl's name, Martha named her baby Victoria, Tori for short, after the little girl she babysat years earlier. Even though Martha could see the disappointment of the baby being a girl on Steve's face, he began to bond with her shortly after they arrived home from the hospital. Martha explained that another trip to the hospital a month later eliminated the possibility of more babies.

Martha continued with her chronology of events and Bill continued typing. Martha stated that in December 1983, she walked into Tori's bedroom. Tori was only fourteen months old at the time and Martha was shocked to see her adolescent son, Ronnie, from her previous marriage with his pants down and lying on top of her daughter. He was in the act of sliding his penis back and forth on Tori's diaper and ejaculating when she walked into the room. Bill needed no further explanation. He now knew what Martha meant in her previous statement when she said, "Oh no, not again." Martha said her son was immediately removed from the home and placed in a mental health facility until he could be dealt with through the juvenile authorities. Luke was only three-and-one-half years old when this occurred. After Martha removed Ronnie from the home, Luke got the courage to tell his mom that Ronnie had also been 'playing with his (Luke) private parts.'

There was no doubt in Bill's mind that Martha must have been torn during that ordeal. One child was the perpetrator and two children were the victims. On one hand, Martha wanted to stand by her teenage son and get him psychological help; while on the other hand, she had to protect her two little ones. Yet, she had the courage to do the right thing – to stand up and protect her children who could not protect themselves. To make her decision more difficult, Steve was begging Martha the entire time to not send her son to jail, but to put him in some kind of home. Steve's theory was that if she sent her son to jail, this would make her son an animal with an animal's mind. Steve's pressure on Martha was almost unbearable, but she knew she must do the right thing for her innocent children, who were victims of a very serious crime. Her son went to a mental health facility. Again, Bill wished more mothers had this kind of courage.

Martha continued her chronology of events, explaining that they bought their house on Rosewood Street in 1984. It needed a lot of remodeling, which began in May 1987 and continued until Spring 1988. As Martha mentioned the remodeling, Bill thought of Tori's statement. Tori stated that she was four years old and their house was being remodeled when her father began molesting her. Martha had just provided a timeline that included dates for Bill to chronologically document when Tori's molestation began. Bill mentioned Tori's statement to Martha, and she said Tori was correct. Steve had a conveyor/roller system that was about fifteen feet long and about three feet off the ground to assist him in remodeling the house. Martha went on to say that the same conveyor/roller system was installed in the workshop area of their current residence.

Bill smiled as Martha corroborated Tori's statement. So many people do not give credit to little children for their intelligence. Many believe that little children have vivid imaginations and make up stories of being sexually abused. This seasoned investigator knew better. He had seen children as young as three years old, at the local children's advocacy center, during their forensic interview, tell their story of molestation in very precise detail. Bill continued Martha's statement as he thought of one of his favorite sayings and he shares it with audiences at his child abuse seminars, "Children deserve the right to be heard, and, children deserve the right to believed!"

Martha then began telling Bill about the warehouse at 649 Martin Street being bought in late 1985 or early 1986. She told how she and Steve brought bicycles for Tori and Luke to ride inside the warehouse because it was so big. She described the ramp inside the warehouse where a vehicle could be driven inside the building, just like Tori described in her statement. Bill continued typing and Martha explained that Tori liked to go with her dad to the warehouse. She cleaned up the office area for her dad and also helped him do carpentry work. Martha said that Luke did not care to go to the warehouse because it was boring. Martha continued with her statement, telling Bill that about the time this warehouse was purchased, Steve also owned a 1988 blue Chevrolet pickup truck that had running boards on it. This was the same truck that Tori described in her statement, Bill thought, where her father had had her stand on the running boards while he stood on the concrete floor and molested her. Martha further explained that while they owned this warehouse, they also bought two couches and two chairs. She told Bill that the yellow velour couch should still be in the storeroom at 649 Martin Street.

Tori mentioned in her statement that her father always wore blue jeans, but never wore underwear with them. Bill asked Martha about this and she stated that Steve quit wearing underwear shortly after they married. He told her the seams of the briefs chaffed him. However, she explained, he would wear briefs to church under his dress pants and at night when going to bed. Ironically, neither of these times were opportunities for Steve to molest Tori.

Bill was constantly thinking of Tori's statement while interviewing Martha. It was so important to corroborate as much of Tori's statement as possible. He knew that when this case went to trial, Tori's character, truthfulness, and every word on her sworn statement would be under attack by Steve's defense attorney.

Tori had also mentioned that one of the places her father molested her was at their house in Jasper, Texas. She described the house and detailed the molestation that happened there. Tori also told Bill that the house had burned. Bill knew that if he was to get an indictment against Steve in Jasper, County their district attorney's office would need to know approximately when Tori was molested there. Tori stated that it happened on July 4th, but she did not know if the incident happened in 1988 or early 1989. Bill brought this issue up to Martha. With Tori being in the special crimes bureau lobby, Martha stepped out of Bill's office and walked to the lobby. This break gave Bill the chance to stretch and grab a fresh cup of coffee. Martha returned a few minutes later with the answer. She questioned Tori about when her dad molested her on July 4th, if the house burned shortly thereafter, or if it burned a long time after the molestation. Martha's way of phrasing this question made it easy for Tori to answer. She told her mom that her dad molested her at the house in Jasper and the house had burned very shortly after he did those things to her. Martha returned to Bill's office. The answer the detective needed for possible charges to be filed against Steve in Jasper County was now exact. Tori was molested in that county on July 4, 1989.

Martha continued talking about the house fire in Jasper County. It really didn't have anything to do with Tori's molestation by her father, so Bill stopped typing and listened. He tried to adhere to an old philosophy – 'Listen and you might learn something.' Martha said the house burned while she and Tori were attending a wedding in Ohio. Steve called her and was very jovial on the telephone. He stated that he had made a movie with Luke and it was going to be worth about $50,000.00. Martha said she could not imagine what Steve was talking about, but $50,000.00 was a lot of money. When she and Tori returned from the wedding, she learned about the house burning. Steve got their video camera and filmed Luke in the foreground while the house burned in the background, for insurance purposes. Instead of being elated, Martha said she was extremely upset. The house held a lot of pictures and other memorabilia from her and her sister's childhood, as well as photos and items of all the children. These items obviously meant nothing to Steve, but they were meaningful to her. Steve had explained the fire started with a faulty fluorescent light he installed in an upstairs bedroom. However, the report from the state arson investigator noted the fire's origin was in the kitchen. Martha stated that she questioned Steve about what started the fire and where it started, but of course, he denied it. Martha said that not only was Steve's discrepancy of where the fire started strange, but she told Bill this was not the first suspicious fire Steve was involved with. She stated that when Steve was getting the divorce from his first wife, they owned a three-story house on the shores of Toledo Bend Lake. Martha said the house mysteriously burned about the time it was to be sold.

The story of the fires gave Bill more insight regarding Steve's personality. Bill knew that Steve was the classic type of child molester, one that must be in control and always manipulate a situation. Money had been tight in 1989 and the $50,000.00 check for the house fire was just what Steve needed to take care of their finances. He was also very self-centered, as are most child molesters. The photos and memorabilia meant nothing to him. And, Steve was certainly not going to let some divorce judge tell him what to do with his property. His philosophy was simple – if he couldn't have it, no one would have it. Burning the property maintained his control.

Bill began asking Martha questions about the family vacation that Tori talked about in her affidavit. It was another key point that was in Tori's statement that needed corroboration. Martha remembered the vacation. They left Beaumont in late July or early August 1991. Their first stop on the trip was at a hotel in Fort Stockton, Texas, just as Tori had stated. Martha said their second night on the trip was spent at a hotel in Albuquerque, New Mexico. Martha remembered that Tori and Steve slept in the same bed and she slept in a bed with Luke. She explained that Tori had gotten into one of the beds and had fallen asleep watching TV. She thought nothing of Steve sleeping in the same bed with his daughter. After all, she was only eight years old. Yet, because of past experiences with her sister and her son, Martha still had an inkling of doubt concerning Steve and Tori. Martha told Bill that she was realizing how well Steve was able to manipulate almost every situation to achieve his deviant goals. Martha also recalled that in talking to Tori, Steve had molested Tori in other hotels and in other towns on the trip – in Arizona just outside of the Painted Desert National Park, and in Yuma, Arizona.

Martha stated that Steve began complaining of the neighbors bothering him at their house on Rosewood Street. She really hadn't noticed a problem but he became adamant about moving. They began to look around the Golden Triangle area and found one-hundred-twenty-five acres of land at the dead-end of a road in Hardin County. It was just what Steve wanted. It was a place where he could be alone with his family. Now in looking back, Martha said it was quite obvious that Steve wanted to isolate her and the children from society. Martha stated in her affidavit, "…and we moved from our beautiful spacious house on Rosewood into a thirty-three foot camper trailer…" Steve had decided that he was going to build the house on the 'cash as we go plan.' Martha said they were extremely cramped in the camper, but Steve was the head of the family and his decision for their family was final. He built two outbuildings for the family. One of the buildings was a bathroom and the other was a kitchen. The buildings were built under the same roof but with separate entrances, and the structure was built fifty to one hundred feet away from the camper. He promised his family that he would build the house by February 1993. Martha recalled that Steve didn't pour the concrete for the structure until February 1993. Meanwhile, his family had to live in very cramped living conditions. Martha explained to Bill that Steve had yet to finish the house. This was the house where they were living until a couple of weeks ago, when she caught Steve molesting Tori. She stated that he was building a two-story residence with a two-story workshop, all under one roof. Until she caught him, she had just been wishing he would hurry and get the residential part of the structure finished so she could move out of the cramped quarters of the camper. She missed the spaciousness of her old house.

As Martha and Bill talked, Martha frequently referred to a yellow notepaper tablet that she brought with her to the interview. Bill had told Martha, when he talked with her after Tori's two-day statement, to get a 'yellow tablet' and write down everything she could think of that would help jog her memory when she came in to give her statement. Her notes seemed to be paying off because her statement was quite detailed. Martha remembered that one of the reasons Steve wanted Tori to stay home that Wednesday night instead of going to church was to help him finish up some woodwork in the residential part of the house. He planned to go to West Texas to Buck Sturlock's ranch on the upcoming weekend. Steve did some cabinet work in Buna, Texas, for Buck, and he was interested in having Steve do some extensive work for him on a ranch he owned in Jeff Davis County. Martha continued referring to her notes as Bill typed her affidavit. She told of one instance where her 1982 Mercedes vehicle was taken to a mechanic shop for some repairs. The vehicle was to be sold after the repairs, so that she could get another vehicle. The repairs were made but the vehicle sat on the mechanic's shop for over a year, waiting for a buyer. Martha said that as she looked back, she realized this was a ploy. Except when she and the children were allowed to use Steve's truck, they were trapped with no transportation at the dead-end of a rural road. It was just another way for them to be isolated from the world.

Martha told Bill it was necessary for her to meet with Steve on several occasions regarding issues resulting from their divorce proceedings. Martha said that she always made sure several other people were present for safety purposes. One of those occasions was on July 17, the day before Steve was arrested by Hardin County deputies for his molestation of Tori in that county. She told Bill that during their encounter, Steve made several statements like "I know I've done wrong." He also said, "Satan makes your worst nightmares come true." That night, Steve also stated, "I told you I never wanted a daughter." During their conversation, Martha said Steve told her he knew there had never been any penetration during these incidents with Tori. His defiance returned.

Martha ended her lengthy affidavit by stating that she hoped and prayed that charges were filed against Steve for what he did to their daughter over the past seven years. She then read the nine-page affidavit that she gave over a period of two days. It was lengthy but concise. It gave the history and chronology needed to tell a complete story. Bill took

Martha's affidavit with the same thought process that he took with Tori's – gathering sufficient detail and covering their entire story involving multiple jurisdictions. Bill had taken on a burden that few detectives would dream of. Most detectives would investigate issues in their jurisdiction and leave the victim and their family to travel to the other locations and tell their story over and over. Bill removed the burden from Tori's and Martha's shoulders. He would complete the investigation, make copies of everything, and send a complete packet of criminal documentation against Steve to each jurisdiction involved. It was possible that Steve could be criminally charged for molesting Tori in four jurisdictions in Texas – Hardin County, Jasper County, Jeff Davis County, and Jefferson County. Martha gave a sigh of relief as she completed her signature on the affidavit. Her affidavit had taken two days to complete, as had Tori's. The days had not been concurrent because of other investigations that also demanded Bill's attention, but it was finally complete. Bill notarized the document. It was done. It was August 10, 1994.

Chapter Thirteen

Happy Birthday Bill

During the days that Bill was busy taking Martha's statement, Rick was busy getting the statements he agreed to obtain. Buck Sturlock appeared in Rick's office on August 4 to give his statement to help piece that part of the puzzle together. Buck accumulated his financial wealth the old fashioned way – he worked for it. He worked hard all his life. He entered a partnership with a friend and purchased a service station on the highway to a timber mill. But there wasn't enough work for both men, so Buck bought out his partner. Profits were a little better than expected and Buck began buying up land between his service station and the mill.

A spontaneous combustion fire started inside the mill, at the bottom of a gigantic woodchip pile. The mill's insurer needed the unburned woodchips moved in order to get to the fire and put it out before the fire burned down the multi-million dollar facility. Insurance agents looked no further than the man who owned the small service station a short distance away and who serviced many of the log-hauling semi trucks and trailers that went in and out of the mill on a daily basis. The insurer wanted to lease Buck's land. He asked if they had a contractor to move the woodchips to his property. They did not. Buck saw the opportunity to not only make money leasing his land but also in moving the woodchip pile to his property. Buck landed the contract on both accounts.

Buck contracted every dump truck driver he could find to move the woodchips. He and his drivers and crane operators worked around the clock. The huge pile of woodchips was moved in a matter of days. The fire was extinguished and the mill was saved. After the fire was out, the mill wanted their woodchips back. Buck was just the man to move the woodchips once again. The project made him wealthy overnight.

Buck loved flying and had taken lessons. Part of the property Buck bought around his service station was an old airstrip that had been used by the mill but was no longer needed by the company. After receiving his pilot's license, he refurbished the landing strip and bought his first plane. It was a fast turbo-prop, single engine, six-seat airplane.

Buck also loved West Texas. His first ranch was just outside Marfa, Texas. It was only 15,000 acres, fairly small according to West Texas standards. In a matter of weeks, Buck had a landing strip on his ranch that ran parallel to U.S. Hwy. 90 and bordered the northern fence line of his property. Now his plane made it very time efficient for him to travel between his home and business in Buna and his ranch. Instead of twelve to thirteen hours of hard driving between his home and ranch, Buck now made the trip in less than three hours of flying time.

A couple of years later, another ranch came up for sale. This ranch was 35,000 acres. It was north of U.S. Hwy. 90 and located at the top of one of the Davis Mountains. At an auction in Jeff Davis County, Buck ended up being the top bidder for this very secluded property. He now owned two ranches. It would take some time, but he knew this was where he eventually wanted to move. Some of this second ranch was so desolate that it had not been disturbed, probably since God had created it. This ranch also had a round concrete cistern on it. It was originally used to collect rain water for cattle, horses, and wild animals. Buck's vision was to turn this huge circular piece of concrete into a hunting lodge for paying hunters to come to his ranch and hunt deer and elk. All he needed to do was find a competent contractor willing to spend several months on his ranch working on the lodge's construction.

In his statement, Buck stated he met Steve through an advertisement Steve placed in the newspaper selling some safes. Buck bought some of the safes and did not have any contact with Steve for about a year. Buck said Steve showed up at his Buna office one day and he hired Steve to do some cabinet work in one of the offices. While Steve was busy with that project, Buck mentioned his West Texas ranch to Steve and said he would like to have a lodge built. Steve was immediately interested in the project. Buck explained that the project would probably take about three years to complete and the living conditions were nothing like life in Southeast Texas. Buck said the ranch had limited living facilities and was quite a distance from civilization. Steve told Buck that his two children were home schooled and living in such a remote location would be no problem. Buck told Rick in his sworn statement that he flew Steve and his son to the ranch in his private airplane and let them look over the ranch and the work he wanted done. Buck said Steve liked the thought of living in such a remote location and wanted to show the ranch to his wife and daughter. Buck continued by saying that Steve went back to the ranch with his entire family during the July 4th weekend. This was about five weeks prior to Buck giving his affidavit to Rick. Buck said it seemed that everyone liked the ranch. Buck told Rick about the last time he and Steve talked, and they discussed a timetable for moving his wife and kids to the ranch. Buck stated that was when Steve told him, "She left me." Steve told Buck that Martha filed for divorce claiming he had beaten her and abused Tori. But, of course, Steve denied the allegations to Buck. Buck told Rick that Steve's divorce didn't bother him as long as he was able to do the work at the ranch that he was hiring him to do. Rick asked Buck about a tan jacket and a vehicle that Steve and his family had access to during their visit to the ranch on July 4th, and a dark brown naugahyde-type booth seat that was mentioned in Tori's statement. Buck stated the coat was kept in the vehicle he let Steve use because the weather at the ranch could turn nasty very quickly. He also stated that the dark brown naugahyde booth seats came from a beer joint that closed down on Hwy. 96, and he bought all of the booths in the place for the lodge he planned to have built. Rick completed Buck's statement, and Buck read the document and then signed it. Their interview ended with Rick telling Buck that investigators would need to visit the ranch within a few days.

  On August 6, Martha left June's house and drove to Bill's office to complete her affidavit, and June transported Luke to Kountze to give Rick his statement. Rick noticed that Luke was very quiet-spoken, even timid for a fourteen year-old young man. As he took Luke's statement, Rick began to feel sorry for the youngster. Luke said he used to have lots of fun with his dad. He told Rick that when he was about seven years old and Tori was about four years old that his dad started being mean to him and extra nice to Tori. He told Rick he noticed his dad spending lots of time alone with Tori. He would take her to the two warehouses on Martin Street and they would be gone for a very long time. Luke said he tried to catch his dad and Tori together because he felt something was wrong, but he could never catch them. When they moved to the one-hundred-twenty-five acre place in Hardin County, Luke explained that they had two four-wheelers. He said on many occasions Tori and his dad would take off on both four-wheelers to wooded parts of their property. He told Rick he would run as fast as he could to stay up with them but he couldn't. He said they would be gone for long periods of time and he always felt their dad was doing something wrong to Tori. Luke said that even when they went to Mr. Sturlock's ranch, his dad and Tori would stay gone for long periods of time. When they returned, he asked what they had been doing and his dad said he'd been teaching Tori to drive. Luke said he always felt something wrong was going on between his dad and Tori, and even though, in his own little way he tried to protect his little sister, he felt that he had failed her.

The next morning, Thursday, August 8, Bill sipped his usual morning cup of black coffee as he phoned the police department's I.D. unit. Angela Stone answered and agreed to meet Bill at the two warehouses on Martin Street and the residence at 8890 Rosewood Street. Bill wanted photos of the various places at these locations where Tori stated her dad had sex with her. Angela was accompanied by another I.D. technician, Sharon Pate. They met Bill at 649 Martin Street where the manager of the business, Craig Warner, invited them in. The couch that had been located in the back storeroom was gone, but the storeroom, the ramp, and other locations in the building were just as Tori had described. Angela and Sharon took several photographs of the locations Tori described in her affidavit as being places where her father had sexually molested her. Meanwhile, Bill visited with Mr. Warner and asked about the couch. It seems that when Mr. Warner and his company leased the building from Steve, the couch had become moldy and they had thrown it away. As Sharon and Angela finished their photos, Bill and the I.D. techs went to the next location, 546 Martin Street. A furniture store had leased this warehouse from Steve. Bill spoke with the building manager and explained the need for photos to be taken of locations within the warehouse where Steve had molested

Tori. The manager immediately began worrying about adverse publicity toward his property. Bill assured him there was not going to be publicity about this case in the local media. Nonetheless, Bill, Angela and Sharon waited for the manager to take down every sign that displayed the name of his business. The manager had evidently watched too many police shows on TV, and was worried the name of his business may appear in one of the photos and ultimately be shown on the local 6:00 p.m. news. He may have even thought that one of the photos taken by the I.D. ladies may also appear on the 5:30 p.m. national news. Bill smiled and shook his head as he patiently watched the manager take down signs and banners. With all identifying signs removed, Sharon and Angela went about the job of taking photographs.

As information accumulated regarding the case, Bill was able to begin painting a picture in his mind of this man named Steve Carpenter. Steve wasn't all that different from other child molesters that Bill had investigated. He was a control freak and excellent at manipulating situations to his perverted advantage. During interviews with other victims and perpetrators, Bill had learned that the profiles of many child sexual victims and their perpetrators are very similar to the profiles in this case – just different names and faces.

Bill and the I.D. duo went next to 8890 Rosewood Street. Bill rang the doorbell and Crystal Roosevelt opened the door a few seconds later. She invited them in and Bill explained that, as a legal formality, he would need her to sign a 'consent form' allowing them to take photos of her residence. He explained that the photos could possibly be used as evidence in Steve's trial in Jefferson County. Crystal quickly signed the forms. She then cordially showed them her house. As they went through the residence, Bill constantly referred to Tori's affidavit. As they entered various rooms of the house, Bill would advise Angela and Sharon if the room needed to be photographed or passed over. With the photographs completed for this location in Tori's affidavit, they thanked Crystal and bade her a good day.

The case was slowly coming together. Sharon and Angela would have the photos from the two warehouses and the Rosewood Street house developed the next day. It was now time to concentrate on the Hardin County property. Bill knew Steve was not going to sign a 'Waiver of Search' form and let Bill and other officers search his property voluntarily. Bill thought about getting Martha to sign a waiver, but, he knew a signed waiver from Martha would not hold up in court because she had physically moved out of the house. Even though she and Steve were still married and the house was, by Texas law, community property, the only legal option to search the property was to obtain a search warrant. In order to cover all of the physical details of the house that would need to be included in an affidavit for a search warrant that would be reviewed by a judge, Bill would need to physically see the house. However, the way the house was situated on the property, it would be difficult, if not impossible, to see all details of the house, all of the out-buildings that would need to be searched, as well as areas on the one-hundred-twenty-five acres of land containing areas where Steve may have molested his daughter. There was another way to get the information needed for the search warrant.

Bill called his friend, Sgt. Micah Lytle. Bill and Micah began their law enforcement career with the Beaumont Police Department on the same day, June 6, 1972. Both men spent several years 'working the streets' in the patrol division. They both studied for months for their sergeant's exam. It's not a matter of a pass or fail exam, but how one 'places' that determines promotion. Both men were promoted to the rank of sergeant and became detectives within the department's detective division. Micah was a detective in the division's Property Unit while Bill was a sex crimes detective in the Special Crimes Unit.

Micah had a particular passion in his life that he began nurturing long before his law enforcement days began. It was a love for flying. Micah had been flying since he was a teenager. Now, he was not only licensed as a fixed wing pilot, but also a helicopter pilot. The police department had both types of aircraft. The fixed wing aircraft was a Cessna Centurion 210. It had been remodeled from six to five seats. In its former life, the plane was used to traffic drugs from Belize to the United States. The plane was confiscated by the U.S. Attorney's office and later given to the Beaumont Police Department. The helicopter was manufactured by Bell Helicopter, Inc. for the U.S. military. It was an OH-58 Kiowa helicopter but had the modifications of the 206B Jet Ranger helicopter. This particular four-seat helicopter had seen action in the Vietnam War, but it was now a surplus aircraft. It was decommissioned by the Army, but it was still a very good helicopter for law enforcement use. Only the Beaumont Police Department used the fixed wing aircraft. Beaumont P.D. shared costs, maintenance, and use of the helicopter with the Jefferson County Sheriff's Department in a co-agency agreement.

Bill explained his need for aerial photographs. Micah checked his schedule and the weather. The next morning with clear skies forecasted was three days away, on Monday, August 11. Micah adjusted his Monday schedule to accommodate Bill's request.

Monday, August 11, was a beautiful day. It was also Bill's 47th birthday. Micah's philosophy was simple – any clear day with light winds was a great day for flying. Bill met Micah at the Southeast Texas Regional Airport at 9:00 a.m. The helicopter was housed in a special security hangar. Bill helped Micah roll the helicopter outside the hangar and then stood back as Micah went through his pre-flight checklist. This consisted of checking the outside of the helicopter thoroughly. Micah climbed into the helicopter's cockpit and began checking the craft's instruments. When the final item was checked off the list, Micah gave the word and Bill climbed aboard. Getting to ride in a helicopter had always been an item on Bill's bucket list. To make the ride even better, it was also a pretty great birthday present from Bill to himself. Micah lifted off and headed north.

Micah ascended the helicopter to the proper altitude that had been designated by the controller at the Southeast Texas Regional Airport. Bill gave Micah the address and Micah began to follow the roads and highways below into Hardin County. Micah followed U.S. Hwy. 96 northward through Lumberton, continuing through Silsbee and then turned west as he followed U.S Hwy. 418. Bill was enjoying the view. He recognized his pastor's house located on U.S. Hwy. 418 as they flew over the top of the residence. His pastor, Ralph, enjoyed hosting crawfish boils for his church members. They continued in a westerly direction until Bill recognized the "T" intersection of U.S. Hwy. 418 and Summers Road. Micah lowered the altitude of the helicopter as he turned north following the rural road. It was a dead-end road approximately one and one-half miles long. As the road came to an end, Steve and Martha Carpenter's house and land was to the right. The house could not be seen from Summers Road, but was quite visible from Micah and Bill's vantage point in the helicopter. Micah began flying the helicopter in a wide circle around the house as Bill busied himself taking several photos of the house and out-buildings with the camera he borrowed from the department's I.D. Bureau. Micah increased altitude and Bill took several more photos to show the relationship of the house to Steve and Martha's undeveloped one-hundred-twenty-five acres. Bill wanted to show this undeveloped land that adjoined the house and yard. Tori had stated in her affidavit that her daddy enjoyed taking her on their four-wheelers into the wooded area of their land and having sex with her. Bill wanted to show the relationship of this land to the residence in his photos. The helicopter was quite noisy, and neighbors on Summers Road began coming out of their houses and looking at the helicopter circling the Carpenter residence. As Micah continued flying in wide circles around the house, Bill commented to Micah that the neighbors must be wondering what in the world was going on. Bill took several more photos and then turned to Micah and told him he had enough to get his search warrant. Micah straightened out their flight path from circles to flying in a southerly direction. It was time to head back to the hangar. Both detectives had plenty of work waiting for them back at the police station.

  The flight back to the airport hangar was equally as beautiful as the flight going north. Micah landed the helicopter on the tarmac in front of the hangar. Within a few minutes, he and Bill put the helicopter back on its dolly and pushed it into the hangar. Micah lowered the hangar door and locked it. The two friends returned to their detective cars and drove toward the police station.

  As Bill was driving to the station, he received a call on his cell phone. He answered and recognized the voice of Bobby Palmer, chief deputy with the Hardin County Sheriff's Department. Ben Moore had kept his boss informed of the ongoing investigation between the two agencies. Bill and Bobby were long-time friends and Bill smiled as Bobby asked him if he had been doing a 'recon' around Summers Road. Bill laughed and confessed that he'd been caught. Bobby told Bill the sheriff's dispatchers received several phone calls from residents in the area wondering what was going on. Bill told Bobby he would have the photos developed (digital cameras were not on the market at the time) at the I.D. Bureau while he worked on the paperwork for the search warrant. Bill advised Bobby he wanted to serve the search warrant the next morning. Bobby told Bill he would have plenty of deputies on hand to assist in serving Steve with the search warrant.

Bill arrived at his office and filled his cup with some freshly brewed coffee. He pounded the keyboard to his computer and had the 'search warrant affidavit' completed before lunch. After a quick bite, Bill walked across the railroad tracks to the district attorney's office. A good friend and great prosecutor, Randy Martinez, was in the outer office as Bill entered the waiting area. The friends exchanged greetings and Bill asked Randy if he had a moment to look at the 'search warrant affidavit.' Randy wasn't in trial at the moment and escorted Bill to his office. Bill gave the prosecutor a quick synopsis of the case and the reason for needing the search warrant. Randy agreed that the warrant was needed and he carefully critiqued the document. Randy commented that he would love to try this case in court. He completed his review of the affidavit, handed it to Bill, and said he thought it was a good document.

The Carpenter property was located in Hardin County, so Bill drove to Kountze to the Hardin County Courthouse. Bill called Ben Moore on the way to the courthouse. He needed Ben's help in getting a judge to look at the affidavit and issue a search warrant. Bill entered the reception area of the sheriff's department at the courthouse and asked for Ben. He came from the back offices a few minutes later. Ben had already notified a judge of their need for a search warrant, so the two men climbed the stairs to the second floor of the courthouse. District Judge Leon Garner arose from behind his desk and shook hands with the detectives. After visiting for a few minutes, Judge Garner asked Bill what brought him north of Beaumont. Bill handed the affidavit to the judge and gave a quick synopsis of the case he and Ben were investigating and their need for a search warrant. Judge Garner read the affidavit as Bill and Ben sat quietly. "Good enough," the judge stated as he finished reading the document. Those two words told Bill he had sufficiently shown more than enough 'probable cause' in his affidavit for the judge to issue the search warrant. The judge called a secretary into his office and explained what he needed to be typed onto the search warrant. A few minutes later, the search warrant was brought to the judge. He scrutinized this document just as he had the affidavit. Finally being satisfied that everything was in order, Judge Garner signed the warrant. By law, Bill and Ben had a maximum of seventy-two hours to serve the search warrant on Steve from that moment.

As Bill and Ben exited the judge's office, Ben turned to his friend and said, "Let's go." Bill knew Ben was ready to go to the Carpenter residence and serve Steve with the warrant as quickly as they could drive to Summers Road. Bill had been at the courthouse most of the afternoon and he looked at his watch to check the time. It was 4:00 p.m. and it was his birthday. Bill's wife and fourteen-year-old son planned to celebrate this birthday with supper at his favorite restaurant with a chocolate cake and hopefully a present or two. He explained the circumstances to Ben and both agreed to serve the warrant the next morning.

Bill arrived at his office around 4:30 p.m. He checked for any phone calls needing a returned call before leaving for the day. Bill was a stickler for returning telephone calls, and it was a pet peeve. He didn't like to call someone, leave a message for them to return his call, and then have that person not be professional or courteous enough to call back. To Bill, that was downright rude. Fortunately, there were no messages on his desk. He locked his office door and walked to Lindsey's office. She had no messages for him either. He bade her 'goodbye' and told her he was going to get a few minutes' head start on his birthday celebration.

Fifteen minutes later, Bill was at home and changing into something more casual. Bill and his wife and son were walking out the door to go to dinner, and his cell phone rang. He recognized Bobby Palmer's voice as he answered. Andy told Bill that he needed to get to the Carpenter residence right away with the search warrant. Bill told

Bobby it was his birthday and he and his family were walking out the door to celebrate. Bobby informed Bill that his deputies and an ambulance had just arrived at Steve's house. Steve shot himself, and someone, possibly a neighbor called 911, and an ambulance and a deputy had arrived at his house moments later. Bill knew what he had to do. He had no choice. He told his wife and son to go and enjoy celebrating his birthday at his favorite restaurant without him. He got in his detective car and drove north.

Bill was in the car only a few seconds when his cell phone rang. It was Martha. Bill could hear her voice quivering as she asked if he knew that Steve shot himself. Bill told her about Bobby's call and that he was on the way to their house as they were speaking. He could only imagine what was running through her mind as she described a phone call from Steve to her cell phone. She was outside June's residence when the call rang to her phone, which was inside the house. June answered the call from Steve a short time earlier. Martha told Bill that Steve began the conversation pleading with June to get Martha to talk to Tori and get her to recant her story. In Martha's words, Steve told June he had been in prayer all day and that God had forgiven him and he needed for his family to forgive him too so they could all be together once again and live happily ever after. Martha said June told Steve "You're asking the wrong person." It was fine to ask for and receive God's forgiveness, but he also was going to answer to the law for what he had done to his daughter. Martha thought the tone of June's voice was odd when she said "You're asking the wrong person." She would find out why later. Martha said that Steve continued to beg for everyone to get Tori to recant her story. He made the statement that it was Tori's fault if their family was torn apart because of her refusal to tell the police that she lied about him molesting her. Martha said it made her angry for Steve to insinuate that everything was Tori's fault. Bill told Martha that Steve was a master manipulator. Most child molesters are quite good at manipulating innocent and naïve members of their family, as well as many people in their community. Martha's voice continued shaking as she told Bill that Steve told June that he would kill himself if he couldn't have his family back together. Bill told Martha he would call her when he arrived at their house. He knew that residence had long ceased being a 'home.'

Several plain and uniform cars from the Hardin County Sheriff's Department were parked at the Carpenter residence when Bill arrived. He found Bobby Palmer and was told that Steve went to a neighbor to call for help. He had already been placed in an ambulance and was on the way to St. Elizabeth Hospital. Bill asked how bad Steve had wounded himself. Bobby described a shoulder wound. The chief deputy stated it did not appear that Steve was trying to commit suicide, but rather, it appeared he was trying to invoke sympathy. Bill told Bobby of the conversation he had with Martha on his drive to the residence, which reaffirmed Bobby's thoughts.

Bill had the search warrant in his pocket for Steve's residence. The warrant covered not only the residential structure, but also the outbuildings, and the entire one-hundred-twenty-five acres of property. Bill had planned to serve Steve with the warrant the next morning, after he enjoyed his birthday dinner and evening with his family. But that plan was blown. It was time to serve the document.

Bill briefed all of the officers and deputies present regarding the contents of the search warrant. Everyone needed to look for any and all evidence of Tori's sexual abuse. Officers received their assignments and dispersed from the meeting in the front yard of the residence. Teams of officers spread out covering the one-hundred-twenty-five acre wooded area. They were looking for a needle in a haystack. They were looking for any possible clue of Steve sexually molesting Tori at certain locations. They were looking for an indention in the ground on one of the many trails throughout the wooded area where Steve had buried a tissue he used to wipe himself after molesting Tori. Photos were taken throughout the house, especially the upstairs bathroom where he had last molested Tori. Photos were also taken of the camper the family lived in until construction on the house finally allowed it to be habitable.

Darkness began to set in and caused the officers in the wooded area to finally call off their search. They found indented places on some of the trails. The indentions could have easily been caused by Steve jamming his heel in the ground and burying a tissue. But the tissue was nowhere to be found. It could have been torn apart by birds building nests or a raccoon taking it as a prize. Just because the tissue could not be found, it did not deter the officers from believing Tori's story.

Deputies, officers, and I.D. technicians slowly called back into service and left the residence. Bill and Bobby were ready to leave. Bill removed Steve's copy of the search warrant and placed it on the credenza just inside the front door. They locked and closed the front door. The house was secure. They had done all they could do to find the truth in the case at this location. Tomorrow was another day. And there was much more work to be done on the case.

Bill arrived at his home. His wife and son had returned from enjoying his birthday dinner. He smiled as he saw his chocolate birthday cake on the counter with a couple of pieces missing. He was starving. They had gotten him a great meal. It was in the fridge in a 'to go' box. After a few seconds in the microwave, the food was ready and Bill was enjoying his dinner. It was quite an interesting birthday and definitely one he would remember.

Chapter Fourteen

Road Trip

On Tuesday morning, August 13, Bill arrived at his office and settled behind his desk for the day's work with a cup of black coffee. Monday had been quite a day. All of the day's events had to be documented in his supplementary report for the case. But, before he started typing, he called St. Elizabeth Hospital to check how Steve was doing from his gunshot wound. Steve was not there. He had been checked out of the hospital and transferred to John Sealy Hospital in Galveston due to his lack of insurance. Bill called John Sealy and went through their stringent security network to learn Steve would be a patient there for several days. Bill also learned that Steve's lung nearest the gunshot wound collapsed on the way to Galveston from Beaumont. After Bill's call to Galveston, it was time for him to get busy pounding on the computer keyboard.

Bill's phone rang about mid-morning and he was glad for the break. It was Rick Lucas. He heard about Steve shooting himself and Bill filled him in with the details, including being transferred to John Sealy Hospital and the collapsed lung. If Steve was looking for sympathy from these two investigators, he was looking in the wrong place. Bill also told Rick they couldn't find the tissue in the woods and so they had mainly taken photos to document locations inside and outside the residence where Tori said Steve molested her. Rick then said, "Well, I guess it's time for a road trip." He told Bill about the information he'd gotten through Buck Sturlock's statement. Both investigators agreed that every piece of corroborating evidence they could muster would help seal Steve's judicial coffin. They also agreed that Steve was willing to do anything to get himself off the hook. Both of them remarked about Martha's resolve to not give in to Steve's pity party. They were proud of her and wished more mothers were this protective of their children.

Every detective loves a good 'road trip' when he can verify to his supervisors that it is needed in pursuit of an investigation. Beaumont P.D. had one particular detective that was notorious for finding ways to incorporate road trips into his investigations. His nickname was 'Interpol Allen.'

Bill walked to the other side of the second floor of the police station looking for his pilot, Micah Lytle. Micah was in his cubicle working on some of the cases he was assigned to investigate. Bill told Micah about the potential road trip. The pilot checked the long-term weather forecast against his schedule. The next Monday, August 19, looked like a good time to fly. Now all Bill needed to do was get his road trip okayed by the 'brass.'

Bill gave his Lieutenant, Chad Brown, an update on the case every day because it was so extensive. Chad was always in for a 'road trip' and he tried to figure out a way so he could go too.

A lot of work had to be done the next few days. Bill knew he would be gone the first three days of next week, so he stayed busy for the day updating the files of the many other cases he was assigned to investigate.

Bill was about to leave for lunch on Thursday, August 15, when he received a call from Martha. Her voice was shaking as she told Bill about two bouquets of flowers that were delivered to June's house. One bouquet was delivered for Tori and the other bouquet was for her. The receipt for the flowers was attached to Martha's bouquet. The bouquets were ordered at 9:49 a.m., on Monday, August 12, the day Steve shot himself. It had dawned on June that if Steve had killed himself the bouquets would have been delivered, in all probability, on the day of his funeral. If he had not killed himself, it would be Steve's hopeful way of seeking pity from Martha and Tori and getting Tori to recant her story. It was more of Steve's manipulation. Bill calmed Martha and told her about his conversation with Rick Lucas and their plans to go to Buck Sturlock's ranch on Monday. He assured her that he and Rick were doing everything they could, as fast as they could, so that he could present his case to the Jefferson County District Attorney and get another warrant on Steve. Her voice calmed. She knew Bill was doing everything possible to put Steve behind bars again. She knew she must stay strong.

Bill continued work on some of his other cases for the rest of the week, and it was 5:00 p.m. Friday before he realized it. There never seemed to be enough time each week to adequately investigate the cases he and other detectives were assigned to solve.

Bill and Micah met at the police station on Monday morning and drove to the hangar at Beaumont Municipal Airport where the Cessna Centurion 210 was kept. Rick arrived at the hangar while Micah was completing the final check of the plane. Luggage was stowed in the rear of the plane. It was pretty obvious that Rick's long legs dictated that he would stretch out across two of the back seats while Bill rode up front with Micah. The weather was beautiful – not a cloud in the sky. It was a great day for flying. A few minutes later they were airborne and westward bound.

The plane's headphones allowed the three men to talk back and forth as they flew. The clear sky made the men marvel at how beautiful everything was at 10,000 feet. The plane did not have an air conditioning system, however, Micah maintained an altitude where the air circulating through the aircraft's ventilation system was a comfortable temperature. Bill looked over his shoulder and Rick's six-foot-ten-inch frame spanned the width of the plane. Rick was holding a fancy looking camera and he would take photos periodically. Bill mentioned the camera and learned that Rick was a photography buff. He had also brought the camera along to take photos of possible evidence found while on the trip. Much of their flight time was spent without talking. They were enjoying the beauty of the Texas landscape.

Micah directed the plane toward Del Rio. A couple of hours later, he descended the plane and landed at the Del Rio International Airport. People might think the airport is a large facility because it is listed as an international airport. In reality, it is a small commercial, non-hub airport with flights that do fly into Mexico. The aircraft needed refueling and everyone welcomed the opportunity to stretch their legs. Except for Rick, of course, whose legs were stretched across the fuselage throughout the flight. As the trio was climbing back into the plane to disembark, Rick made an interesting request. He asked Micah if he could fly along the northern edge of the Rio Grande as they flew toward Buck Sturlock's ranch. They learned that Rick was also a canoeing buff and belonged to a canoeing club. He told Bill and Micah that he had probably canoed the Rio Grande thirty times, but he had never had the opportunity to photo the river from the air. "No problem," Micah replied as they settled in once more.

A few hours earlier, the men left the flat plain of Southeast Texas behind and now they were viewing the mountainous and rugged terrain of the Rio Grande River from above without ever leaving their great state. As Micah gained altitude and began to fly west northwest, they looked out of the plane and could see the beautiful Amistad Lake. They flew west of the lake and Micah kept the plane a few hundred yards north of the Rio Grande River. Rick was busy taking photographs of the canyons that outcropped into the river. Rick began calling out the names of the canyons to Micah and Bill. He said his canoe club had paddled the river many times and they had often gotten out of their canoes and hiked into many of the canyons, marveling at their beauty. One of the canyons' names stood out from the rest – Rattlesnake Canyon. As they continued their journey, Micah told the others that they were on radar. He said that both the Mexican government and the U.S. government were probably tracking their plane, not knowing if they were drug dealers or who they were. Micah pointed out the top of a plateau. It looked like a highway about 200 to 300 yards in length with a beginning and an ending. Micah told them it was a drug distribution air strip.

Their flight continued along the northern edge of the river until the river took a southwestern turn toward the Big Bend National Park. Big Bend is one of the least visited national parks in the United States. Yet, it is one of the most beautiful but rugged parks in the country. If a person wanted to get away from the hustle and bustle of the big city or the daily grind and vacation in a wild, remote area of Texas and the United States, Big Bend National Park would be a great choice.

Micah kept the plane in a westerly direction until he saw a state highway going north and south. He knew this was U.S. Hwy 385. Buck Sturlock's directions were for them to go to Marfa, Texas. Micah continued in a westerly direction until he saw another north/south highway. By looking at his map, he knew this road was Hwy. 118. He continued westbound flying over Turkey Peak. A few minutes later he arrived at another north/south highway. He knew this was U.S. Hwy. 67. He turned the plane northbound and saw the small town of Marfa straight ahead. As Micah flew over Marfa, he turned the plane eastward along U.S. Hw. 90. This is the same U.S. 90 that runs east and west through Beaumont. It was hard to believe that they had left the Beaumont Municipal Airport beside U.S. Hwy. 90, where the elevation was sixteen feet above sea level and they were now on the same highway in Marfa, where the now on the same highway in Marfa, where the elevation was over 4,000 feet above sea level, and, they were still in Texas.

After turning right on U.S. 90, Buck Sturlock's directions were for them to look for a runway that parallels the south side of U.S. Hwy. 90, about two miles east of Marfa. The runway was on his ranch. The directions were clear enough. A few seconds after turning east, Micah spotted the runway. It was not made of concrete or asphalt. Rather, it was a dirt runway that had been leveled and smoothed for landings and departures of small aircraft. Micah made a flyover to determine if one end of the runway was better than the other for landings. A few minutes later, Micah guided the plane as it touched down on the western end of the runway. The plane was safely on the ground. It was 12:30 p.m.

The western end of the runway had a hangar and Buck Sturlock's plane was safely stored inside. Cell phones were not a common commodity at the time. Buck Sturlock had been told they would arrive around noon, but was nowhere to be seen. So, the wait began. At 1:00 p.m., the detectives were getting a little concerned, and they were getting pretty hungry. The airplane was their only means of transportation. They weren't in a position where they could traipse down to a local restaurant in Marfa for a bite to eat.

The crew-cab one-ton dually truck came from the backside of the mountain just south of the runway. Two men got out and shook hands with the detectives. Rick and Sturlock knew each other and shook hands. Everyone else introduced themselves. Sturlock said they lost track of time because he and Jesus, his foreman and the other man in the truck, had been viewing his buffalo herd. He said this 15,000 acre ranch was named the Buffalo Gap Ranch, and he had a buffalo herd grazing on the other side of the mountain. Speaking of time, the detectives told Sturlock it was time to eat. They were starving. Sturlock didn't have a watch and asked for the time. It was 1:15 p.m. Sturlock told them to hop in the truck. They had to hurry because the only restaurant in town would close in fifteen minutes.

Sturlock parked in the dirt parking lot and everyone exited the truck and entered the restaurant. It was not a name brand chain restaurant. It was a family owned restaurant that served breakfast and lunch, and the men had barely made it. The grill was still on and hamburgers were ordered all the way around. A few minutes later, the men were chomping down on some of the best hamburgers, fries, onion rings, and sweet tea that could be served anywhere in Texas. Those burgers would have put most hamburger chain restaurants to shame. With their hunger quenched, the men exited the tiny restaurant a few minutes later. They were ready to head to Sturlock's 35,000 acre Davis Mountain Ranch. A little girl had been sexually molested there six weeks earlier and possible evidence was there waiting to be discovered.

Sturlock drove north on Hwy 17. The terrain was beautiful and rugged. The land was flat along Hwy. 17 with mountains in the background. The prairie grass was a golden color, probably from the lack of rain in this part of West Texas and the hot August days. The pasture to their right seemed to go on forever and animals could be seen a quarter of a mile away. Upon closer inspection, the men could see that these animals weren't cattle, they were pronghorn antelope. The detectives stared at these magnificent creatures. This was an animal that was not seen in Southeast Texas. They continued north through the small but historic town of Fort Davis. It would have been fun to visit the historic sites in the West Texas town, but, duty called. A couple of miles later, Sturlock turned through a gate onto private property. He was asked if this was his ranch, and he replied, no, they would go through three separate ranches before they got to his. He explained that these ranch owners had to give a right-of-way through their ranches in order for him to get to get to his ranch.

The road to Davis Mountain Ranch was made of mountain gravel and rock. Only one vehicle could traverse it at a time. It was smooth occasionally but quite rough most of the way. As Sturlock headed the truck higher and higher up the mountainous terrain of Casket Mountain, he pointed out Star Mountain several miles away to their right. They passed a road maintaining machine that sat beside the road. Sturlock stopped and let Jesus out and then continued driving. He explained that the piece of equipment was his. He'd purchased it at a county auction in East Texas and then brought it here to help maintain his road to the ranch. Sturlock drove around one mountain curve and sitting on the side of the road was a beautiful mule deer buck chewing his cud as he relaxed beside a mountain tree shading him from the August sun. The men saw more and more deer as they continued their journey. They were nearing the front gate of the ranch when a herd of elk bolted from the watering trough beside the gate. Sturlock explained that throughout the entire Davis Mountain range in West Texas are resident herds of elk as well as mule and white tail deer. As they drove through the gate, Sturlock pointed out a corral that was beside a barn. He explained that he had a calf in the corral a couple of weeks ago but it had been killed by a cougar. The trip from Hwy. 17 had taken over one and one-half hours. They were near the peak of Black Mountain, elevation 7,544 feet above sea level.

  The ranch house was a simple structure. It was not a fancy structure. The steps going into the house had a small porch covering that had a hole in it. One of the bedrooms had bunk beds in it to accommodate several people. The rest of the house was simple, yet comfortable. Jesus had started a roast in the crock-pot that morning. Its aroma permeated throughout the house. The front yard was surrounded by a cyclone fence.

  Rick asked Sturlock which vehicle Steve used when his family visited the ranch about six weeks earlier. A green-colored Jeep was pointed out that was parked in a row of other vehicles beside the gate of the cyclone fence that led into the yard and to the front door of the residence. Bill and Rick walked with Sturlock to the convertible vehicle. In the back compartment of the vehicle lay a brown coarse fabric field jacket. Rick asked if this jacket stayed in the vehicle. Sturlock stated that it did. The jacket appeared to be an exact likeness to the jacket

Tori had described that her dad had gotten from the back of the vehicle and then placed it on top of the dusty booth seat at the building under construction where her dad had molested her on the ranch. Rick advised Sturlock that it was necessary to confiscate the jacket for evidence. Sturlock had no problem with it and Bill had him sign an evidence confiscation form acknowledging that his property was taken in furtherance of the criminal investigation against Steve.

Jesus arrived at the barn and ranch house on the road maintainer. After parking it beside the barn, he entered the residence to check on the roast and other items he was preparing for supper. It was too late to go to the lodge building under construction. It was only 5:00 p.m., but, it could get dark very quickly in the mountains. So, everyone grabbed a chair that was on the porch and enjoyed the beautiful, rugged mountain scenery. Jesus exited the house and walked to the barn. A few minutes later, he exited the barn toting a five-gallon bucket filled with something. He walked to a trough that was outside the fence of the front yard. None of the detectives had noticed the stainless steel vessel until Jesus began making a lot of noise as he poured the bucket's contents into the six-foot structure. Jesus put the bucket back in the barn and then went back in the house to check on supper. The detectives determined that Jesus had put out some feed for cattle or horses that were roaming in the pasture surrounding the house. About ten minutes later, Micah, Bill and Rick noticed little heads popping up on the horizon and down the hill from the house. The heads got larger and their bodies took form as they came closer to the house. It was a beautiful herd of mule deer. The largest was a five-by-five monster mule deer buck. He ambled up to the trough and began eating from the trough as did several mule deer does and a couple of yearling bucks. No one moved. Everyone marveled at the beauty of the wild animals only a few feet away that had come to supper like a domesticated herd of cattle. The herd of deer stayed at the trough until every grain of food was gone. Each of them slowly left the trough and ambled fifty to a hundred yards away. They laid on the ground and began chewing their cuds in peaceful bliss on the mountainside.

"Supper's ready," Jesus announced to everyone. No one had to tell these guys twice. The hamburgers of lunch were long gone. Everyone grabbed a seat at the dinner table and dug in. With supper coming to a close, everyone was groaning about having eaten too much. Jesus busied himself cleaning the table and washing the dishes. Everyone ambled back outside to marvel at the beauty of the light slowly fading away. The sky was magnificent as the stars began to shine. Everyone commented about how many more stars were visible at 7,000+ feet above sea level and with no city lights to dull the view.

Jesus was up before everyone Tuesday morning. The aroma of a hearty breakfast of bacon, eggs, biscuits and hot coffee had everyone out of their bunks in no time.

With breakfast out of the way, it was time for Bill and Rick to get busy. It was time to go to the partially-constructed lodge. Sturlock drove the detectives to the lodge building which was about two miles from the ranch house. Along the way, Sturlock stopped the vehicle beside a steep embankment along the road. He told them about falling down the ravine in a vehicle and almost dying there a couple of years earlier. After the story, they continued to the lodge building. Sturlock explained that the structure used to be a water cistern with a concrete wall about four feet high. It was used to feed and water cattle and horses on the ranch. A couple of years earlier, Sturlock had the idea of putting a metal roof over the cistern and enclosing it to make a rustic lodge to house hunters who paid to hunt on his ranch. The roof was partially complete. Someone had also begun to put up framework for doorways, and some lights, piped water, and other necessities had begun being put in place to make the structure livable. Rick got his camera and Bill got his notepad from Sturlock's vehicle. Sturlock was always a busy man with more things to do than he had time to do them. He told the detectives to do whatever they needed to do. He had to go and check on a waterline that was causing him some problems farther up the mountain. He would be back later to get them. Or, now that they knew the road between the house and lodge, they could walk back if he was not back in a timely manner to get them. With that, he drove off ascending the mountain.

The detectives got busy with what they do best, finding evidence and solving cases. Rick began taking photographs of the partially constructed lodge. His first photos were fifty to one hundred yards from the lodge. It was a large structure and Rick wanted to get the lodge in its entirety plus items that were within ten to twenty yards of the lodge's outer structure. It took him several minutes to walk around the lodge, taking several photos as he circled the building. As he finished the outer photos, he moved closer to what would become the windows of the lodge. He walked around the outer perimeter of the building taking photos from every window. When he finished this task, he and Bill entered the structure.

Rick took photos of the inside of the lodge from left to right as they entered the doorway. They had already seen the six booth-type seats positioned against the south inner wall of the lodge. Three tables were positioned between the booth seats, similar to being in a restaurant. The seats were covered with dark brown naugahyde, just as Tori had described. Rick moved to the center of the building. He turned from left to right, taking photos from the center of the building, looking outward. He and Bill now focused on the booth seats and tables. The seats were covered in a thick layer of dust. The two men looked closely at each seat. The dust on the seats was uniform in its covering, like a grayish-white blanket, that let the dark brown tint of the naugahyde material show through.

Looking at the seats from left to right, seat five was different. The layer of dust was disturbed, but it was not brushed as if someone had wiped the dust with a hand or some object. Rick and Bill could see that something had been placed on the seat and dust, and then removed. They looked very closely. Suddenly they both became ecstatic and could not believe their discovery. They could see the exact imprint of the seams of the coarse fabric coat that had been in the back of the Jeep that Steve had driven while touring the ranch. They could also see the outline of the two rows of stitching from a seam that was in the coat. Bill and Rick had just discovered the exact booth where Steve had placed the coat on the booth seat six weeks earlier, and layed back, made Tori climb on top of him, and he sexually abused her. The discovery was nothing short of a miracle. What were the odds that a hard rain or wind had not disturbed the dust where the coat had been placed? What were the odds that a squirrel or raccoon had not walked through the lodge and disturbed the dust where the coat had been placed?

Rick took several photos of the coat's image in the dust. One of the most notable photos was when Rick reached in his pocket and pulled out a nickel. He placed it beside the dust depicting the seam and stitches and took several photos. They did not have a tape measure with them, but the photos with the nickel next to the images in the dust gave their proper dimension. Bill then placed the jacket next to the images of the seams in dust. It was a perfect match. Rick took several more photos. The investigators knew they had to tell Tori's story to several district attorneys. If Steve was indicted in as many as four criminal jurisdictions, then Tori's story would possibly be told to four judges and juries. They knew photos were one of the best ways to tell Tori's story. The smiles on Bill and Rick's faces wouldn't go away. They had just put the final evidentiary nail in Steve's coffin.

Rick had planned ahead. He knew that an offense report and investigation needed to be made in reference to Tori's sexual molestation in Jeff Davis County. He contacted one of his Texas Dept. of Public Safety investigator colleagues, Trey Rogers. Trey was stationed out of the Midland, Texas, district office. He had a huge territory to cover in conducting and handling his investigative case load. Trey had to drive almost two hundred miles from his office just to reach Buck Sturlock's ranch, but he also knew he would get to see his long-time friend.

Satisfied that they had taken enough photos and enough measurements for their prosecution against Steve, the two men decided to leave the partially constructed lodge. Sturlock had not returned from his task of working on his water line, so Bill and Rick started walking toward the house. About a mile down the road, they heard Sturlock's jeep coming up behind them. He had completed his task. They climbed aboard and the three men headed for the house. It was time for lunch. Everyone hoped that Jesus had another great meal prepared.

As Bill, Rick, and Sturlock drove up to the ranch house, the aroma of lunch permeated the air. The men had just sat down to lunch when they heard a car approaching. Sturlock looked and saw a gray car come to a stop by the other vehicles outside the fence. Rick looked out the window and smiled. It was his friend, Trey. He made it in time for lunch. He opened the door and shook his friend's hand. Rick escorted Trey inside the house and introduced him to everyone at the table. Jesus set another place at the table for Trey. The conversation during lunch was quite lively with all sorts of stories being told.

Sturlock told the men he would like to show them his ranch after lunch. Bill, Rick, and Trey conducted their investigative meeting as soon as they each finished a scrumptious piece of Jesus's chocolate cake. Trey completed the paperwork necessary to file Tori's report in his jurisdiction. He said goodbye to everyone, especially his long-time friend Rick, and then he headed back down the ranch road. He had to get back to Midland. The other investigations he was working on demanded his time.

The three Southeast Texas detectives did not plan to return to Beaumont until the next morning. With lunch and police work out of the way, they were ready for Sturlock's tour. Sturlock switched vehicles for the ranch tour. He had modified a convertible four-wheel drive vehicle by putting a seat on top of the back compartment of the SUV. This new seat allowed the occupants to sit higher and see better than sitting in the traditional back seat. It also made the vehicle a little more top-heavy in the rear area of the vehicle. Sturlock drove with Micah riding shotgun. Bill and Rick took the elevated back seat.

Sturlock drove down one back road and then another. They traversed up one hill and then another. At one point Bill noticed something white against the green and brown foliage. Whatever it was looked to be at least two miles away from their vantage point on top of the mountain they were driving on. Sturlock explained that the white object was the roof of the partially constructed lodge they investigated that morning. Rick had his camera along and took several photos. The thought that struck Bill at that moment was there was nothing here for miles upon miles except mountainous terrain.

Steve had moved his family from a beautiful home on Rosewood Street in Beaumont to one-hundred-twenty-five acres at the dead-end of a rural road in Hardin County without a home to live in. They stayed in a cramped thirty-three foot RV camper so he could be in a more isolated area. Then Steve wanted to move them to West Texas to live in a vast area isolated by miles and miles of wilderness so he could have more control over his family and to continue his perverted deeds against his daughter. That was Steve's plan until Martha came home a little too early one evening a few weeks earlier. If he had not been caught that night, he may have been able to commit his deviant acts against Tori well into her adulthood. But that wouldn't happen now. He had been exposed.

After Rick had taken several photos of the lodge and its remoteness, Sturlock continued on the tour of his ranch. The terrain was rugged, yet beautiful. Sturlock would drive down a hill and through a dry creek bottom and then climb the embankment on the other side. It seemed like an easy task. But Bill and Rick's combined body weight made the vehicle a little back-end heavy. On several occasions, they would lean forward to put their weight in the center of the vehicle to keep it from flipping over backwards. Sturlock left the barely marked roadway on one occasion and drove about half-a-mile through a flat prairie area. He stopped and got out. It was time to stretch. He walked to a large hole in the ground and began telling the guys that he and his son had gone exploring one day and the hole opened into a cave. He said they explored the cave with long ropes tied to them for safety on several occasions, going deeper and deeper each time. He explained that it became apparent that the caves or caverns were quite deep and went for quite a distance underground. Sturlock said he got in touch with some people at the University of Texas in San Marcos. A team of spelunkers came to the ranch and investigated the caves. After extensive spelunking, the explorers concluded that the caves very possibly traveled underground, linking up with Carlsbad Caverns in New Mexico, a distance of almost two hundred miles.

Sturlock got everyone back in his SUV and they were off again. Several jackrabbits were spotted running to get out of the vehicle's way. A jenny-jackass and her newborn baby were spotted a few yards to the side of the road. She watched warily as the vehicle stopped long enough for Rick to take a couple of photos. About a quarter-mile down the road, they saw the jack. He was a typical stubborn jackass as he stood in the middle of the road. He never moved. Sturlock finally put the vehicle in gear and went around him. He must have figured that it was his road and anything and everything could just go around him.

The exploration trip continued several more miles. Toward the back of Sturlock's ranch, he showed his guests a residence on top of a mountain about three to four miles away. It looked like a medieval castle. Sturlock explained he was not sure exactly where his ranch boundaries were. He had never explored his entire ranch. Some parts of the ranch were inaccessible and may have never seen a human footprint since God created it, he explained. While they were admiring the castle several miles away, Sturlock noticed that the sky behind the castle was turning from a beautiful clear sky to a darker blue. He told the detectives they should probably start heading back to the ranch house because it looked like a storm was brewing. He turned the vehicle around and they began retracing their steps. The skyline behind them got darker and darker. Sturlock increased his speed where it was safe to do so. At one point, one of the men asked Sturlock what he was going to do if the storm hit before they got back to the ranch. West Texas storms can be very violent at times, and he said he would probably park the vehicle and all of them would squeeze under it to escape from the wind, rain, and possible hail. He then told them their next worry would be that the dry creek beds that they crossed earlier would now be swollen creeks and extremely dangerous to cross until the water subsided. With that explanation, he drove faster.

The clouds overtook them. It was about 5:00 p.m. but appeared to be after dark. Someone asked how far it was to the ranch house and Sturlock answered frankly that he didn't know. He was not that familiar with the road they were traveling. The wind began to pick up and at times was blowing thirty to forty miles per hour. Sturlock went around one more hill and the lights of the ranch house shown below. What a relief to everyone. Sturlock traversed down the hill and parked the vehicle next to the cyclone fence. Drops of rain were starting to fall as the men entered the ranch house. Less than two minutes later, the rain was coming down in sheets. Everyone thanked the good Lord for holding off the rain until they had reached safety. With that, everyone sat down to the dinner table to a delicious supper, listening to the rain falling relentlessly outside. It continued to rain most of the night.

    Wednesday brought another beautiful morning. The rain and clouds were gone. It was a beautiful day for flying. After another great breakfast, the detectives packed their suitcases and were ready to leave the ranch. It was a memorable trip. Sturlock drove them down the mountain to their plane waiting below. Micah performed his pre-flight check of the plane. Sturlock did the same with his plane as he needed to fly home to Buna to take care of business and family matters. With the gear safely stowed in the rear of the plane, Micah warmed up the engine. They said their goodbyes to Sturlock, thanking him for his assistance in their investigation and his warm hospitality. Their one regret was that there was no time to see Sturlock's magnificent buffalo herd on the other side of the mountain. Micah taxied the plane to the end of the runway and then gave it the gas. A few seconds later and they were eastbound, destined for Beaumont. As they were climbing in altitude, a second plane flew alongside them. With a grin and a wave, Sturlock literally passed them on the fly. His plane was faster than theirs.

Chapter Fifteen

Stalking

While Bill, Rick, and Micah were busy in West Texas, Steve was busy in Southeast Texas. He was discharged from the hospital in Galveston. A church friend drove to Galveston and brought him home. His truck was still there. The house was locked by law enforcement when they finished serving the search warrant. He entered his home and looked around. He saw his copy of the search warrant on the credenza just inside the front door. He searched his residence and nothing appeared to be missing. He grinned with satisfaction and realized it was time for him to get back to work. He rubbed his shoulder. It was still tender to the touch where the bullet had entered his upper chest. This messy, trivial issue of him having sex with his daughter had gone on long enough. It was time to get his family back home.

Steve had tried begging and pleading with Martha to get Tori to recant her story to the police. He didn't realize how stubborn his wife could be. He must have been too easy on her in programming her to submit to his wishes, whims, and desires. He acknowledged to himself that he would have to correct that when everything was back under his control at home.

He had closed their joint bank accounts and withdrawn all of the money. He had also cancelled all of their credit cards that had both of their names on them. His mind was at work on how he could squeeze Martha into submission a little more.

The day Greg took Martha to the bank and caught Steve in the bank lobby had been quite traumatic. After leaving the bank, Martha and Greg stopped at a gas station and filled his truck with gas. Martha had decided to rent a car to help disguise her movements. She knew Steve was probably trying to find where they were hiding. Martha tried to use the same credit card she used to buy gas when she was with Greg, but it didn't work. She called the credit card companies and explained their situation. She found out very quickly that the credit card companies didn't care. All they wanted was their money. Martha tried to get a few credit cards in her name but every one of the companies denied her application. She had worked in Steve's business. Now she was finding out that he was getting all of the notoriety for their company, especially from places like credit card companies. It was as if she had never worked at all.

Martha realized she was fortunate to have help from her sister-in-law. June's home was a safe place because Steve did not know where his sister lived. He knew she and her husband lived in Beaumont, but had no idea where. During the day, June and her husband, Frank worked at their separate law firms. Their home had an alarm system. June also had a housekeeper that was at her home daily. When Martha needed to leave the house, Luke and Tori stayed out of sight inside the house with the housekeeper. Martha also kept her truck in June's closed garage when she did not need to go out.

The weekend was coming up and June suggested that they all go to her and Frank's lake house for the weekend. It seemed like a great idea. It would give all of them a chance to get away from Beaumont and relax for a couple of days. That Friday evening, June and Frank loaded Luke and Tori in their vehicle and headed north to their lake-front home at Sam Rayburn Lake. Martha needed to visit with Greg before going to the lake to meet June, Frank, and the kids. She had to travel west on Hwy. 418 to get to Greg's home. This county road was the one her residential road intersected with. As she was traveling westbound on Hwy. 418, she noticed a vehicle approaching her at a high rate of speed. Instead of passing her, the vehicle stayed behind. Martha realized it was a truck and not a car. Her heart suddenly jumped in her throat. The truck was identical to Steve's new truck. The driver of the truck started flashing the truck's lights from bright to dim several times in an attempt to get her attention. When the lights were on dim, she was able to identify the driver as Steve. Martha realized that Steve would very likely ram the back-end of her truck if she didn't pull over and stop. As the vehicles came to a stop of the side of the road, Steve exited his truck and approached Martha's truck window. She rolled her window down only a few inches instead of down completely. She didn't want Steve reaching into the truck and grabbing her. He told her he wanted to see the kids. Martha flatly told Steve no. In a panic, Steve told her that he knew if he could talk to Tori, that he could talk her into recanting her story. Martha looked at him like he was crazy and flatly told him no again. Her mind was racing and she so desperately wanted to tell Steve what she really thought of him. She wanted to tell him what a despicable pervert he was. She actually began to feel sick to her stomach to even be near him. She realized she was the one in control at this moment, not him. Her attorney, Tim Landry, had instructed her to be in control and not blurt out what she really thought of Steve if they were ever together. Steve told her he only wanted to have his family back together. Martha knew this was a lie. He didn't care about his family. He only cared about himself. If he had his family back together, she knew he could continue controlling everyone, and they would be right where he had left off. As hard as it was, she held her tongue. She maintained control of the situation. She was scared to death of Steve. She was shaking inside, but her voice was firm. Martha told Steve she needed time to think. She knew this statement gave Steve a glimmer of hope. This statement caused him to back off a little, instead of pressing harder. She told him to leave them alone so she could think. Steve promised that he would not bother them but wanted to meet Martha and talk in a few days. He walked back to his truck as she drove away.

    Martha watched the rear view mirror more than the road ahead. He was still following her. She reached the end of Hwy. 418 at U.S. Hwy. 69 in Kountze. She did not want Steve following her to the lake. Her children were there. Steve and the whole family had been to June and Frank's lake house on several occasions. Instead of turning right and heading north to Warren, she turned left, heading through Kountze toward Lumberton. She did not want to turn in a northerly direction toward the lake at all. His headlights had been about half a mile behind her. As she traveled south, she saw him stop at the intersection and then turn around. He evidently figured that any further following would be futile. Still shaking from the experience, Martha breathed a sigh of relief. As she passed through Kountze she turned east on Hwy. 327. She traveled east to Silsbee looking in her rearview mirror most of the way. Steve did not appear to be anywhere in sight. She drove through Silsbee, and hit the loop and turned north on U.S. Hwy. 96 and headed to the lake. She drove as fast as the speed limit would allow.

It was well after dark when Martha arrived at the lake house. She hugged Luke and Tori a little longer than usual. They thought nothing of it, oblivious to what their mom had just gone through. When they went outside to catch fireflies, Martha took the opportunity to tell June and Frank what had happened on her trip to the lake. Martha hoped that not going in the direction of the lake house after her encounter with Steve, would not give him an indication of their whereabouts that weekend. Everyone felt it was a safe weekend for everyone to relax.

An old saying is that 'All good things must come to an end,' and that included the safe weekend at the lake. Everyone returned to June and Frank's house. Martha kept noticing her truck not running right, but she thought she may have bought a tank of bad gas. When she went to start her truck on Monday morning to run a few errands, the truck wouldn't start. The motor would turn over, but it would not start. She had Frank look at it before he left for work. A few minutes later he turned to his sister-in-law and informed her that the vehicle had been tampered with. His statement took her breath away. When they returned from the lake, she parked her truck in June and Frank's garage and closed the door, just as she had done since she began staying there. There was no way anyone could have tampered with the truck at June and Frank's. There was only one place the truck had been out in the open – the lake. Frank opened the cover to the gas tank and unscrewed the tank cap. He showed her where it appeared that sugar had been poured into the gas. It had apparently not been so much that she couldn't drive home, but it had been enough to clog her fuel pump, or fuel lines, carburetor, injectors, or all of them. Martha could hardly stand. It was as if all her strength was draining from her body. Steve had stalked her again, and he found her and ruined the truck, the only decent piece of property she owned. She had planned to sell the truck and get a more economical vehicle.

She contacted her truck buyer and he was still interested in buying the truck. He offered her twenty-five percent of what she should have gotten for the vehicle. It was going to cost thousands to remove the gas tank, replace the fuel pump, replace all of the fuel lines, rebuild the carburetor, and replace a few more parts that Steve's deed had destroyed. He had beaten Martha once again. He hadn't physically beaten her, but she was emotionally beaten. Steve's act would have broken most women. Most women would have bowed their head in defeat and humiliation and gone back to their spouse to be abused more than ever. But Martha was not most women. She was still alive. Her children were still safe. No matter what Steve did, Martha was determined to see that he paid dearly for all he'd done to Tori.

Martha wasn't the only one that was determined to see Steve pay for what he'd done to Tori. Ruining Martha's truck made June mad. How dare he to come onto her property at the lake, sneak around in the middle of the night, and pour sugar in the gas tank of Martha's truck. June knew this was her fight too, because of what her brother had done to her many years earlier. She cleared her afternoon schedule, picked Martha up, and they went car shopping. They found an economical car that would be a great vehicle for Martha and the children. Martha was back in business.

Martha called Steve and set up an appointment for her to visit their house. Most of their clothes and other belongings were still there. She didn't want to go there alone, and she didn't want Steve to see her new car. She chose a day when Greg was off work and could pick her up from June's house and take her to confront Steve.

Martha and Greg arrived early on a Wednesday afternoon. Steve was waiting for them. Greg gave his mother a little bit of breathing room, but he stayed close enough to protect her if needed. Martha walked through the house and into the back room of the partially constructed structure that was their living area. While she was walking, Steve kept trying to touch her. She told him she needed time before she could allow him to be affectionate toward her. Every time he touched her, she sickened and felt like her skin was crawling. They walked past the dining table and Martha saw all of their credit cards spread out on the table. Steve saw her looking at them and he said he was able to track her movement each time she tried to use one of the cards. He said he cancelled all of the cards and the credit card companies called him every time she tried to use a card. He said he knew she tried to rent a car and make other purchases. He smugly told her that each time a credit card company called him, he told them she was unauthorized to use the card, and if the company allowed her to use their card, he would consider it theft.

They walked outside and sat in the front porch swing. Greg was watching them from a short distance away. Steve told Martha that he never cheated on her. Martha never spoke a word but she looked at him like he'd lost his mind. She thought, how can he say that? Did he not think that having sex with their daughter was not cheating? He told her he had stated that he never wanted a daughter several times before she got pregnant with Tori, during the pregnancy, and even when Tori was born. Steve continued explaining to Martha in his warped thinking, that God had given them a daughter. He said it was a sign from God that it was okay and she was a gift. Martha knew that Tori was a gift from God, but she was certain that God had not given Tori to them to satisfy Steve's perversion. He continued telling Martha that he never loved anyone as much as he loved Tori and she belonged to him. Martha let him ramble. Steve told Martha that he tried not to do things with Tori but he couldn't help it. He said he had tried to have venomous snakes bite him. He also injected mercury in attempt to kill himself so that he would no longer do (perverted) things to Tori. But, that had not killed him either, and he took it as a sign that everything was okay. Finally, Martha asked Steve why he thought Tori was a gift from God. Steve rambled on even more, saying he knew what he had been doing to Tori was wrong, but he kept on and on. Martha listened as Steve would say one thing and then contradict himself. Martha knew it was time to go. She got some of their clothes together and had Greg put them in his truck. Martha needed money. Steve had taken everything dime they had. She didn't beg, but she did ask Steve for some money for the kids. He pulled a $20.00 bill from his pocket and gave it to her. He told her he would give her more later. She and Greg left. Steve never gave Martha another penny.

Martha and Greg went to the house one more time about a week later. Steve was waiting. Martha got more of their clothes and placed them in Greg's truck. She and Steve wound up sitting in the swing again. Steve promised her, once again, that everything would be okay if they could just get back together. He promised Martha that they would move to a location where no one knew them, but she needed to get Tori to recant first. Martha tried to keep things calm and told Steve she would think about it. But in her mind, there was no way she would ever get back together with him. She asked Steve for some money again. He ignored her request.

As Martha started walking toward Greg's truck, Steve admitted that he thought he found his sister's house and thought that was where they were staying. He admitted that as he was lurking around in the neighborhood where he thought June and Frank lived, a Beaumont police officer slowly drove by. Steve said the officer turned his patrol car around to follow him. Steve said he sped up, trying to get away from the officer, and the officer turned his red and blue lights and siren on to get Steve to stop. He said he started zig-zagging through several residential streets and somehow he managed to elude the officer. He told her that he never went back to that area. Martha didn't say a word. As she got into Greg's truck for them to leave, Martha made a mental note to thank Sgt. Bill Davis for having the police department make special patrols around June's residence for their protection. It paid off for them.

Chapter Sixteen

Jail

On Thursday morning, August 22, Bill and Rick arrived at their respective offices and got to work. They began assembling their documentation and evidence together to present to, not one district attorney's office for prosecution, but to several district attorney offices throughout the state. Working investigations in real life are not like what is depicted on a television show. Real investigations require lots of paperwork, and huge amounts of documentation. All of this is done in order to fulfill the Fourth Amendment to the Bill of Rights of the U.S. Constitution. All police officers must go to a basic law enforcement academy to become a peace officer as directed in the Texas Code of Criminal Procedure (C.C.P.). In fact, all law enforcement officers in Texas, under the Texas C.C.P. Article 2.12, are defined as 'peace officers.' This means that all officers from the Texas Dept. of Public Safety highway patrol troopers, to Texas Rangers, to sheriffs and their deputies, to chiefs of police and their officers, to constables and their deputies, to school district police chiefs and their officers, to game wardens, and a host of other defined officers, all are state licensed 'peace officers.' There are occasions when officers may be out of their jurisdiction, but they continue to have arrest powers throughout Texas in certain situations, due to them being state licensed peace officers. After completing the basic police academy and becoming a peace officer, the learning process, just like any other profession, never ends. Officers must continue to attend schools to learn the laws and how to perform their job under the constantly changing laws of local, state, and federal governments. Officers must learn that the court trial of a defendant does not begin when an investigation is accepted by the district attorney's office and everyone walks into a courtroom. A trial begins when a crime is committed. It continues throughout the criminal investigation. Upon completion of an investigation, an officer submits his investigation documentation to an assistant district attorney in charge of accepting investigations for prosecution from officers. That assistant district attorney, or in some small jurisdictions, the district attorney, then scrutinizes every piece of documentation presented to them in the case file to make sure none of the constitutional rights of a defendant(s) have been violated. In most cases, district attorneys view these case files in a very simple manner. If something was documented properly, it happened. If something material in that case was not documented properly under the rule of law, then that piece of evidence or situation did not happen. The amount of probable cause in the evidence and documentation is then scrutinized. The district attorney or assistant district attorney, referred to on many occasions as the prosecutor, must make sure there is sufficient probable cause to not only get an indictment from a grand jury, but ultimately to have a judge or jury find this person guilty of the crime(s) committed and assess sufficient punishment for what was done to a victim so that justice, to some degree, is served. As the investigative and judicial process is explained to officers while in their basic academy, they are constantly reminded that attorneys, both prosecutors and defense attorneys, as well as judges will scrutinize their work. These attorneys and judges may not be on the local level. If a defendant and his attorney wish to appeal the verdict or punishment issued by the original court, the facts and documentation and legal points may be appealed. Now, all of the facts, evidence, and rules of law that came into play during the original trial, will be scrutinized by appellate judges throughout the Texas judicial process. This means an officer's work could ultimately end in the hands of the justices of the Texas Court of Criminal Appeals, the highest criminal court in Texas. Some investigations may also go through not only a state court or state appeals courts, but also to the federal court system. In certain situations, such as a capital murder trial where a defendant is sentenced to the death penalty, the case will not only go through the state appellate process, but may also enter the federal court system. If a capital murder incident is upheld throughout the state appellate system, it will, by law, then enter into the federal court system. Now, the appellate process could go through an original federal court. If that federal judge upholds the ruling through the state court system, a case could then be sent to an appellate federal court. If this federal appellate court upholds everything, the case goes all the way to the U.S. Supreme Court.

These future officers in the basic academy, also known as cadets, as well as veteran officers, are constantly aware that the people scrutinizing their work, attended law school and most have many years of experience within the judicial process as attorneys and judges. A good example of the judicial process is presented by Sgt. Bill Davis in his must-read, first true-crime novel, *So Innocent, Yet So Dead*. The original trial of that capital murder case began in a local district court. The judicial process ended twelve years later with an appeal to the U.S. Supreme Court to stay the execution of the convicted murderer of a ten year-old child. The Supreme Court justices refused to hear the case, and the man was executed.

Steve sexually abused his daughter in four jurisdictions in Texas. Bill wanted to see that Steve was indicted in all four jurisdictions. He contacted one of his law enforcement acquaintances in Jasper County where Steve and Martha had once owned a house. This county is located near Sam Rayburn Lake, one of the state's prime bass fishing lakes. Lewis Drake was an investigator with this county's district attorney's office. After a short telephone conversation of checking on how each other were doing, Bill went straight to the point. He explained Tori's case to the investigator. Lewis told Bill to send the case file to him and he would review it with his district attorney.

After finishing the phone call with this investigator, Bill called Trey Rogers in Midland. He made sure that Trey's paperwork on Tori's molestation at Sturlock's ranch was ready. He advised Trey that he was compiling all of the paperwork from the four jurisdictions and would be mailing it to him within the next few days. Trey also gave Bill the telephone number of the chief investigator for the Jeff Davis County District Attorney's office. Trey felt that because this case was so complex, it would be a good idea if Bill spoke with Adam Gomez, the chief investigator, and explained the complexity of the case that would be coming his way within a few days.

Bill asked for Adam Gomez as the receptionist for the 83rd District Attorney's office in Alpine, Texas, answered the phone. As Bill worked with the people in the 83rd District Attorney's Office, he discovered that they covered a lot more territory than just one county for this judicial district. He learned that the 83rd Judicial District covered not only Brewster County, but also Jeff Davis County and Presidio County. Chief Criminal Investigator Adam Gomez answered the call. Bill introduced himself to the investigator and told him about the investigation that would be coming to him by way of DPS Investigator Trey Rogers. Gomez was very interested in Bill's description of the case. His district attorney, Mr. Brian Ramirez liked prosecuting cases like this. He felt if he could get criminals like Steve, who liked to hurt innocent children, off the street, then he had done his job and made the 83rd Judicial District a safe place for his constituents.

With telephone calls out of the way, Bill returned to the job of creating not just one stack of papers for the Jefferson County District Attorney's office, but a separate stack of papers for the Hardin County District Attorney's Office, Jasper County District Attorney's Office, the Jeff Davis County District Attorney's Office, and for the department's case file. Bill and the Xerox machine in the police department's Special Crimes Unit stayed very busy for hours on end. In the midst of making all of the copies of the case files, Bill grinned as he thought of police shows on television. Citizens never see this part of police work as they watched their favorite police dramas.

Bill also called Martha. He told her of the successful trip he and the others had at Sturlock's ranch. He needed them to come to his office. Tori needed to identify the coat they brought back from the ranch as evidence. Bill knew this might be traumatic for Tori. He knew that seeing this coat might bring back negative memories of what her father did to her in that partially built lodge on that West Texas mountaintop. He would be sensitive. He would be professional. But he needed to show it to her.

Martha, Tori, and Luke were punctual, as usual. Bill stopped his copying project and greeted them in the lobby. Bill only needed to visit with Martha and Tori. Martha brought Luke with them for safety purposes. She knew Steve was still trying to find them. She didn't want Luke to be 'stir' crazy at June's house and venture outside. It would be her luck to have Steve driving through the neighborhood trying to find them and spot Luke.

Bill had discussed Tori's case with a friend of his, Randy Martinez, one of the felony prosecutors at the Jefferson County D.A.'s office. Randy liked Bill's idea to go back as far as Tori could remember in documenting the sexual molestation by her father. However, Bill did not go into extensive detail involving the last molestation in Jefferson County. Randy also wondered about Steve's sexual relationship with Martha and if there was any correlation between him having sex with Martha and him having sex with their daughter.

While Martha waited in the lobby, Bill escorted Tori to his office. He showed her the Carhartt-style brown coat they retrieved from Sturlock's ranch. Tori told Bill the coat looked identical to the coat her dad put on the dark brown colored bench at the lodge at the west Texas ranch. She said he put it on the dark brown bench to keep from getting dirty from the dust that was on the bench. Bill and Rick had also taken photos of all of Sturlock's vehicles at the ranch. Tori immediately pointed to the vehicle she and her father drove to the lodge at the ranch. Bill made a mental note to include in his notes that would go to all the prosecutors that Tori picked out the same vehicle from which Sturlock removed the coat when Bill, Rick, and Micah visited at the ranch. Sturlock had told them he always kept the brown coat in that particular vehicle. Bill then asked Tori if she remembered the last time her father molested her inside the city limits of Beaumont. He purposely asked Tori if the last time Steve molested her was at their residence on Rosewood Street before they moved to Hardin County. Tori corrected Bill, telling him the last time was at the warehouse her mom and dad owned on Martin Street. She told him the last time he molested her in Beaumont was in the first half of November 1993. She stated that her mom and dad were moving some office furniture out of the building to get it ready for the new tenants who leased the building. As they entered the building, her dad checked a couple of answering machines for messages. He went to a bathroom located downstairs and got some toilet paper. Tori told Bill that when she saw her dad get the toilet paper, she knew what was going to happen. As they walked upstairs and entered her dad's office, he told her to take off her pants. Almost like being a robot, Tori said she removed her tennis shoes and then her jeans and panties. He then had her sit on the right side of the black couch that sat against the wall. Tori then described to Bill how her dad sexually molested her with penetration of her vagina with his finger, oral penetration, and penile penetration for the next several minutes. After Steve's ejaculation into a piece of the toilet tissue, he instructed Tori to get dressed, and they left the building a few minutes later. Bill completed Tori's statement. She read it and then signed the affidavit as being true and correct. Bill now had specific answers to the who, what, when, where, how and why regarding Steve's last sexual molestation of Tori in Beaumont. This affidavit was enough to prosecute Steve for the first degree felony charge of Aggravated Sexual Assault of a Child.

Martha's affidavit began a few minutes later. She was able to answer Bill's questions about the building on Martin Street and established that she and Steve had control over the building during the first half of November 1993. Not wanting to be very personal but needing to be, Bill asked Martha if she would share some information about her sex life with Steve. She started at the first of their relationship. She was a petite young woman, thin and almost looking like a teenage girl. She described how Steve wanted sex with her all the time. She told Bill that Steve did not like to have vaginal/penile penetration until the very end of their sexual activity. She described how Steve liked to place his penis between her legs and rub his penis between the labia of her vagina. She said he would do this until just before his ejaculation. He would then penetrate her vagina and ejaculate seconds later. Bill never said a word, but kept on typing. Martha had just described the exact way Steve had sex with Tori, except for the full penetration seconds prior to a climax. Martha also told Bill that Steve hardly ever wanted to have sex with her when she was pregnant with both Luke and Tori. Martha said she needed stitches following the natural births of Luke and Tori, but that didn't matter to Steve. Immediately upon returning home from the hospital on both occasions, and still having stitches, Steve wanted and demanded to have sex with Martha. She said Steve also wanted to have sex with her every time she was ill, running fever, etc. Martha told Bill that it seemed like the sicker she was, the more Steve wanted to have sex with her. There was one occasion, Martha said, that she was so sick, she was hallucinating. Steve demanded and had sex with her every day and twice on one day during this illness. Martha said that one of Steve's sons from a previous marriage was killed in an accident. The night he received the call of his son's death, Steve hung up the phone and immediately told Martha he wanted sex.

Tori's first recollection of her father sexually molesting her was when they lived at their home on Rosewood Street. Tori described having some 'conveyor belts' in the house. Bill had asked Martha to go back through her notes and documents and look for an approximate date when those 'conveyor belts' would have been in their house. She replied that the 'conveyor belts' were actually roller platforms used by carpenters, and the rollers were in their living room from May 1987 to January 1988. Tori turned five years old that September. Martha's dates corroborated Tori's statement that her first recollection of her dad molesting her was when she was four years old, while the 'conveyor belts' were in the house.

With both Tori and Martha's affidavits signed, Bill had one more request. He wanted photos and not just any photos. Bill wanted those jurors to see more than the eleven year-old Tori. Bill wanted them to see her when the molestation began – when she was four years old. Bill wanted photos showing Tori's age when the molestation began and each year thereafter until the molestation ceased. Bill and his partner, Gene, had achieved a ninety-eight percent conviction rate in court for cases they investigated and were accepted by the district attorney for prosecution due to their ability to think like the suspect, to think like the defense attorney, and to reason what may be going on in a juror's mind. Tori was only eleven years old. Some people in our communities see young girls in a different light, thinking of them as physically looking and sometimes acting older. Some people attempt to rationalize that the child instigated a sexual incident with someone much older. Bill did not want jurors to view Tori as just an eleven year-old young woman they could literally see in a courtroom. He wanted them to see this was a child, not only at eleven years old, but at the age when Steve first began molesting his little girl. Many people are 'visual' people. They are people that may not understand or comprehend descriptions of someone or something using only words; however, these same people can be shown a photo or drawing of something or someone and understand completely. As Martha, Luke, and Tori were exiting the lobby, Bill reminded Martha that he needed the photos of Tori for every year from four to eleven years of age. He explained, again, that he wanted the judge and jury to see this child at every age from the first to the last time Tori was sexually victimized by her father. Martha told Bill she was working on getting the pictures. Some of the photos needed were in their house, where Steve was currently living. She told Bill she would have access to those pictures as soon as he did his job and arrested Steve and got him out of their house. Bill understood. He knew what he had to do.

As Tori, Luke, and Martha left the Special Crime Unit's lobby, Bill returned to his office. He took the coat that had been taken as evidence from Buck Sturlock's ranch and placed a Beaumont Police Dept. evidence tag on it. He took the elevator from his second floor office to the evidence division of the police department, located in the police building's basement. Perhaps the architects who designed the police station in the mid-1970's and the persons with final approval of the building's design were unfamiliar with the flood-prone Southeast Texas area. The approved design of the police station included an underground basement. Basements are quite unusual in coastal locations, especially in areas that are mere inches above sea level. Bill thought about this as he entered the basement and handed Sturlock's coat to one of the evidence division staff. He returned to his office. He still had lots of work to do. Other cases also demanded Bill's attention during the next several days.

Bill was at the copy machine in between cases. The stacks of paperwork for each jurisdiction where Steve committed crimes against Tori grew steadily. He began working on his 'probable cause' affidavit. The district attorney's office likes this document. It is a summary of the entire investigation and it develops the 'probable cause' that is required by the U.S. Constitution's Fourth Amendment to the Bill of Rights. Bill began the document with a chronological history of receiving a call from Ben Moore with the Hardin County Sheriff's Department. Bill described the Hardin County incident where Martha came home and caught Steve as he exited the bathroom and descended the stairs from molesting Tori seconds earlier. Bill quoted the statement Steve made to Martha, "It's not what you think. It hasn't been going on very long. You don't realize how many other people do this." He continued the affidavit with Tori's statement to Lucy Carrier at Amelia's Place. She said her father molested her at their home in Hardin County, but that he had been molesting her for a very long time and many of the incidents occurred while they lived in Beaumont. Bill continued the 'probable cause' explaining Tori's lengthy affidavit where she stated that her father first molested her at their home in Beaumont around May 1990. Bill also described how Steve molested Tori at the two warehouses in Beaumont from 1991 to November 1, 1996. Bill knew this would be the date that the district attorney's office would use for their 'on or about' date for Steve's warrant and indictment. Bill also included in the affidavit that Tori was not the first child Steve had molested. He documented the sworn statement from Steve's younger sister, June Green. He described how Steve performed penile/vaginal intercourse on June when she was only three years old and he was thirteen years old. Bill included Martha's description of how Steve had sex with her, which was identical to how Tori described her father had sexually molested her. Bill finally concluded his 'probable cause affidavit' stating, "Based on the above information, I respectfully request that a warrant be issued for the arrest of Steve Elton Carpenter, white male, for the charge of Aggravated Sexual Assault, a First Degree Felony." Bill signed the document in front of Mikayla Wright, a Notary Public for the State of Texas, who was also one of the secretaries in the police department's detective division.

Most district attorneys want an investigation to be completed by the law enforcement agency when the investigation is submitted to their office. There are exceptions to this rule. For instance, there may be a murder investigation underway and a detective needs a warrant on a suspect that is a flight risk. The detective submits his investigation to the district attorney's office, indicating that in his evaluation, there is sufficient probable cause that a crime or crimes were committed. Then, the prosecutor in that office will review the case. If that prosecutor believes sufficient probable cause exists, a formal complaint will be issued. The formal complaint and a copy of the detective's 'probable cause affidavit' will then be taken by that detective to a justice of the peace. The justice of the peace, a state magistrate, will review the documents to make sure probable cause has been met in accordance with the Fourth Amendment of the U.S. Constitution's Bill of Rights, and the proper legal complaint in accordance with the Texas Penal Code against the suspect(s) has been issued. The judge then issues a warrant for that suspect. The detective can then arrest the suspect, hopefully before he absconds to parts unknown. However, the D.A.'s office usually wants the case completely finished before it is submitted to the grand jury for their decision to indict, or not indict this person on the felony charges they have been accused of committing.

    Bill's investigation against Steve was in this situation. In photos alone, Bill was waiting for Angela and Sharon with the department's I.D. Unit to process over one-hundred-sixty 8 x10 inch photos. He was also waiting for Rick Lucas to furnish his photos from Sturlock's ranch. Bill was also worried that Steve was a flight risk. Steve's stepson, Greg, had worked with Steve in their construction business. Greg moved on and was working for another construction company. Some former co-workers informed Greg that Steve was suddenly not showing up for work, becoming evasive and was not sleeping at his home. Steve was living in the homes of relatives and friends, and was staying only a night or two at each location. Greg told his mom that Steve was becoming very elusive. Martha conveyed this information to Bill. He had seen this type of behavior and action before from suspects who knew an arrest was forthcoming. Steve was getting ready to run. Maybe Steve was thinking of running to Sturlock's ranch in West Texas. He would have 35,000 acres where he could hide out. Or maybe he would run to Mexico. He could be across the border in about six hours. In any situation, time was not Bill's friend on this investigation.

    Generally, the investigations Bill submitted to the D.A.'s Office were almost always complete and ready to be sent to the grand jury and on to trial. In this case, Bill prepared another document to accompany the case file he would submit to the D.A.'s Intake Unit. He created a document informing the D.A.'s office that the investigation was very complex. He documented that the victim had been sexually molested in four separate Texas counties in the past seven years. He further documented that the paperwork he was currently submitting contained all affidavits that developed the probable cause that Steve was the suspect in this molestation. Bill then listed five specific items that would be submitted to the case file in the near future. The first additional item listed was Bill's supplementary report that would chronologically bring this complex case together. The second item was the photography from the various crime scenes in the four counties where the crimes occurred. The third item was the photography of Tori from four years old to eleven years old. The fourth item was the Hardin County Sheriff's Department offense report of Steve's attempted suicide on August 11. And the fifth item listed was a completed copy of the search warrant served on Steve's property on August 11. Bill also mentioned that the environment surrounding this case was very volatile due to Steve's act of violence, even though the violence was self-inflicted. Law enforcement officers learn early in their career that persons who may be suicidal, can also be homicidal. Bill was worried, if Steve found Martha, Tori, and Luke, that he may be desperate enough to kill all three of them and then commit suicide. Bill was doing everything he could to prevent that. Five o'clock p.m. came and went. Bill kept typing. He kept copying. Finally, he was through. The case was ready to present to the D.A. It was time to get a warrant. It was time for Steve to go to jail – again. It was August 27, 1994.

Bill arrived at his office the next morning and poured his cup full of black coffee. As he sipped the savory liquid, he called Martha. He told her he would be walking to the D.A.'s office in a few minutes and would be requesting a warrant on Steve. He told her to get in touch with Greg and try to monitor Steve's location throughout the day. It was Friday, and Bill did not want to give Steve the advantage of having two weekend days to get a head-start on absconding from the area.

The trip from the police station to the courthouse took only a few minutes. It was a quick walk from the back door of the police station, across the railroad tracks that separated the two buildings, to the entrance of the courthouse. It was usually a quick hike, unless a train happened to be on the tracks, then it was not a quick trip. It involved getting into a car and driving several blocks to an underpass, traversing it, and driving on a different street to the courthouse parking lots. Bill was fortunate this Friday morning – there was no train.

    Bill entered the lobby of the courthouse, spoke to several people he knew, and then stepped into the elevator. A few moments later the elevator doors opened to the third floor. Seconds later he said 'hello' to Stephanie, the D.A.'s receptionist. Bill told her he needed to file a case. A few minutes later, Randy Martinez, the chief intake prosecutor came to the waiting area and invited Bill in. They walked to Randy's office and Bill handed Tori's case to him. "My goodness," Randy exclaimed as he took the folder that was over two inches thick. Randy would not take the time to read all of the paperwork at that moment. It was not time for trial. The veteran prosecutor scanned Tori's twelve-page affidavit. He carefully read Bill's 'probable cause affidavit' and the supplementary report stating that five more important items would be added to the case file soon. There was no doubt in Randy's mind that Steve had sexually penetrated his daughter from four years old to eleven years old. He felt that Bill had sufficiently documented the probable cause needed for criminal charges to be filed against Steve. Randy wrote the 'formal complaint' by hand and gave it to Bill, and then Bill gave the 'hand written complaint' and the 'probable cause affidavit' to Randy's secretary, Jacquie. A few minutes later, she handed the typed 'formal complaint' to Randy. He signed it and gave a copy of the 'formal complaint' to Bill, along with a copy of the 'probable cause affidavit.' It was time to see the judge.

    Bill left the D.A.'s office and went to the ground floor of the courthouse. Justice of the Peace Carl Davis, one of two J.P.'s housed in the courthouse, was in and busy conducting a wedding in his courtroom. The judge's senior secretary, Lana, greeted Bill as he entered their office. He handed her the paperwork from the D.A.'s office. Lana had known Bill for a number of years and knew his paperwork involved someone being victimized by some type of sexual crime and it was time for a warrant. She read Bill's 'probable cause affidavit,' shaking her head in sadness that someone would commit such a crime against an innocent child. For that innocent child to be that person's own flesh and blood was beyond her comprehension. Yet, Lana had been the judge's secretary for several years and admitted there were not many things that surprised her anymore from the viewpoint of dastardly deeds committed by perverted criminals. She scrolled a blank warrant into her typewriter and began typing. Just as she finished, the judge walked into the office area from his courtroom. He had pronounced the couple, man and wife and they had left his courtroom to hopefully live happily ever after. Judge Davis (no relation to Sgt. Bill Davis) was a highly respected justice of the peace. He was a police officer for a number of years. He then went from city police officer to an investigator for the district attorney's office. Working with prosecutors fascinated him and prompted him to enter law school. He received his law degree and worked a few months longer. As Justice of the Peace Howard Ellis announced his retirement, Carl announced his desire to fill the position. Working for a major law firm on civil issues, or working in some specialized field of law did not interest Carl. He had been a public servant for too long. He wanted to continue working for folks in the community. The Jefferson County Commissioners Court appointed Carl to fill Judge Ellis's unexpired term. When his first election came around, he won handily.

  The judge and the detective shook hands as Lana completed typing the warrant. Judge Davis invited Bill into his chambers and began reading the 'probable cause affidavit' and 'formal complaint' against Steve. Bill watched him closely, not interrupting. As the judge finished reading the documents, Bill began telling him about Steve stalking the family, shooting himself, and possible preparations to flee the area and possibly the country. Bill told the judge he felt Steve was an obvious danger to himself and the innocent members of his family. Judge Davis took all of this into consideration. He made a note on his paperwork to have a 'protective order' placed on Steve when Bill arrested him and brought him back to his courtroom. Bill also advised the judge that Steve had already been arrested in Hardin County for his alleged sexual crimes against Tori and that he had promptly gotten a local bail bondsman to post his $50,000.00 bond. All Steve had done was give the bondsman ten percent, or $5,000.00 cash, from cleaning out his and Martha's bank accounts, and he was once again a free man, pending trial in that county. Depending on what judge received Steve's case on his docket, Steve could easily be out on bond in Hardin County for one to four years before the case ever went to trial. A person is always innocent until proven guilty in a court of law. Steve was walking around, an innocent man by law, to stalk, manipulate, and coerce Martha and Tori. Steve was hoping that his manipulation and coercion would become so unbearable, they would cave and ask all of the district attorneys where he was charged to drop the charges against him. Steve forgot one factor in his equation – a bull-headed detective that was not going to let him achieve his goal. Bill asked the judge to consider a high bond in light of all of the coercive things Steve had done since posting bond in Hardin County. Judge Davis was very aware of the Eighth Amendment of the Bill of Rights of the U.S. Constitution, which guaranteed citizens to not be issued excessive bail. However, considering how quickly Steve made a $50,000.00 bail with no problems, and considering the coercive tactics that Steve committed since being freed on bail in Hardin County, the judge knew it was also his duty to protect innocent citizens, especially victims and their families. Judge Davis signed the warrant. He thought for a moment and then documented Steve's bond at the top of the warrant. He handed the warrant to Bill who thanked the judge for his time. As he exited the office he looked at the bond –$120,000.00. Bill couldn't wipe the smile off his face. "Let's see Steve get out of jail on this one," Bill thought.

  Bill walked back across the railroad tracks to his office and immediately called Martha. She was almost speechless as she realized Steve was about to go back to jail. And this time, it was going to be much more difficult for him to get out on bond. But, where was he? Bill needed Martha's help. Steve had not been staying at home. Martha told him she put in a call to Greg for help. Hopefully Bill would know where to serve the warrant on Steve in a matter of minutes.

  Most of the time, legal affairs are not quick and easy. And most of the time, the legal matters seem to take forever for those who are not lawyers. Friday morning, August 27, was no exception. Bill's stomach was growling as he talked with Martha. Their telephone call ended and he left the police station. It was time for lunch.

Bill just finished his lunch when his cell phone rang. It was Martha. Steve was hiding out at the homes of two friends from their church. One of those families was Mr. and Mrs. Mark Jenson. They lived in Lumberton on the Chance Cutoff Road. Greg contacted his friend, Officer Bradley Richards, with the Lumberton Police Department. Greg gave Bradley a description of Steve's truck and the two families who were letting Steve stay with them. Within an hour, Bradley found Steve's truck parked inside the garage of the Jenson's home. Someone at the home must have needed to exit the home through the garage and had left the garage door open. Finding Steve had been too easy.

Bill drove north. He asked the dispatcher to call Lumberton P.D. and request Officer Bradley Richards to assist in serving the arrest warrant on Steve. The officers met at the school district's office located on Hwy. 96 and exchanged greetings. Bradley led the way to the Jenson residence. Bill's detective car was unmarked. Bradley's patrol car was clearly marked. The two officers had barely stepped out of their vehicles when two men and a woman opened a door leading from the house to the garage and began walking toward the officers. Bill had been given a photo of Steve by Martha as well as a mug shot from the Hardin County jail by Major Moore. Steve was the second man walking toward them and Bill 'locked in' on him. Mr. Jensen began telling the officers he and his wife didn't want any trouble. He continued saying he and his wife had been 'laying hands' on Steve and praying for him. Bill was almost oblivious to Jensen's statements. He had tunnel-vision. Bill stepped around Jensen and immediately ordered Steve to put his hands on the vehicle they were standing beside and "back up and spread 'em." Bill was watching Steve's every move. He was making sure the suspect's hands were visible at all times. Steve owned guns and he was cunning, manipulative, and now desperate. No one knew if he would try to end everything in a blaze of glory, committing 'suicide by cop.' Steve wasn't dumb. He knew when to fight, when to run, and when to comply. He quietly put his hands on the hood of the vehicle. Bill stepped behind Steve while Bradley covered him to make sure Steve didn't make any sudden furtive moves. Bill patted down his suspect for weapons.

There were none. Bill retrieved his handcuffs, placed them on Steve's wrists, and then locked them so they wouldn't tighten and cause injury. "Steve Carpenter, you are under arrest for Aggravated Sexual Assault of a Child," Bill boldly proclaimed, and he led Steve to his car. As Bill seated Steve in his car and secured the seatbelt around him, Bill smiled with satisfaction. He hoped Steve Carpenter had just taken his last breath of free air.

    Legal issues still needed to be completed. Anytime someone is arrested in a county different from the county with venue over the alleged crime, the suspect must immediately be taken before a magistrate in the county where the arrest took place. That magistrate must then advise the arrested person of the charge against them. The suspect then has their Miranda Warning administered to them by the judge so they will know their rights. Bill was unaware of who and where the local justice of the peace might be located. Bradley knew where the judge's office was, and Bill followed him. A couple of minutes later and the officers parked their vehicles in Judge Phil Graves' parking lot. The three men entered the justice of the peace office and Bradley said 'hello' to everyone. Bradley introduced Bill to the judge's staff and informed them that a prisoner needed to be warned of his rights. The judge's staff member named Grace began filling out the proper document needed for Steve to be warned of his rights. A couple of minutes later and they were in front of Judge Graves. Bradley stood to Steve's left while Bill stood to his right. The judge asked Steve several questions for identity purposes and then told him to listen carefully. Judge Graves then told Steve he had been arrested for the charge of Aggravated Sexual Assault of a Child, a first degree felony. He then proceeded to explain the Miranda Warning to Steve. The judge told Steve he had the right to remain silent and not make any statement at all. The judge continued telling Steve that any statement he made may be used as evidence against him at his trial. He asked Steve if he understood this right, and Steve answered, "Yes, sir." The judge continued explaining that he had the right to have a lawyer present to advise him prior to or during any questioning. The judge again asked Steve if he understood this right. Steve answered, "Yes, sir." The judge continued by telling Steve that if he was unable to employ a lawyer that he had the right to have a lawyer appointed to advise him prior to and during any questioning. Again the judge asked Steve if he understood this right, and again Steve stated, "Yes, sir." Finally, Judge Graves told Steve that he had the right to terminate or stop any interview at any time. For the last time, the judge asked him if he understood this right. Steve answered in the affirmative again. The judge looked at Bill and asked him to un-handcuff Steve. With the handcuffs removed, Judge Graves had Steve put his initials beside each one of the Miranda rights listed on the document and then had him sign at the bottom of the page. Judge Graves also signed, dated, and timed the document and gave a copy to Bill. Steve was re-handcuffed, and it was time to go to Beaumont.

After saying 'goodbye' to Bradley and thanking him for his help, Bill and Steve headed to Beaumont. No questions were asked. No statements were made. That would come later. The only voice heard in Bill's detective car was the dispatcher and other officers as they communicated on Bill's police radio.

One stop had to be made before Steve was booked into jail. Bill drove into the Jefferson County Courthouse parking lot and parked. He exited the car and walked around to the passenger's side. He helped Steve out of the car and explained they were going before another judge, the one that issued the warrant, and he was going to get his rights read to him again. They entered Judge Davis's office and informed Lana that the man the warrant had been issued for earlier that day was in custody and his rights needed to be read to him. Bill escorted Steve to Judge Davis's courtroom. A few minutes later, the judge entered the courtroom through the back entrance and seated himself on the judicial bench. He looked over the documents and then went through the same process that was done a few minutes earlier in Judge Graves' courtroom, but in a different county. A few minutes later, Judge Davis identified Steve and read each of Steve's rights, pausing after each right and Steve answering in the affirmative that he understood each of his rights. When the judge completed reading Steve's rights, he had Bill unhandcuff Steve so that he could sign the document. Steve and the judge signed the document, and Steve was re-handcuffed. Bill received a copy of this document to be placed in his file with a copy going to the multiple district attorney offices involved in this case. Bill and Steve exited the courthouse and walked to Bill's car. Steve was safely seated and belted in the passenger's seat. They were en-route to their final destination, the Jefferson County Correctional Facility – jail.

A few miles south of Beaumont and Bill exited Hwy. 287. He drove to the 'book-in' gate and pressed a button. A voice came over the speaker and Bill announced himself and said he had a prisoner. The gate opened quickly and Bill drove inside the compound and parked. He assisted Steve out of the car for the last time. They walked to a locked metal door and Bill pushed another button. The door opened and they walked into the jail compound. Bill removed his .40 cal. Glock from its holster and placed it in a gun box. He locked the box and placed the key in his pocket. Jill, the female jailer, unlocked the barred door as soon as she observed that Bill's weapon was safely locked in one of the lock-boxes. No guns were allowed inside the jail area. As the two men approached the counter, Bill removed Steve's warrant from his pocket. He filled out his part of the warrant showing that it had been executed, and handed it to Jill. With the warrant in hand, jail personnel would take care of booking Steve into the facility. Bill retrieved his gun as he exited the jail, got in his vehicle, and drove away. Steve did not.

Bill called Martha as he drove back to the police station. He couldn't wipe the grin from his face as he told Martha that she could sleep comfortably that night. Steve could not hurt her or her children. He was in jail under a $120,000.00 bond. She was in tears with relief. This is what Bill lived for – helping and protecting people, and trying with all his might to see justice was served toward the victimized. But, the judicial part wasn't over. It had just begun.

Steve looked through the bars of the holding cell. One of the jailers would be taking his mug shot and fingerprints in a few minutes. He would then be assigned a cell and be nothing but one of over 1,100 inmates in the facility. It wasn't Steve's first time to look through the bars of a cell. He had that pleasure when he was booked into the Hardin County jail a few weeks earlier. But, he was in and out of that jail in a matter of hours. This jail stint may be a little longer, he thought. Steve's manipulative mind was already at work. He would get Martha and Tori to recant before long. He would have them back under his wing and control before long. He smiled as he thought it was only a matter of time. And, in his warped mind, he rationalized this had to be the will of God. Well, it probably was. Just not in his favor.

A couple of weeks after Steve's arrest, a local attorney, George Stewart, was assigned to defend him of the charges against him. Mr. Stewart was a very experienced attorney and was board certified in criminal law. Bill knew Stewart well. They were friends – outside the courtroom. Bill was glad Steve had been appointed a very competent attorney. That way, Steve would have no appeal regarding incompetent counsel when he went to prison for molesting Tori.

Chapter Seventeen

Post Arrest

So much had happened to Martha, Tori, and Luke in the few short weeks since Martha walked in on Steve and caught him just after he sexually molested their daughter. He was now in jail. Maybe everything would be better. The news media is usually careful to protect the identity of juveniles involved in crimes, whether or not they are victims or suspects of crimes. Yet, the media has access to certain documents such as arrest summaries, probable cause affidavits, and offense reports through the federal law dealing with open records. One of the local television stations, whose ratings were below the other local stations, broadcast Steve's arrest of molesting a child. In their news cast, Tori's name was not mentioned, however, the television reporter let it slip that the victim was the perpetrator's daughter. Tori was Steve's only daughter. Now everyone knew who made the outcry that landed Steve in jail.

Martha needed help for herself and her children. She needed financial help because Steve took every cent of money they had. She needed physical help. June was there for her and the children providing a safe haven for them to live. June also helped by getting a second-hand car for her to drive. Tim Landry, her attorney for the divorce, was also helping in a legal manner. Martha a nd her children were Christians and they turned to many of their church friends for help. Some were very supportive and great 'prayer' friends. Many were gossips. Some of the adults invited Martha and the kids to their homes for Bible study and prayer. For over two years, these were the people they socialized with.

Some of the kids were nice and supportive for Luke and Tori. The pair had gone to their church school except for the past year when Steve persuaded Martha to school them at home. Tori's birthday was about three weeks after Bill arrested Steve. June threw a birthday party for Tori and invited her old school friends. This was the first real contact they had with Tori since word got out about what her father did to her. Instead of being supportive of their friend, most of the girls wanted to know the details of how her father molested her. Tori had begun to notice boys, and her classmate, Nick, was so cute. She had a crush on him and flirted with him every chance she got. He was a typical boy that hadn't noticed girls yet, so Tori didn't know if he liked her or not. Nick came to the party. Tori naively thought she could trust him. She shared a few of the horrible things her father did to her. Instead of being caring and sympathetic toward Tori, he crudely tried to touch her the same way she described her father's actions. Tori was crushed. Luke and Tori learned very quickly who their real friends were.

Angela and Sharon walked into Bill's office the Wednesday morning after Bill arrested Steve. They carried a large brown 10 x 13 inch manila envelope filled with one-hundred-sixty 8 x 10 inch photographs. The two forensic technicians had been very busy in the department's 'dark room' developing the photos for Bill's case. He thanked them for their hard work and immediately opened the envelope. It took a while for Bill to sort through all the photos and categorize them according to each location where Steve molested Tori. After getting the photos in order, Bill knew his next task – back to the copier. He patiently made four copies of each photo – one copy for each district attorney in whose jurisdiction Bill hoped to have criminal charges brought against Steve. Once that was finished, Bill returned to his office and laid out the four stacks of affidavits and documents he previously made for these jurisdictions. Now he added the photos to each stack. With the old cliché that 'a photo is worth a thousand words,' everyone could now see the locations Tori had described where her father molested her.

Bill called Lewis Drake, the investigator for the district attorney in Jasper County. He wanted Lewis to be ready for the large envelope that contained Tori's case. Bill told him it should arrive in a couple of days. Bill immediately called his contact in West Texas, Adam, with the Jeff Davis County District Attorney's office and advised him the case file would be en-route later that day. Adam stated he had already prepped his D.A. to be ready for the case from Southeast Texas.

It was time for lunch. Bill left his office with both hands full. One hand carried his briefcase, and the other hand held four large envelopes. Bill decided FedEx was the best way to go. This would travel quickly, and he could track each envelope if needed. Bill stopped by the local FedEx office after lunch. He handed over the packet for Jasper County and for Alpine Texas whose jurisdiction covered Jeff Davis County. The cases were on their way. Bill hoped more felony charges would be stacked against Steve in the near future.

Bill drove north and was at the Hardin County courthouse a few minutes later. The secretaries in the sheriff's department looked up as Bill knocked on the locked door. They immediately recognized their law enforcement friend and allowed him entry into their office. He asked for Major Ben Moore. Ben was in his office and heard voices. He walked into the lobby and motioned for Bill to come in. Bill entered Ben's office and handed a thick envelope to his friend. The last time the two detectives met was when Steve shot himself and they had to quickly run the search warrant on the property. Bill briefed Ben on the current events of the case, including Steve's arrest on the Jefferson County warrant a few days earlier. They visited a few minutes and Bill looked at his watch.

It was getting late in the afternoon, and Bill had one more stop to make before he was finished for the day. He drove to the Jefferson County Courthouse in Beaumont. He rode the elevator to the third floor, went to the district attorney's office, and asked for his friend, Randy. A few minutes later his prosecuting friend entered the waiting area and escorted Bill to his office. Bill handed the last of the four folders to Randy, explaining that the envelope contained a copy of the warrant Bill served on Steve, copies of the search warrant that was served on Steve's property, and copies of the one-hundred-sixty photos involved with the case. Both Bill and Randy agreed that other documents regarding the case could arise. However, for all practical purposes, the case file was complete. It had been a long day.

On Friday, September 20, Bill returned to his office from lunch when Martha called him. Steve had been in jail for three weeks. This was twenty days longer than when he was in jail the first time. Martha explained that she had been working with her son, Greg, to move from June's house back to her own house. She checked the mail that morning and found a large envelope had been delivered from Steve. She told Bill she opened the envelope and found a long drawn-out letter from Steve trying to manipulate and persuade her and Tori to have charges dropped. The next day, Martha went to Bill's office so he could read the letter and determine if the letter could possibly be used as evidence against Steve. Considering all possibilities, Bill thought the district attorney's office may want to consider an extra felony charge of 'tampering with a witness' or at least show a jury at the trial how Steve tried to manipulate or coerce Martha and Tori into submission and have the charges dropped. As Bill read the letter, he could only smile and shake his head as he saw how Steve was doing everything possible to get out of jail and get his family under his submission once again. The letter consisted of seven pages. The first page simply stated, "May God give you wisdom and peace to do the 'rite' thing. I love you Martha." Bill noticed in the letter that Steve had difficulty in spelling correctly. The next page began with him telling Martha how he thought of her and the kids 'nite' and day. He told her how he was making his last appeal for her help. He said that "outside of your help, I have no hope of the charges going away." Steve told her that he had repented (to God) of everything he had ever done wrong in his life. He then went on a multi-page dissertation of all of the good things they had done as a family for God and others. Throughout the letter he kept reminding Martha of the incidents he was referring to by saying, "Do you remember?" He admitted he had gotten away from God, but reminded Martha, "You are guilty of this also." The one sentence that really got to Bill stated, "I beg you please to recant your story to Hardin County and Beaumont. Do whatever it takes to convince them that you made it up and rehearsed Tori." Steve then reminded Martha of people in the Bible who were rewarded by God for lying. He reminded Martha that Rahab the harlot lied to the soldiers at Jericho to save the lives of two Israelite spies and was rewarded by being in the blood line of Jesus. Steve made his final twisted plea to Martha saying, "I don't approve of lying but this will save our marriage and you will be rewarded for it much, by God himself." He finished the letter pleading, "May God Bless you and give you the courage to do this thing for our marriage and my life. I love you with unending love that was given to me by God himself. Please love me, please." Steve had pulled out all the stops including coercion, lying, pleading, and twisting God's word for his own selfish use. Bill looked up from the letter to Martha and used one word to ask a question. "Well?" Martha replied, "I hope he spends the rest of his life in prison, and Tori feels the same way." Bill looked at her and said he would do his best to make her wish come true.

In October 1994, Bill was in his office and received a call from Martha. She wanted him to know she received a call from the district attorney's office in Jasper. The D.A. investigator to whom Bill sent Steve's case file to, telephoned Martha, and the investigator and district attorney wanted to visit with Tori to review some of the facts of the case before they presented the case to their grand jury. Bill asked Martha to call him after the interview and let him know how it went.

Martha called Bill again two days later. Her voice was shaking. He could tell instantly that something was wrong. Martha said they had just left the district attorney's office in Jasper County. She told Bill the investigator and the district attorney kept Tori in a room for over four hours. She said that Tori was sitting on the passenger's side of the car, crying and was in a fetal position. It seemed that their interview had turned into a interrogation. They wanted Tori to go into details about her molestation by Steve. Bill had done the same thing, but Tori said she could tell that Bill really cared about her and her feelings. He had been gentle and professional when he interviewed her. She told her mom that the two investigators gave her the creeps and she felt that all they wanted was for her to tell them the grotesque details of what her dad had done to her. Bill was upset. What these two men had done to Tori was exactly why the local children's advocacy center had been created – so the child would not have to retell their story multiple times. This was why Bill spent so many hours with Tori when he took her statement – so she did not have to tell her story over and over and over. In their minds, Tori, Martha, and Bill strongly felt the two men accomplished nothing except to re-victimize Tori.

When hard times come, a person finds out who their true friends are. A friend that stood by Martha and the children was Teresa. She had been their main counselor and prayer warrior. Martha mentioned to Bill in one of their numerous conversations in the fall and winter of 1994, that Teresa said Steve confessed to her about molesting Tori. In December 1994, Bill requested Teresa to come to his office. He had needed to take a statement from her and her information could be vital to the numerous investigations concerning Steve throughout the state. Teresa told Bill how her family and the Carpenters became friends, through not only church, but also her husband and Steve had worked together on various contracting projects. She said when Steve came by their house to talk to her husband she noticed that he seemed to be troubled, and she said she always counseled and prayed with him. Teresa said that on July 27 or July 28, Steve called and said he was in trouble. She asked Steve what was wrong and he replied that he had been sexually abusing Tori and Martha had caught them. Bill questioned Teresa to make sure he had written down correctly what she had just said. This was very important. Teresa was not a police officer. She did not have to give Steve the Miranda Warning and make sure he understood his rights. He had voluntarily confessed to sexually molesting his daughter to a friend. Teresa said that she asked Steve how long he had been molesting Tori and he said he had not been doing it very long. She got the impression from him that he had only been molesting Tori for about a year. Teresa told Bill she later found out that Steve had been molesting Tori since she was about four years old or younger. He obviously downplayed the length of time he had been molesting Tori so it wouldn't look so bad on him. Steve then asked Teresa if she would go and pray with Martha and Tori and persuade them to drop charges against him. Bill informed Teresa he would add her name to the list of people Steve tried to manipulate in order to get out of jail. Steve had told Teresa how he loved Tori and that she was his baby and she loved him. Steve then made a profound statement. He said, "Teresa, I never had to force her to do anything." Teresa told Bill she was speechless when Steve made that statement. She said she did not know how to even respond to him. She acknowledged that Steve had just implicated some of the blame of him molesting Tori, on the child. He had just insinuated to her that somehow, his eleven year-old daughter had been a voluntary party to his sexual acts with her, rather than her being a victim at the hands of her natural father. Teresa stated that during the Thanksgiving holidays she and Martha were talking and Martha realized that Bill probably did not know about Steve confessing to her. Teresa said that was when Martha said she needed to make sure Bill knew of Steve's phone call to her. Teresa also told Bill she assumed that Steve had done the right thing and confessed to him about molesting Tori. Bill responded that Steve had never confessed to his crimes against Tori except to insinuate his guilt on several occasions to Martha. Teresa was surprised when Bill told her the magnitude of importance her affidavit was. Bill told her she was the only person, so far, that Steve had blatantly confessed to and outright stated that he sexually molested Tori. In a state of panic shortly after the investigation began to unfold months earlier, Steve had made a full confession, but several months passed before his confession came to light and was properly documented.

Thanksgiving was over and holiday shopping was in full swing. Bill was busy working on another case he'd been assigned to investigate when he got a telephone call from the Jeff Davis County District Attorney Investigator, Adam Gomez. His district attorney was preparing to present Tori's case to their grand jury on December 18 and wanted Bill to travel to Jeff Davis County and testify. Bill was always ready for a road trip opportunity. He requested that Adam fax a grand jury subpoena to his office right away. Bill knew his supervisors would not approve a road trip without a subpoena. Bill received the subpoena via fax a few minutes later. He was commanded to appear before the Jeff Davis County grand jury on December 18, 1994, at 10:00 a.m.

Bill went to the detective division and found Micah Lytle. He inquired if Micah was available to fly him to Alpine on Wednesday, December 17, for testimony before the grand jury the next day. As usual, Micah was up for flying, especially when the weather was pretty. Micah cleared his calendar and was ready for the trip. Along with the subpoena, Adam sent Bill a note saying that he checked and there were commercial flights that would accommodate Bill's trip to Alpine. If Adam was willing to pay for fuel, which would be less expensive than air fare, Bill could utilize Micah and the department's confiscated drug plane. Bill called Adam with the inquiry. It was a deal.

Wednesday morning was a beautiful day with clear skies. Bill and Micah met at the airport hangar where the department's plane was housed and loaded their gear into the plane. Micah fueled the plane the day before to make their time more efficient. It was always breathtaking to watch the Texas landscape from above as it goes from flatland to mountains. Adam was waiting for them as they landed at the Alpine airport. They exchanged greetings and loaded into his vehicle for a short trip to their hotel. Adam had work to do and informed Bill that he would pick them up the next morning at 9:00 a.m. As Adam drove away, Bill and Micah realized they were afoot. Their tour of Alpine would be limited to how far they wanted to walk.

Bill and Micah awoke early the next morning and readied for their morning in Alpine. They decided to eat breakfast at a restaurant that was about two hundred yards from their hotel. After looking over the menu, both men decided to eat a hearty breakfast. Micah ordered scrambled eggs with sausage and toast. Bill ordered eggs with bacon and toast. They knew they might not get to eat lunch until after they returned to Beaumont. They finished their breakfast and walked back to the hotel and were waiting when Adam arrived. Micah was dropped off at the airport so he could re-fuel the plane and be ready to go as soon as Bill completed his testimony. Bill and Adam continued on to Alpine's historic courthouse in the heart of the city. The handsome courthouse and matching jail were erected in 1887 shortly after Jeff Davis County was organized. It is said the bricks and lime for the mortar were burned in kilns locally. Interestingly, no one seems to know who the building contractors were.

Bill was called and he entered the room where the Jeff Davis County grand jury was seated. After being sworn in, the district attorney gave the grand jurors a brief summary of the history of Tori's case and how Jeff Davis County became a part of this complex criminal episode. Rural areas like this mountainous region of Texas don't see many investigations like this. Several of the grand jurors asked Bill questions so they could picture in their mind this father molesting his daughter inside a partially built hunting lodge in the middle of a ranch in a remote wilderness area. When all questions had been asked and answered, Bill was excused. The grand jurors had all the information they needed to vote on whether to 'no bill' Steve of the crimes he allegedly committed against Tori, or to indict him of the crime of Aggravated Sexual Assault.

Adam drove Bill to the airport where Micah was waiting. He had already loaded their luggage in the plane and was ready to go. They said their goodbyes to Adam and climbed into the plane. A few minutes later, they were airborne and eastbound. Bill began to feel queasy during the flight. Maybe, he thought, it was indigestion from breakfast. However, the feeling didn't go away, it intensified. They were about one hundred miles from Beaumont and Bill was feeling was so bad that he told Micah he might need to make an emergency landing. Being several thousand feet in the air was not like being on Interstate 10 and being able to pull into the nearest convenience store for a necessary stop. Micah announced to the air traffic controller that he was beginning his descent. Bill was in a cold sweat. The plane's wheels finally touched the runway at the Beaumont Municipal Airport. Bill's door to the plane was open as the wheels came to a halt and he was in the building's restroom in seconds.

Later in the afternoon, Bill called Micah to see if he was sick. Bill thought maybe he had contracted a virus. As they talked, they realized Bill had eaten one item different from Micah at breakfast that morning. Bill had contracted food poisoning. He told Micah he would be sure to order the sausage the next time they had breakfast at that restaurant.

A couple of days after returning home and recovering from his food poisoning episode, Bill called his friend, Adam. Bill was told that Steve was indicted that afternoon for Aggravated Sexual Assault of a c\ Child in Jeff Davis County. It was a satisfying feeling for Bill. He now had Steve indicted in not one, not two, but three counties in Texas for sexually molesting Tori. Bill immediately called Martha and told her the news. This indictment gave her, Tori and Luke even greater peace of mind that Steve would never hurt them again.

The holidays were over and Martha got to work on getting all of the documents needed to file a joint income tax return for 1994 for her and Steve. Following hours of tedious work, she had everything ready. She made a visitation appointment at the jail to see Steve. She needed him to sign the income tax form so she could get their taxes filed in a timely manner. He refused. Steve was still working every possible angle to make Martha's life so miserable that she would finally relent and have Tori recant her story. He was so wrong about her.

On May 15, 1995, Steve was indicted for Aggravated Sexual Assault of a Child in Jefferson County. This indictment was the third indictment against Steve for sexually molesting his daughter. Bill called Martha again and told her the good news. It gave her and her children even more peace that Steve would never hurt them again. Bill wished there had been one more indictment. Steve had also molested Tori in Jasper County, but that county's district attorney would not present Tori's case to their grand jury. He would not give a reason why. Bill had hoped for four indictments against Steve. There should have been four. But, three out of four wasn't bad. It was time for trial.

Chapter Eighteen

Luke's Story

Many people see a story on the nightly news or in the newspaper, or on social media and only look at the person who has been murdered, assaulted, or the victim of a child abuse incident, and think of that particular individual being the only one victimized or affected by the crime. Crimes affect entire families, communities, our country, and even the world. On September 11, 2001, a coordinated terrorist attack killed 2,996 people, including the nineteen hijackers. This act of terror affected almost 3,000 people directly, causing their deaths. But this terrorist act also affected the families of all of the victims who died on that horrific day, and it also affected the entire world.

Steve victimized Tori. The crime not only affected her, but their entire family. Martha was obviously affected. Tori was her child, her baby. People so often forget about the others – family members who are directly or indirectly affected by criminal acts within the family. Victimization also includes brothers and sisters.

Luke was two and one-half years old when his little sister, Tori, was born. To him it was fun having a little sister. As she got older, he played with her and they had a very close bond. He played the role of big brother well, always protecting his little sister. Tori was born in a hospital in Beaumont because Martha's doctor was there, but the family resided in Jasper County. Their father didn't seem to mind playing with them and being a good dad. They moved to their house on Rosewood Street in Beaumont while Tori was still quite young. Luke told Bill that he started noticing his dad being mean to him when he was in the first grade. He was seven years old and Tori was four-and one-half years old at the time. He didn't understand; it was like his dad went from being a 'good' dad to a 'bad' dad. Even though his dad was being mean to him, Luke told Bill that he was still obedient to his father. One day some kids asked Martha why Luke never got in trouble at school. She replied that even though Luke was quite young, he was a Christian. She continued telling the boys that Luke believed in obeying the Bible and honoring his father and mother. As Bill and Luke talked, Luke said he was in the second grade when he met the love of his life. Her name was Carley. She was his first true love. Steve found out that Luke had a girlfriend and Steve made him sit beside him as he called her parents. Luke said he was devastated as he listened to his father tell her parents that his son was trying to get into their daughter's pants. With tears in her eyes, Carley told Luke the next day at school that she could not talk nor be around him anymore.

Luke told Bill that after they moved to Rosewood Street his dad used his brother's warehouse on Ninth Street. Luke said his dad kept his equipment there for the construction jobs he worked on. Luke stated that on several occasions, Steve took both he and Tori with him to the warehouse. As they arrived at the building, Steve told Luke to wait outside the building. Steve also told Luke to be very careful. He said that this part of Beaumont was a very bad neighborhood and he hoped Luke would get kidnapped. He said Steve would then take Tori inside the warehouse and lock Luke outside the building. Luke said he was scared, but he was also worried about his little sister. He said something didn't seem right about his dad being alone with his sister like that.

Steve and his brother did not get along very well, so Steve bought a warehouse on Martin Street. Steve told Luke to be careful because this warehouse was in a bad part of town also. To substantiate that this warehouse was in a bad neighborhood, the bodies of two black males were found on the new property not long after Steve started using the building. The first body was discovered by Luke one day when he accompanied Steve to the warehouse. Luke said he was riding his bike at the warehouse and he found the body of a black male in the grass beside the ramp that led into the building. Luke said he always felt his dad killed the man because the night before the discovery of the body, his dad left the house saying the alarm was going off at the warehouse and he had to go check and make sure everything was okay. Luke said his dad called the police and officers were everywhere within a few minutes. A few weeks later, Luke found the second body in a weeded area on the property. He remembered that this body smelled as horribly as the first body he discovered. Luke said he tried to talk to the police officers and tell them that he found the bodies, not his dad. He also tried to tell the officers that he thought his dad killed the two men because on several occasions his dad displayed racist tendencies toward black people when he and his dad were alone. Luke stated that his dad had an Uzi semi-automatic machine gun, and he liked to drive through black neighborhoods at night with his window down yelling at people and pointing the gun at them. Luke said that not only did his dad dislike black people, but he also had a fascination with Hitler. He watched anything he could find on TV about Hitler. He also possessed a German army helmet and a Hitler youth knife, and he was very proud of both items. Luke told Bill that on both occasions when police officers were at the warehouse investigating the deaths, they were not interested in talking to him. He tried to talk to them but the officers told him they needed to talk to an adult. After all, he was just a seven year old kid. Bill thought as Luke told him this story that sometimes people need to listen to what children have to say. Bill also thought, "Children have the right to be heard, and, children have the right to be believed."

Steve was friends with a local police officer and enjoyed doing 'ride-alongs' with him. The friend lived in Beaumont when he and Steve met and then he moved to a farm outside a small community about forty miles west of Beaumont. The friend had Steve do an extensive and expensive remodeling job on the farm house. For some reason, this officer, who was in charge of the narcotics unit of his department, had Steve install two safes in his home. One safe was located in the bathroom in the cabinet under the lavatory. The second safe was installed in the closet of one of the bedrooms. Months after the remodeling project was completed, Steve was visited at the warehouse by two FBI agents. They questioned Steve about the remodeling he did at his friend's farm and wanted to know if he knew anything about drugs or money being stored at the farm. Steve mentioned that he installed a safe inside the residence, but he never mentioned the second safe. Luke had been at the warehouse that day. As the agents left the warehouse, Luke tried to talk to them. He tried to tell them he was with his dad at the friend's farm during the remodeling project. He tried to tell the agents that a second safe had been installed. But they didn't listen to him and left the warehouse property. Luke said this was the third time he tried to reach out to officers to tell what he knew, but none of them listened. He was totally discouraged. A short time later, there was a big FBI raid on the officer's property. A SWAT team was called out because the man barricaded himself inside his home, claiming he was being held hostage. To prove he was a hostage, one of his fingers was cut off and thrown out the door to prove the point. The officer wasn't being held hostage. He cut off his own finger in attempt to throw the FBI off-guard, but it didn't work. Eventually the officer surrendered. As the man was arrested, his home was also searched pursuant to a federal search warrant. The incident was all over the news. Only one safe was discovered.

In an interview years later, Luke told Bill that only two officers had ever listened to him. The first officer was Rick Lucas. And the second officer was Bill.

The stress of Steve being mean to Luke really started to bother him. He began to have problems at school. It wasn't learning related or attentive problems. He had accidentally soiled his school uniform, and, it happened on several occasions. Martha told Bill that Luke was potty-trained as a small child, so these accidents were very uncharacteristic of him. His teacher and fellow students could smell it. Luke had to be humiliated by it. Martha said she begged Steve to let her take Luke to a doctor but he wouldn't hear of it. She said Steve didn't believe in doctors and told her that "God would heal him, if he was to be healed." But Martha believed in doctors. She knew that God created doctors and gave them the ability to medically heal people, and she knew something was very wrong with her child. She was usually subservient to her husband, but her child's health was at risk and problems were being caused at school. An appointment was made and Luke was examined by a doctor. The diagnosis was something she had never heard of. Luke was suffering from 'encopresis' due to stress and nerves. Bill smiled as Martha told him this story. Bill presented child abuse programs throughout the country and often informed his audience about this medical problem called encopresis and that it is caused by stress or poor diet. Bill always asked his audience who was in charge of a child's stress and diet. The answer – Parents!

Bill explained that encopresis begins with a child being constipated. When the constipation is not correctly dealt with, it turns to impaction. Sometimes the stool becomes so impacted that it can be almost as hard as concrete. The stool is usually quite large and then it stretches the colon to cause rectal distention. The impaction and distention now causes the rectum to be less sensitive and a person can't feel when they have to go to the bathroom. Bill continued by telling Martha that many parents, because they have never heard of encopresis, give their child the wrong medicine, a laxative. The stool becomes semi-solid and can leak around the impaction, causing involuntary leakage and soiling of clothes. Bill said many parents think the child was too lazy to go to the bathroom, which resulted in them soiling their clothes. Martha listened as Bill told her that many parents whip or even beat their children for soiling their clothes, thinking the child could have prevented it, when in reality, the child didn't even realize what had happened. Bill said he had investigated cases where a parent's ignorance of medical problems affecting their children resulted in the child being abused. Martha said that the doctor instructed her to give Luke a stool-softener. When the impaction was finally passed, Martha said it was the diameter of a goose egg. Martha said that when they left the doctor's office, Luke was very excited. He hugged her and thanked her for getting him a good doctor.

  Tori was about to start pre-kindergarten and Martha knew she could not be with her daughter every moment to protect her. Martha also knew that one way to protect her little girl was through awareness and education. She bought a tape about good touches and bad touches for Tori and Luke to watch. She tried to get Tori to watch the tapes on several occasions throughout the summer, and even after school started. But every time Martha tried to get Tori to watch the tape, she would look away, or play with something, or walk out of the room. She refused to watch the tape. Finally, Martha sat Tori down and warned her to tell someone she trusted if anyone ever touched her in a way that made her feel uncomfortable. Martha told Tori if anyone, a stranger, her uncle, step-brother, cousin, dad, or anyone ever touched her in the bra or panty area, to be sure to tell her or someone she trusted. Luke said he walked up behind Tori later that day after their mom had had her talk with Tori.

When she turned around, he immediately saw that Tori had cut a huge section of her bangs. When he asked her why she had done it, she hung her head and said she didn't know. A few days later, Tori was in a school Christmas play. Her part in the play was one of the angels. Luke said his little sister was an angel and was perfect for the part, except for her missing bangs. Luke told Bill that Tori's refusal to watch the tape and then cutting her bangs after their mom had had her talk with Tori made him even more suspicious that his dad was doing something sexual to his little sister.

Years later, Tori told her mom that when she talked to her about being touched sexually and named off several possible people that might do that to her, she only heard one person being named. Yes, it was her dad. She told her mom she became angry that what her dad was doing to her was wrong. Not knowing what to do, she acted out her anger by cutting her hair. As Bill heard this, it reminded him of so many young people who self-mutilate, such as cutting themselves or hurting themselves in some other way. So many times these young people act out their anger due to them being a victim in some way. Someone needs to ask them, "What's wrong?" Be prepared. They may tell you.

Steve had a backhoe at the Martin Street warehouse that he used on construction sites. Luke said that his dad liked to put him and Tori in the bucket of the backhoe and let them ride in the bucket. Sometimes their dad would drop the bucket suddenly making them feel like their stomach jumped into their throat. Luke said it was not fun riding in the bucket, even when Tori was with him. He did not like riding the rides at the annual fair either, but his dad told him to get in the bucket on these occasions, and he did. He said he did not want to be a disobedient child. Steve knew Luke hated riding in the bucket and this was one of the ways Luke believed his dad liked to terrorize him. One day his dad had him ride in the bucket by himself. When he dropped the bucket this time, he dropped it really fast causing Luke to hit his head on the top part of the bucket. Luke said it hurt very badly. He felt woozy, but he remembered his dad looking at him, grinning, and telling him that he had done it on purpose. Steve helped him out of the bucket and laid him on the floor of the warehouse. Luke said he felt his head where he'd hit the metal bucket and there was a large bump. Martha was at their home on Rosewood Street and Steve called her and told her there had been an accident. Luke said their mom arrived at the warehouse a few minutes later and saw his injury. She began yelling at Steve, asking why he had not taken Luke immediately to the hospital and then called her to have her meet them at the emergency room. Luke said his mom and dad helped him off the floor and assisted him to his mom's car. Luke said she left the warehouse and took him to the hospital emergency room for treatment. Going to the hospital was very rare for their family because their dad's philosophy was "If it was meant for you to be healed, that God would heal you." Luke ended the story by telling Bill that his dad never came to the hospital to check on him. He stayed at the warehouse – with Tori.

For the next five years, Luke told Bill that it seemed his dad spent more and more time alone with Tori. Luke said he wanted to go to the warehouses with his dad and Tori, but most of the time, his dad would make him stay home doing chores while only he and Tori went to the warehouse for whatever reason. Luke said that at first, his dad and Tori went by themselves occasionally. As the years progressed, the two of them went by themselves more and more. Luke mentioned that on many occasions, Tori would ask her dad if Luke could go with them. He always replied that Luke had chores to do and couldn't go. Many times when Steve and Tori returned home, Tori had a sack full of candy. Luke said she always shared it with him.

Luke said his mom and dad bought the one-hundred-twenty-five acres of property in Hardin County in the early part of 1992. When the one-hundred-twenty-five acres was purchased, his mom and dad decided that year that mom would home-school he and Tori instead of going to the Christian school they had been attending. He was now in the eighth grade and Tori was in the fifth grade. Home-schooling gave the family more flexibility in their daily routines.

Luke liked going to the land and walking through the woods. Many times Steve would assign chores to Luke. He said he would hurry with the chores as quickly as possible so that he could be with Tori. Many times when he finished, he discovered his dad had already taken

Tori for a walk in the woods. Luke said that he would run the trails in the woods trying to find them, wanting to protect Tori.

Their dad bought two four-wheelers a few months before the land was purchased. On many occasions, Steve would ride one four-wheeler and Tori would ride the second one. They would leave Luke afoot. He said he would run as hard as he could to catch up with them. Many times he would get close to finding them and he would hear the four wheelers start up and Tori and their dad would go deeper into the woods. Many times it took him an unusually long time to find them. Several times he found them and Tori would look at him with a sad look on her face. He said it really bothered him and he felt that somehow he had let his little sister down, but he didn't know how at the time. Luke told Bill that Tori told him after everything was exposed, that he had almost caught their dad in the act of molesting her several times when he came upon them in the woods.

As they cleared the land and began to build their house, Luke said that his dad seemed to intentionally commit meaner and meaner deeds toward him. At the time, Luke was twelve years old and Tori was nine and one-half years old. Before buying the land, the abuse Luke received from his dad was verbal and emotional, except for the incident involving the backhoe at the warehouse a few years earlier. After purchasing the land, the abuse also became physical. Luke said he was playing by a tree one day and his dad sneaked up behind him. Luke heard a thud and looked at the trunk of the tree that was less than a foot from his head. He immediately recognized the knife blade sticking in the tree beside his head as his dad's. He whirled around and saw his dad grinning only ten feet away.

Luke loved to shoot guns and he and his dad would set up targets in the woods along one of the trails. They practiced shooting at the targets with their rifles. Luke said he had an SKS military rifle. His dad had a M1 Garand rifle that he purchased at a gun show. One day after shooting several bullets at their target that was over one hundred yards away, Luke walked to the target to see how well he had 'grouped' his shots. As he was counting the holes in his shooting group, Luke said he was startled at the deafening sound of a rifle being fired and he could hear the bullet whistling past his head. He looked at his target and saw an extra bullet hole that could not have been more than six inches from his head. He whirled around and saw his dad holding the rifle and grinning. Luke said he was leery that one day his dad would shoot him and this incident was no exception. He knew his dad counted the number of shots he'd fired and thought he was out of ammunition. Luke had become so wary of his dad that he always carried extra bullets or an extra knife hidden in one of his pockets. After looking at Luke and grinning, Steve looked and saw that his semi-automatic rifle had jammed. After he unjammed the rifle, Steve looked back at Luke who had his rifle in one hand and a bullet in the other hand. Luke said his dad's smile quickly disappeared when he saw that his son was not out of ammunition and could defend himself.

Luke said he also loved to go hunting. He and his dad would get their rifles and go deer hunting on their land. Many times his dad would tell him to go down one trail while his dad went down another trail. Luke said he had become very leery of his dad, fearing that his dad wanted to kill him and make it look like an accident. On one of their hunting excursions, Luke said he and his dad got to a fork in the trails and he went one way and his dad took the other trail. The two trails met farther in the woods. Instead of hunting, Luke said he waited and then started trailing his dad. He was very stealthy as he eased through the woods. He finally found his dad. Luke said that instead of his dad looking down the trail that his dad had just walked, his dad was looking down the trail that Luke would have been walking on. Luke said he observed that his dad had his high powered rifle pointed in the direction he would have been walking. Luke said he felt if he had not been suspicious and if he had walked down the trail his dad had told him to walk on, he would have been killed that day. Luke looked at Bill and said he knew his dad was trying to kill him on several occasions. He even confessed that he thought several times about killing his dad. He said it was self-preservation. The only reason he didn't kill his dad was because he didn't want to be arrested and taken to jail.

A few months later Luke and his dad had to use scaffolding to do some work on the outside of the second story of the house. He noticed that the boards they had to walk on were loose, but that was usually the case with scaffolding boards. While they were doing their work, his dad began pushing him. Luke said after his dad pushed him several times, he began to push back. His dad then hit him with his fist so hard it knocked him backward. Before he could regain his balance, his dad stepped toward him and shoved him as hard as he could, knocking him off the two-story scaffolding. Luke said they had been using machetes to clear saplings and other brush from around the house. It was common for a one to three¬ inch stick-up to be protruding from the ground where they had cut the saplings. He landed on the ground with one of the stick-ups deeply bruising his right kneecap.

When Luke and Steve arrived back home for supper, Martha noticed Luke was limping as they entered the house. She immediately asked what happened. Before Luke could respond, Steve said, "Aw, we were just fooling around and he got a little hurt." Martha said that as she looked at Luke, he looked away and said nothing. She figured there was not much to it since Luke did not say anything.

A few weeks later, Martha saw Luke getting ready to take a bath and he was not wearing a shirt. He had a large bruise in the middle of his back. She asked him what had happened. He told her he was working with his dad earlier in the day. His dad got mad at him and threw a hammer at him. He turned away from his dad just in time to avoid the hammer hitting him in the chest. Martha said she hunted Steve down on the property and gave him a piece of her mind for hurting her child. She said Steve shrugged his shoulders and told her they were playing and he got a little hurt. Luke told his mom years later that Steve also shot at him with a nail gun on several occasions. He was hit with the nails on many times, but never at close enough range that would have caused serious injury or death. Luke said he was always far enough away that the nail would be very painful when it hit him, but it would not penetrate his skin. He would always turn and see a sleazy, sneering look on his dad's face. It was as if to say, "I can kill you at any moment."

The knives, the guns, the nail guns, and the verbal statements from his dad toward him made Luke realize he needed to be alert at all times. He said he and his dad would get into fights and his dad tried to inflict pain and injury on him. Luke said he learned to block and deflect punches thrown at him by his dad. He was worried that if he became aggressive, his dad would have him arrested. Luke said that so many times he wanted to kill his dad so the abuse would end. He said he knew he would go to jail if he killed him and he didn't want to ruin his life that way. Luke said his dad came into his bedroom at night on many occasions and hovered over him. He always layed very still so his dad would think he was asleep. Because the years of abuse seemed to be getting worse, Luke said he never knew what to expect and he prepared himself for the worst. For years he went to bed with his hunting knife under the covers with him.

Luke told Bill that for many years he lived every day with the 'dark' dad, the 'ugly' dad. People at church and friends saw the other side – the nice guy, the hard working guy, the good dad, the great husband, the Christian church going man that was always friendly. As Luke found out about Tori's molestation, he realized that not only he, but also his sister saw the 'evil' guy. It was like Steve was two different people.

When Martha caught Steve molesting Tori, Luke said he did get the chance to talk to officers, but because the focus was on what their dad did to his sister, he never told anyone of the abuse he suffered from his dad for many years. Luke said that as the trial began to unfold, he kept waiting for someone to talk to him about the abuse he suffered. He felt that his dad should pay for what he did to him too, but he said he was never asked. He also admitted he was not familiar with the judicial process and throughout the trial he felt it was not the time to tell his story. Luke said he expected he would get a chance to tell his side of what happened and kept expecting someone to ask him if he had also been abused.

Luke finally got to tell his story – in this chapter. Luke was Tori's big brother by two and one-half years. He was also her knight in shining armor. He was her hero. As their mom drove them to meet Greg at Walmart on U.S. Hwy. 69, Tori snuggled next to Luke, his arm around her, holding her tight. Her secret was finally out. She could rest. Luke's suspicions were true. His mind was racing. He wished he could have caught his father molesting his sister days, weeks, months, even years earlier, and stopped the abuse much sooner. He had not been able to. But now his dad was finally caught. One thing was for sure, neither his dad nor anyone else would ever hurt his little sister again. Not if he could help it.

Chapter Nineteen

Court

Many people believe a trial begins when a jury is seated, the defendant is seated at his/her table with their defense attorney, the prosecuting attorney is at his table, and everyone stands as the judge enters the courtroom and the bailiff declares that court is now in session. While this is technically true, the trial actually begins when the crime is committed. Bill had taught veteran law enforcement officers about child abuse and sex crimes investigations at the regional police academy for almost twenty years when he investigated Tori's case. He stressed to officers that every investigation they conduct has the potential to go to trial before the U.S. Supreme Court. This is why Bill taught officers to begin each investigation deliberately, meticulously, and to leave no stone unturned. He encouraged officers to play 'devil's advocate' by having another detective review the case, searching for any loopholes left for a defense attorney to exploit at trial. Bill and his sex crimes detective partner, Gene, did this exercise on many of their cases. This exercise was one of the main reasons their conviction rate was so high on their cases that were accepted by the D.A.'s office.

Many times the trial involving a crime never takes place because there is insufficient evidence or facts to sway the district attorney's office to accept a criminal investigation and send the case to the grand jury for indictment. Hundreds, possibly thousands, of people have asked Bill how he could investigate thousands of child abuse and sex crimes incidents. Their main comment was that it must have been horrible. Bill always replied that the cases are horrible, and he always emphasized that someone has to speak up for the child or rape victim, and God picked him to do the task. Bill also stressed that while all of the cases are horrible, he always received great satisfaction in solving each and every case. Although he could not undo what was done to a child, he could work hard enough to finally end the abuse and hurt and then help the child and innocent family members put their lives back together. Bill also emphasized the cases that bothered him most were not the horrific incidents. The worst cases were the ones when he knew without a doubt who committed the crime, but he did not have sufficient facts and evidence to prove the case to the district attorney's office and in a court of law. He knew who committed the crime, but for now, he could not prove it, and, for the time being, he could not stop that child's abuse.

With some crimes, there is never a big trial because the defendant pleads guilty to the charge. The judge then orders a pre-sentence investigation which is conducted by the probation department. The probation officer requests a criminal background investigation on the defendant and receives a recommendation of punishment from the prosecuting attorney and the defense attorney. Many times the probation officer will contact the detective who completed the criminal investigation and ask for their opinion on sentencing. When the probation officer's investigation is complete, he makes a recommendation for punishment to the judge. Most judges go along with this recommendation and punish the defendant according to what is recommended.

Bill had just left his office at 5:00 p.m. one day and received a call from his sister-in-law, Wendy. In between sobs, she told Bill that she had just spoken with her granddaughter-in-law, Stormy. Wendy's granddaughter, thirteen year-old Misty, had gone to Stormy and made an outcry to her that her father (Wendy's son, John) had been sexually molesting her for years. Misty's mother, Clara, worked out of town for an international corporation twenty out of thirty days every month. When Clara left for work, he would make his daughter move from her bedroom to the master bedroom and would molest her until Clara returned approximately three weeks later. It was too late in the day for Bill to contact the law enforcement agency that needed to handle Misty's investigation. Bill asked Wendy to bring Misty to his house for protection. Clara and Stormy arrived at Bill's home late that night. Both of them were scared of Mark and what he might do to them if he found out that Misty told their 'secret.' There was one person Mark was scared of and respected. Yes, it was Bill. Mark knew Bill would protect Clara and Misty at all costs. The next morning, Bill called a detective with the proper agency. A warrant for Mark was issued late that evening. A plan was drawn up to lure John out of his mobile home the next morning. At about 7:30 a.m. on the following day, Bill, his wife Mary, along with Clara and Misty, sat in Bill's truck parked on the main highway a short distance from the side road of John's mobile home park. An undercover deputy was parked in the mobile home park, and two uniformed sheriff's cars were parked on the highway. Mary made a call to her nephew and said her car was broken down in the grocery store parking lot and she needed his help. He was a good 'shade tree' mechanic and he would do anything for his aunt. Within three minutes, Mark exited his mobile home with one of his sons. Bill handed a pair of binoculars to Misty. Mark drove from the side road to the main highway. The undercover car was behind him. As Mark drove onto the main highway, the uniformed sheriff's cars activated their emergency lights and siren and Mark pulled to the side of the highway. Bill told Misty to watch closely. His precious thirteen year-old niece watched through the binoculars as her father exited his truck. Misty bounced up and down on the back seat of Bill's crew cab truck and watched the deputies handcuff her father. "Do you see him?" Bill asked Misty. "Yes, sir," she replied. "He's taking his last breath of free air," Bill exclaimed to her. Misty put a sign in her bedroom that night. It read, "I can finally sleep free." Two weeks later, Clara called Bill. She, Misty, and all five of her sons were troubled. They wanted to know when Mark's trial was going to start. After all, two weeks had already passed and trials on TV never take that long. Bill chuckled and told Clara that they had watched too many police shows. Later that day, Bill met with Clara and all of her children. He explained that investigations like Stormy's may take months to years before ever going to trial. He told them that the wheel of justice turns slowly. At first the wheel turns quickly. Misty made an outcry. A detective conducted his investigation and turned it over to the district attorney. A warrant was issued, and Mark was arrested. The grand jury indicted Mark. Following that point, Bill explained, the wheel of justice would turn much slower. Everything was up to the judge's court docket as to when their father's trial may be scheduled. Bill asked all of his nephews to promise they would go to counseling. Each of them needed counseling because they had been beaten by their father and threatened with death if they revealed to their mother, or an anyone else, what he was doing while she was away at work. All of them were also angry. They were sure their father was sexually molesting their little sister, but they were unable to prevent it from happening. Bill told them they could help their little sister most by going for counseling. They all promised. More than a year later, Mark pled guilty to the charge of "Continuous Sexual Abuse of Young Child or Children" and began serving a thirty year prison sentence. Under this charge, Mark will not get out of prison for good behavior. He must serve his sentence day for day. His children learned that a criminal investigation and the judicial process does not occur in a day or two, or a week or two. They learned, in the end, that justice usually prevails. They also learned that no matter how much time their father spends in prison, it will never be long enough to heal the pain he inflicted on his family. Wendy made sure her granddaughter received counseling. None of the boys followed through with their promise to seek counseling.

Tori's case was set to go to trial on Judge Barnes' docket for Monday, July 14, 1995. It was three days shy of the one-year anniversary when Martha walked in and caught Steve seconds after he molested Tori. The crime victim's advocate, Crystal, called Martha a couple of weeks earlier and scheduled an appointment for her, Tori, and Luke to meet her in the lobby of the Jefferson County Courthouse. As a witness, a person is always apprehensive, sometimes even terrified about testifying. One of the ways to lessen some of the courtroom fear is to introduce potential witnesses to a courtroom. Crystal met Martha, Luke, and Tori in the courthouse lobby and she explained that Judge Barnes was in a trial and they would not be visiting his courtroom, however, there were other courtrooms they could visit. Crystal escorted the trio through the lobby, past the restrooms, and into a small hallway that housed the offices and courtrooms of the county's two justices of the peace for Precinct One. As they entered one of the courtrooms, Martha remarked that it was smaller than she had imagined. Crystal explained that courtrooms are much smaller than what is depicted on TV, although Judge Barnes' courtroom was much larger than the room they were in. Crystal pointed out the judge's bench, the witness chair, and the court reporter's location. She showed them which table was for the prosecutor and the defense attorney and where Steve would be sitting during the trial. She showed them the chairs where the jury would sit to hear and see all of the testimony and evidence. It was easy for Tori, Luke, and Martha to see the benches where the spectators watching the trial would be sitting. Crystal explained that all of them were potential witnesses in the trial and they would not be allowed to hear each other's testimony. They would be admonished by the judge to not discuss their testimony with anyone except their respective attorney. She told them there were special rooms for witnesses where they would be placed to wait their turn to be called to the courtroom to testify. Martha remarked to Crystal that her description of courtroom procedure was certainly different from what was depicted on TV.

Throughout the summer of 1995, June kept her niece and nephew busy working at her office. Tori and Luke stayed busy filing papers for the lawsuits June was involved with. Steve's trial was one week away when Randy called Martha. He needed to review Tori and Martha's testimonies before the trial began. Tori's interview with Randy was scheduled for the Wednesday before the trial began. June took time off from her busy schedule to take Tori to see her prosecutor. Tori thought the prosecutor reminded her of an oversized teddy bear as Randy introduced himself to her. They sat in his office for over an hour as Randy talked with her about her testimony. He tried to assure her that everything was going to be fine. Tori was still nervous. It was her first time to ever testify. "He has probably been in a courtroom a ca'zillion times," she thought.

Martha's interview with Randy was the following day. She brought her notebook with all of her notes. She read over them several times the previous day. He introduced himself to Martha as she sat across his desk from him. He began by discussing her divorce from Steve and how the defense attorney, Stewart, was making an issue of it. He told Martha that Stewart would probably stipulate that she and the kids did not want to move to the top of a mountain in West Texas, so she filed for a divorce and prompted Tori into making false allegations against her father. Suddenly, Randy's phone rang. Martha could tell the call was about another case that was assigned to Randy for prosecution. The call seemed to last a very long time. It finally ended, and as Randy was turning his attention back to Martha, the phone rang again. That call continued for over an hour. Martha waited patiently. As the last call ended, Randy reminded her to listen to each question and think about her answer before giving it. He ushered her back to the lobby. The interview was over.

On Monday morning, Judge Barnes entered the courtroom and looked at all of the prosecutors and defense attorneys who awaited his reading of the week's courtroom docket. Ten cases were set for trial in his courtroom for that week. He read aloud the first case set on the docket. It was a burglary of a business case. The prosecutor announced they were ready for trial. The defense attorney announced they were ready to accept a plea bargain for the defendant, and the case was resolved in a matter of minutes. Judge Barnes announced the second case on the docket. It was a robbery case. The defense attorney and his client also accepted a plea deal. The judge moved on to the third case on his docket. It was a murder case. Both the prosecution and the defense announced they were ready for trial. This trial would probably last most, if not all week. Seven cases were still on the docket. All of them would be reset on Judge Barnes' court docket. The new court date was several weeks away. Seven victims and their families had psyched themselves up for a trial. Having their cases postponed was a terrible disappointment for each of them. Tori's case had been eighth on the docket.

Martha called Randy's office the following week. He was busy in court, but she was able to visit with his secretary. Tori's case was reset for Monday, August 11. Randy was usually very busy the week before a court date, so he didn't have time to interview Tori and Martha again. He asked his secretary to call them and remind them to be ready for trial in a few days. They were fifth on the judge's docket, and they were cautioned to be ready. Their case may, or may not make it to trial. An aggravated assault case involving a shooting was second on the docket and it appeared the defendant was not going for a plea.

The docket was read by Judge Barnes on Monday morning. The robbery case was set first on the docket, and a plea was accepted. The judge moved on to the second case. The defense attorney announced they were ready for trial. Randy's secretary called Martha and told her Randy believed the aggravated assault case would take no more than two days to try. The secretary told Martha to stay by the phone for Tuesday afternoon or Wednesday morning. The secretary called again Wednesday morning. The trial had ended Tuesday afternoon but the third case on the docket was going to trial and Tori's case would be rescheduled again. By now, Martha, Tori, and Luke were beginning to understand the court system a little more. They realized that even though your case may be set for trial on a certain day, it does not necessarily mean it will actually go to trial on that day. They were feeling the emotional ups and downs of the judicial system.

Martha learned the next week that Tori's case was reset for Monday, September 8. They were now third on the judge's docket. As that Monday morning arrived, they were ready for trial. They all thought they would surely go to trial this week, and their emotions were high. Each of them had gone over their testimony countless times in their mind. They were ready. The first case on the docket entered a plea. The second case went to trial. They were devastated again. Tori was crying and distraught. Martha was upset and trying to understand this criminal justice system that seemed to re-victimize the victims and their families again and again. She turned to the only person she knew that had not let them down. Bill answered his phone and recognized Martha's voice. Her tone told him that she was very upset. He was unaware that the case had been reset for a fourth time. He listened to Martha as she vented her frustrations. Giving up and dismissing the case was not an option for Martha or Tori, but they didn't understand the judicial system. They were tired of working up to an emotional high preparing for trial and then having the rug pulled from under them, and they were looking for some answers. Bill pushed back and stopped working on paperwork regarding another investigation. A victim and their family needed his help. Bill asked Martha if he could share a true story with her, and she agreed to listen. He told her the young lady's name was Brandy and she attended his church. She was the victim of an incestuous relationship, and her step-father was the suspect. Brandy's victimization did not begin when she was a small child like Tori. Brandy's victimization began when she was eleven years old. She was scared to tell anyone because her step-father had threatened to kill her mother if she ever told. Bill told Martha that Brandy's molestation continued until she was nineteen years old. He continued, telling Martha that he was the greeter at his small church, and every Sunday when Brandy arrives for church he gets the biggest hug in the world from Brandy's little daughter, Tracy, who is a product of the incestuous crimes committed against Brandy. Bill told Martha that Brandy's case was not reset four times like Tori's had been. Brandy's case was reset fifteen times before it went to trial. He said there were many occasions when Brandy would come to church and he would greet Brandy, Tracy, and Brandy's little boy, Brandon, at the door. After getting hugs from the children and them going on to children's church, Brandy would begin to cry and tell Bill how her case was reset for the umpteenth time. She was so frustrated that she decided to call her prosecutor the next morning and drop the charges against her step-father. She said she couldn't handle it anymore. Bill told Martha that he always let Brandy vent her frustrations, then he asked her how she felt about letting her step-father get away with victimizing her for over eight years. Bill then brought up the civil side of the law to Brandy. The step-father was not only Tracy's grandfather, he was also her father. Bill told Brandy that if she dropped the criminal charges against him, he could hire an attorney and pursue custody of Tracy since he was biologically her father. Bill told Martha that the civil issue gave Brandy the courage to hold up to her criminal case being reset fifteen times. He ended the story by telling Martha that Brandy's step-father was serving fifty years in prison for the crimes he committed against this innocent girl. There was a pause on the phone. Martha told Bill it was a good story and to not worry. They would all be ready for trial the fourth, or the fourteenth time it was reset.

  Martha called Randy's secretary after she hung up from talking to Bill. She discovered Tori's case had been reset for Monday, October 6. Tori's case was first on Judge Barnes's docket.

The judge entered his courtroom promptly at 8:30 a.m. Monday morning. He told everyone to be seated and told his assistant, Ms. Jones, to begin the week's docket call. "Carpenter vs. The State of Texas," she proclaimed. Randy stood and stated, "The State is ready, Your Honor." George Stewart was present in court and proclaimed, "The defense is ready, Your Honor." The judge then ordered them to be ready for trial at 1:30 p.m. that afternoon, and the court continued calling out other cases on the week's docket.

Martha, Luke, and Tori awoke that Monday morning and prepared to leave for the courthouse, but then they waited. They waited for the phone to ring, and they waited. They all jumped when the telephone suddenly began to ring. Martha answered. It was Randy. "Meet me at the courthouse at 12:30 p.m. for a final briefing," he instructed. "We'll be there," Martha replied. The time had finally come. They all had butterflies in their stomachs. Tori's story was about to be told.

Martha parked in the courthouse parking lot. She and her children were in the district attorney's lobby on time. Randy arrived a few minutes later and took them to his office. He told them the first thing that must be done as the trial process began was to pick a jury. He explained that in legal terms, the jury selection process is called "voir dire." He stated that as soon as twelve jurors were picked they would be seated in the jury box. They would then stand and be sworn in as jurors. The formal charge would be read and Steve would stand with Stewart and answer to the charge. If he pled guilty, the trial would take a turn and go straight to the punishment phase. If he pled not guilty, then the trial would begin with Randy calling Tori to the witness stand. He also explained they would probably not be allowed to hear each other's testimony. They told Randy they thought this was strange because the trials on television always had the witnesses sitting in the courtroom and hearing testimony from other witnesses. He smiled and explained that was not the way trials are conducted in the real world. A few minutes later they walked toward the courtroom on the second floor of the courthouse. Randy showed them the witness rooms and they took a seat. It was time to wait once more.

Randy put his papers for the trial in order at the prosecutor's table. Stewart did the same at the defense table. People gradually walked into the courtroom and took a seat. A bailiff handed numbers to them as they entered the courtroom. At 1:30 p.m., the bailiff arrived and announced that court was in session and everyone rose from their seat. Judge Barnes entered and took his seat at the bench. He instructed everyone else to be seated. Then, one by one, the people sitting in the courtroom gallery began to be questioned. All of them, thirty-two in all, were potential jurors. They were all asked if they knew of someone that had been the victim of child sexual abuse. Several of them raised their hands. A male member of the jury panel stated he had a relative who had been the victim of sexual abuse by another family member. He stated that nothing had been done legally to this person and he felt he could not be fair and impartial. Another member of the panel also had a relative, a niece, who was the victim of sexual abuse. She said the defendant was the niece's brother. She stated that even though she experienced this incident in her family, she felt she could be fair in rendering the proper verdict in this case. Another lady in the panel who had raised her hand was asked to tell of the incident she was referring to. She said she was the victim of child sexual abuse and the defendant in her incident was also a family member and that nothing was ever done legally. She stated she felt she could also be fair in rendering the proper verdict. Another lady that raised her hand stated she had also been a victim of child sexual abuse. She said nothing was done to her perpetrator legally, but she also felt she could render a fair verdict. Lastly, a fifth person, another lady, raised her hand. She stated that her mother had been a child sexual abuse victim and the perpetrator had also been a family member. She also felt she could render a fair verdict in the case.

As Bill heard from those who raised their hands from the group of thirty-two individuals, he was reminded of the national statistics of child sexual abuse. One in three females and one in six males will be sexually abused in some manner prior to their eighteenth birthday (U.S. Dept. of Health & Human Services). It was interesting to note that this group of thirty-two randomly selected individuals was exactly in line with the national statistics.

After questions were asked by Randy and Stewart, the jury selection began. Jury selection is done by a process of elimination. Eight members of the jury panel were dismissed for one reason or another. When twenty-four remained, Stewart got to strike six members for no reason at all. Maybe he didn't like their looks or maybe he didn't like their profession. His reasons did not matter. He got to strike six people from the panel. Likewise, Randy did the same. As their numbers were called, individuals walked to the jury box and sat down. Of the thirty-two individuals who were the original jury panel, the jurors holding #3, #5, #6, #8, #9, #12, #13, #15, #16, #24, #26, and #27 were seated. As #27 arrived at the jury box, they were all asked to stand and Judge Barnes swore them in as jurors. Judge Barnes turned to Steve and stated, "The defendant will stand. The State will read the indictment." Randy then began to read the formal indictment against Steve. The indictment stated that the grand jurors indicted Steve related to an incident on or about November 1, 1996, in Jefferson County, State of Texas, where he sexually assaulted Tori, also called the complainant, being younger than seventeen years of age, by intentionally and knowingly causing the penetration of the female sexual organ of the complainant by inserting his male sexual organ and that she was younger than fourteen years old. This indictment constituted a felony charge of Aggravated Sexual Assault. Judge Barnes turned to Steve and stated, "Mr. Carpenter, you've heard the State read the indictment. Do you plead guilty or not guilty?" Steve, still standing, said four words, "Not guilty, Your Honor." The judge acknowledged his plea and ordered him to sit. He then turned to the jury and began giving them instructions. He told them court would be held from 8:30 a.m. to 5:00 p.m. until the trial was over. He added that sufficient breaks throughout the day and for lunch would take place. He told them they could not talk to anyone about the case. He also admonished them to not read anything about the case while they were a juror, not to go to the scene, to listen carefully throughout the trial, and to see the bailiff if there was a problem. He also told them they could take notes, but they were not allowed to take their notes into the jury room when they began deliberations. After giving the jury their instructions, the judge adjourned court. There were some legal matters he and the two attorneys needed to discuss in the judge's office. Martha, Tori, and Luke were sent home to wait another day for their day in court.

Judge Barnes was a very punctual individual and convened court promptly at 8:30 a.m. on Tuesday. The jury was not seated because the judge and two attorneys had to provide testimony about legal issues they had discussed the day before. Having these legal issues entered into the court record, the jury was brought in and seated. Tori, Luke, Martha, June, Teresa, and Bill were in the courtroom gallery. Judge Barnes turned to Randy and asked him if he would like to make a brief opening statement to the jury. Randy acknowledged that he would and began by stating he believed the evidence would show a tragedy. He continued by saying that the evidence will show something that, although we all realize it happens, none of us want to really face the fact that it does happen. Randy continued telling the jury the evidence should show how Steve isolated himself and Tori for the sole purpose of sexually abusing her. He told the jury the evidence would show how difficult it is for a young girl, barely a teenager, to talk about this kind of thing happening to her. He continued, stating "The evidence would further show how difficult it is for a mother of this child to talk about the sense of shock, horror, and betrayal that she felt upon finding out what was going on with her husband and her own, their very own, flesh and blood."

Judge Barnes turned and said, "Mr. Stewart, would you like to make yours (opening statement) now, or wait until they rest?" Stewart stated he would make a statement. He turned to the jury and said "There's a popular radio personality who has a saying, "That's the rest of the story." He continued by saying, "There's going to be evidence to show there's a lot more to this." He then alluded that all of this criminal episode was being brought on because of a divorce. He continued stating that there was a large amount of property and the evidence would show that one person ended up with all of that. He ended his opening statement stating, "Look at motives, look at bias. Thank you."

Bill sat in the gallery and soaked in all that Stewart had just stated. In essence, Stewart wanted these twelve jurors to believe that

Tori, Martha, and Luke were going through all the rigors of a police investigation, and now all of the pressures and humiliation of a public trial and having to testify to all of the sordid details of a sexual abuse allegation against Steve, just to acquire a few acres of land in a divorce. Bill shook his head in disbelief. Did Stewart really believe these twelve jurors were that gullible? Did he really believe these twelve people would buy into the scheme that Tori would allow herself to be put through this kind of trauma just to help her mother get a divorce and send her dad to prison? Bill smiled as he thought, no, this was the only meager defense Stewart could muster. Let the testimony begin.

As Stewart sat down from his opening statement, Judge Barnes turned to Randy and stated, "State may call its first witness." Randy stated, "State would call Victoria Carpenter, Your Honor." As Tori rose from sitting beside Martha, and began walking toward the witness chair, Stewart rose and stated, "Your Honor, we would invoke the rule at this time." The judge turned to the jury and explained that the rule had been invoked. He stated that basically meant that defense counsel is asking that all the witnesses who may testify have to remain outside the courtroom so that one witness cannot hear the testimony of other witnesses. Judge Barnes then stated that all witnesses for the State or defense must leave the courtroom at that time. Martha, Luke, June, Teresa, Bill, and other witnesses that had been notified they may have to testify, exited the courtroom. One person that was not going to be a witness was Crystal, the crime victim's assistance representative who had been with Tori as she gave Bill her statement. Crystal sat on the front row. She purposely sat in an opening between the corner of the prosecutor's table and the podium that was positioned between the defense and prosecutor tables. The podium was where the attorneys were to stand during most of their questioning of a witness. Tori could easily see Crystal from the witness chair. Crystal's presence helped to calm Tori as she sat in the chair waiting for the questioning to begin.

Tori's testimony began with Randy asking her to state her full name and she did. He asked her if he and she had talked and she said, yes. He asked her if at any time had he told her what to say and she said, no. He asked her if he told her she must tell the truth about everything that happened to her and she said, yes. He asked her how old she was and she replied, thirteen. She explained she had just become a teenager only a couple of weeks earlier and told her birth date. Tori stated her family, her dad, mom, brother, and she lived at a residence in Hardin County. Randy asked Tori the names of her family members and she stated their names. When Tori named her father's name, Randy asked if her father was in the courtroom. Tori said, yes. Randy asked Tori to point to her father and describe what he was wearing, and she did. Randy stated, "Your Honor, may the record reflect the witness has identified the defendant?" "The record will so indicate," Judge Barnes replied. Randy asked to approach Tori from the podium and Judge Barnes granted it. Tori had begun crying. Randy asked, "Why did you start crying, Victoria?" She answered, "Because it hurts me to see him." Randy now centered his questioning on the incident for which Steve had been indicted. It was one of the many incidents where he sexually assaulted Tori at the warehouse located at 546 Martin Street. Randy showed Tori a photo of the outside of the warehouse that was taken by the police department's I.D. technicians, Angela and Sharon. It was marked State's Exhibit #1 and entered into evidence for the trial. Randy asked, "Victoria, there in the building at 546 Martin Street, did your father ever sexually molest you there?" She answered, "Yes." He asked, "On one occasion or more than one occasion?" She answered, "More than one." Randy then focused his questioning on Steve's office located on the second floor of the building. Tori described that Steve would always lock the office door and usually check the answering machine. On the occasion she was testifying to, she said he then went to the bathroom and got some baby wipes or toilet paper. Randy asked, "Victoria, frankly, when your dad went into the bathroom and got baby wipes or he got toilet paper, frankly, what did that tell you was going to happen?" Tori answered, "That he was going to molest me." Randy asked, "You were eleven years old. How long had this been going on?" Tori answered, "As far back as I can remember." Randy turned his questioning to the black couch in the office and Tori explained her dad moved the black couch from office to office for several years. She explained he kept rags on the shelves in the office and he got one and placed it on the couch.

She explained he would lay a rag on the couch, have her sit on it, and also use it to clean himself and her after he abused her. Tori testified he would tell her to get naked and he would then start rubbing her. Randy asked her where and she stated, "On my vagina." He asked Tori if she remembered first having a talk with her mom about things like that, that a girl is supposed to learn from her mom. Tori answered, "About age four." Tori explained her mom told her no one should touch her there because it was not right. Randy asked Tori, knowing it was wrong for someone to touch her there, "Did you ever tell anybody about it?" Tori answered, "No." "Why?" Randy asked. Tori responded, "Because I was afraid he'd either hurt me or he would hurt my family or something totally wrong would happen." Randy asked, "Even though this is your dad. Right?" Tori nodded affirmatively. Randy told her she had to answer aloud and she said, "Yes." Randy asked, "Did he ever tell you to keep it a secret?" Tori answered, "yes" on two occasions he told her not to tell anybody. Randy now turned his questioning to the actual molestation. He asked Tori about Steve rubbing her on her vagina and she explained that he penetrated her with his finger. Randy asked, "How could you tell he penetrated your vagina with his finger?" Tori answered, "Because he would jab his finger in me and it would hurt." Randy asked her what happened next. Tori described how he would rub her breasts and then put his mouth on her vagina, rubbing his tongue on her. Randy then had Tori explain how her dad would then place his male sexual organ in contact with her female sexual organ. Tori described how her dad would lie on the couch and have her sit on top of him. She described how their sex organs would be in contact with each other and he would move back and forth until white stuff would come out of his penis. She said he would quickly clean himself up with the rag. Randy needed to get this testimony into evidence because this was the legal description of what constitutes sexual assault.

  As Tori was testifying and having to describe in great detail the sex acts her dad had inflicted on her, the courtroom door quietly opened. From Tori's viewpoint, she saw about twenty young people, about the same age as she was, enter the courtroom accompanied by two adults. She quickly figured it was a school field trip that had entered the courtroom. They were going to hear her describe the sexual acts she had to endure. Her mind quickly told her there were several courtrooms they could have gone to. Yet, they entered the courtroom where she was testifying. She knew Randy would have never approved anything like this. She quickly concluded it was a scheme by her father's attorney to embarrass her to the point she would cave in and be too embarrassed to testify. She later found out that her guess was right. This classroom had been the idea of Stewart and his hope was that she would be so embarrassed she would stop testifying and his client would get off due to Judge Barnes having to declare a mistrial. Stewart guessed wrong. The students made Tori mad and even more determined to get the truth out. As each question was asked, Tori looked at Crystal sitting on the front row. Crystal had a positive and comforting look on her face as her eyes met Tori's. Her testimony suddenly became even more articulate than ever. Stewart's maneuver failed.

Randy continued his questioning of Tori, but now changed his questions to Steve molesting her in their home when they lived on Rosewood Street. Stewart constantly objected to Randy's questioning being extraneous. Judge Barnes had to stop and have a hearing in his office with the attorneys. It gave Tori a chance to calm herself and collect her thoughts to continue her testimony. It gave the jury a chance to have a coffee and restroom break. About twenty minutes later, the Judge overruled Stewart's objection (which Stewart would later use in appeals to the 9th Court of Appeals and on to the Texas Court of Criminal Appeals), and resumed testimony. As Randy resumed his questioning, he asked Tori if her father molested her once or many times in their home. She answered, "Many times." It's sad to think that for so many children, their home, which should be their safe haven, the place where they feel safe and not threatened, turns out to be their 'hell on earth.' Randy continued his questioning by asking Tori where Steve molested her in the home. She answered naming her bedroom, the bathroom the family shared, in the closet in the hallway, in the bathroom by the back door, and the upstairs bathroom. This meant that almost every room in that home had an unpleasant memory for Tori. He asked her how Steve molested her and she described basically the same way he had molested her at the warehouse. Randy then showed her a photo of another warehouse that Steve leased at one time. Tori identified it and described the many times her dad molested her there, too. He asked Tori if anything stood out in her mind that was different than the other locations. She answered, yes, and then described a yellow couch he had in his office at this warehouse. She described how he had molested her at least three times on that piece of furniture. Tori also described how her father would molest her on or in the pickup truck he drove. The second warehouse had a ramp that allowed him to drive his truck into the warehouse and then close a garage door, securing the facility. She described how he would have her stand on the truck railing. At this height, she described that her waist was even with his waist. Tori then described how he would perform penile/vaginal contact until ejaculation occurred. Randy continued his chronological direct examination by moving his questioning to the family moving to their residence in Hardin County. Randy jumped forward in the calendar of events and asked Tori if something concerned her in the month of 1997. Tori answered that she began her period, her menstrual cycle, that month. She testified she was afraid her father would get her pregnant. Randy moved forward to July 16, and Tori described her father molesting her that evening. Tori said that earlier in the day, her dad asked her to stay home from mid-week church so they could have some 'funzies.' She explained that was his way of telling her that he was going to molest her that night while her brother and mother were gone from the house. Tori articulately described how her father began molesting her on the vanity of the upstairs bathroom in their partially constructed home. On this night, she stated he did something additional to her that he'd never done before. He forced his penis into her mouth. She continued, stating that as he was doing this to her, she heard the front door slam and heard her mother's voice. She described her dad's panic and heard her mom coming up the stairs toward the bathroom as he ran out of the bathroom and down the stairs. She said that as her mom entered the bathroom she was wearing only her bra and panties. Her mom asked what he was doing in the bathroom and Tori said she lied at first in fear of what her dad might do to them. She finally began to cry and admitted to her mom that he had been molesting her. Tori said her mom left the bathroom and she hurriedly got dressed. She ran to the master bedroom window and saw her mom confronting her dad in the yard. Her mom called her and she ran outside to her mom. Tori testified to the jury that her dad told her, "Victoria, I never meant to hurt you in any way." Tori then described how she and her mother left and drove to town and got Luke from church. They then drove and met her brother, Greg. She stated a little later that evening, they drove to the beach to get away from her dad. Randy's last questions asked Tori if she was younger than fourteen years old when all of her molestation by her dad occurred. She answered, "Yes." Aggravated Sexual Assault of a Child, Texas Penal Code Section 22.021 had been established. Randy finished his questioning for the time being. Tori's cross examination by Stewart was about to begin. The Judge ordered a short recess.

As court reconvened, Stewart got right to the point. He asked Tori if she was aware of the divorce proceeding between her mom and dad, and she was. He asked if she knew what her mom got from the divorce. She said she was aware of her mom getting the house and the land and some other things. He also brought up home-schooling and asked whose idea that was. Tori testified it was her dad's idea. Stewart passed the witness. He was done. Maybe he thought it would inflame the jury to harp on the molestation. Maybe he thought Tori had done such an outstanding and articulate job of describing her molestation that any further questioning would certainly cause the jury to find his client guilty as charged. Judge Barnes instructed Tori she could step down from the witness chair. She walked out of the courtroom to the witness room where her mom sat. She fell into the comfort of her mother's arms. She had testified in the presence of her father as to the seven years of 'hell' he put her through. She had done it.

Randy called Barbara Harrison as his next witness. She began her testimony explaining her job of conducting sexual assault forensic examinations and her qualifications. Barbara had been one of the first sexual assault nurse examiners in the Southeast Texas area. She was also the only nurse in Texas that had a non-profit business apart from a hospital that specifically was for forensic evidence collection associated with adult rape incidents and child sexual molestation incidents. Barbara described how she began her examination of Tori with taking a brief statement from her for diagnosis and treatment. This brief statement, Barbara explained, was so that she could do a better examination on Tori. Randy then centered his questioning with Barbara on her genital examination of Tori. He had Barbara explain what a colposcope was and how she used the magnification of the instrument to better examine Tori. Randy then introduced an enlarged photograph of Tori's genital area and had Barbara come from the witness chair and stand by the enlarged photo. Barbara then educated the jury about the female genital area. She had testified many times in other trials and was very good in educating jurors, dispelling myths about the hymen, and describing how her findings led her to believe that Tori had been the victim of sexual abuse. She showed the jury that Tori had a complete absence of hymenal tissue in one location and testified that this loss was consistent with penetration of the female sexual organ. As Randy passed the witness to Stewart, he had to ask Barbara if she found evidence that his client had committed the molestation to Tori. She explained that it had been more than seventy-two hours since the last molestation when she examined Tori and no specific evidence was found by her linking Steve to the molestation of his daughter. Her evidence showed that it was consistent with the history Tori gave her when she began the exam.

    Martha was Randy's next witness. As soon as she took the witness stand, Randy had her point out her ex-husband, Steve, which she did. Randy had Martha quickly testify about her marriage to Steve, their homes, warehouses, and construction business. He finally got to Martha's testimony about July 16, 1997. She described how Tori wanted to go to church that night and how she begged her daughter to stay and help her dad. Martha described how Tori started to cry and finally gave in to staying at home under the pretense of helping her dad do carpentry work. She continued her testimony describing how she returned home after taking Luke to church. As she entered the house, she described ascending the stairs toward the bathroom. She stated that Steve exited through the black plastic bathroom door curtain and had an unmistakable erection underneath his boxer shorts as he descended the stairway. Randy had Martha describe how she observed Tori wearing only panties and attempting to put on her bra when she entered the bathroom. Randy cautioned Martha that she could not testify to Tori's statements, but Martha did testify that Tori told her she had been molested. The testimony turned to her confrontation with Steve in the yard. She testified that he said, "You don't realize how many other people do this," and "It's not what you think." Martha said Steve told her, "You know, I've been having people lay hands on me and casting out demons." He also told her it didn't go on for very long. She testified that he also asked her to just let him go and not file charges on him and he promised he would never touch Tori again. Martha's testimony continued as Randy asked if Steve had an unusual way of having sex with her. In Martha's description of her and Steve having sex, she described her sex with him as being identical to the way Steve had sex with Tori. Randy then turned his questioning to the many letters Steve had sent to Martha. He specifically questioned her about the letter Steve sent her from jail in September 1997. Randy had Martha read to the jury the part of the letter where he asked Martha to have Tori recant her story given to Major Moore and Sgt. Davis. Randy went on to introduce three more letters as evidence where Steve asked Martha to get Tori to recant her story. In one letter, Steve used examples from the Bible how God rewarded people for lying. Martha stated she thought the letter was another attempt for Steve to control them and felt it was threatening. Randy passed the witness to Stewart. He had Martha go through a short family history, how she got the land and house in the divorce, and was receiving all the proceeds through renting part of the property. His questioning was very short and Martha stepped down from the witness stand.

Randy's next witness was Sgt. Bill Davis. Randy had Bill explain how a phone call from Major. Ben Moore got him involved in this complex investigation. Randy asked Bill if he went to the warehouses, the house on Rosewood Street, and the house and land in Hardin County, which he answered, yes. Randy asked Bill, "Now, what was the purpose of you, Detective Davis, going to all of these separate locations involving this one investigation." Bill answered, "Pursuant to my investigation in Beaumont and pursuant to my interview with the child, I realized as I began my interview with her and as other locations became known to me, I knew that either I could send this child to different locations and areas for extra investigations or I could do it all myself in one setting with her, which was my decision to do, to lessen the trauma to the child." Bill then explained that he had the department's I.D. personnel follow him to the two warehouses and the residence on Rosewood Street. He stated he had photos taken of every location where Tori said he molested me here, and here, and here, and so on. As Randy completed his questioning of Bill and passed the witness, Stewart requested and was granted time to read Bill's ten page supplementary report before cross examining the detective. After several minutes of reading, Stewart looked at the Judge said, "We have no questions, Your Honor." Stewart's eyes made contact with Bill's. The look said it all. Bill knew he'd done an investigation that gave Stewart almost nothing to work with. Bill smiled at the defense attorney as he exited the witness stand.

    Teresa was Randy's next witness. As she took the stand and was sworn in, she gave her background information and explained she knew Steve through church. She also identified him sitting next to his attorney. Randy then centered Teresa's testimony to the telephone call she received from Steve on July 26. Teresa said she could tell something was troubling Steve. She asked him if something was wrong and she testified, "He told me that he had been sexually abusing Victoria, his daughter, that he wanted me to call Martha, his wife, and ask her to forgive him and Tori to forgive him for what he had done. He told me that he had gone to Brother Black, which is a pastor in Beaumont who does deliverance, and had been prayed for in deliverance and that he wanted his wife's forgiveness and he wanted her to drop the charges that were against him." Teresa said that "Steve is a man that preached the word of God and it was very shocking to me." Randy asked Teresa if she felt that Steve was concerned about what he had done, or concerned about getting caught. Teresa answered that she felt he was only concerned about getting caught. She said the comment he made to her that she couldn't get past was, "he said he never forced Tori to do anything – he never had to force her to do anything." Teresa said she was shocked at his statement and told him, "Don't you realize how horrible this is?" Teresa also testified that earlier in her conversation with Steve, he said that Martha had caught "them." She felt that Steve was insinuating that Tori was a consenting partner of the sexual episode. Randy asked her why she thought that was an odd thing for him to say. Teresa said, "Well, because she's a child, she's a little girl. She's not a grown woman, consenting adult."

As Stewart began his cross-examination, he immediately asked Teresa if she knew of Steve and Martha's divorce and that she got everything. Teresa commented that she was aware that Martha got whatever she and Steve agreed on. Stewart saw he didn't get anywhere with that question. He then asked Teresa if she had visited Steve in jail. She said, "no," and her cross-examination was over. Stewart had run into roadblocks with every witness.

As Teresa stepped down from the witness stand, Randy addressed the court, "Your Honor, subject to its right of rebuttal, the State of Texas rests." Direct testimony was over. Randy felt he had produced more than sufficient evidence to have the jury find Steve Carpenter guilty of sexually assaulting his little daughter for years and years.

Before Stewart began presenting his defense witness(es) in an attempt to get the jury to find Steve 'not guilty' of the charges, Judge Barnes called a recess. The bailiff escorted the jury into the jury room for a coffee and restroom break. Judge Barnes, Randy, and Stewart retired to the Judge's chambers to discuss legal matters involving the case. All of the witnesses – Tori, Martha, Bill, and Teresa – gathered in the courtroom gallery to relax and visit, but not to discuss their testimony. They were all still under "the rule." Barbara Harrison left the courthouse to attend to business at her office.

Stewart began Steve's defense as court reconvened. He called Steve to the witness stand. After testifying to being a contractor and his ex-wife helping with the business, Stewart asked him about Teresa and their telephone conversation. He asked Steve if he said the statements Teresa claimed that he said. Steve responded, "I did not." Stewart asked Steve if he ever molested his daughter and named each location that had come into question. After naming each location and asking Steve if he molested Tori there, he responded by denying the molestation at each location. Stewart then turned the questioning to July 16. He said he, Martha, and Tori got into a big argument because he wanted to move to West Texas and they did not. Stewart asked Steve if later that night, was there an allegation of an incident with him running through the house in his boxer shorts. Stewart asked, "Well, did that happen?" Steve responded, "No sir, it did not." Stewart even asked Steve about his and Martha's sex life. He asked Steve if Martha's rendition of their sex life was true. Of course, Steve denied it. He said he thought their sex life was wholesome and normal. Stewart asked him where he thought Martha might have come up with these peculiar sex acts. Steve said that at one point, Martha's background was promiscuous. He said she had worked in a topless bar and had live-in friends at her home after her first husband's death. Stewart turned to Steve being arrested in Jefferson County and asked if he wrote Martha any letters while in jail. Steve said he wrote her about one-hundred-fifty letters. When Stewart asked Steve if he ever asked them to recant their stories, Steve said, "I asked them to recant what they had lied about." Stewart ended his direct examination of Steve by asking him, "Did you ever molest her at any of these locations?" Steve answered, "Never."

Randy began his questioning by asking Steve if everyone was lying on him. Steve merely stated he believed everyone was "misinformed." Randy asked, "How is your daughter misinformed about you putting your penis in contact with her vagina?" Steve then said she had probably been traumatized by his wife and sister. Steve said he believed all of this was a conspiracy against him. He went so far as to testify that he and other members of his family were believers and on the side of forces of light. He said his sister and other family members were non-believers and on side of forces of darkness. Randy asked, "And it is because your sister is alive with the forces of darkness that she is getting your daughter to lie about you?" Steve answered, "She opposes me on things." The jury was listening intently. Steve also indicated his brother was a part of the sister's and wife's conspiracy against him and the three of them had contacted some of his potential clients and had taken business away from him.

Upon further questioning by Randy, Steve admitted his brother had moved to Montana and he had not had contact with him in about eight years. Steve also said that Tori was lying about the accusations because she did not want to move to West Texas. Randy asked him if Tori was testifying against him just to keep from moving. Steve quickly answered saying, "Not at all, not at all. She was coerced." He answered saying it was probably his wife and sister. Randy asked how Teresa lied. Steve suggested she also lied after talking to Martha. It was interesting to note that Steve admitted to molesting Tori to Teresa before Teresa ever talked to Martha. Randy continued questioning Steve and asked if he said that someone else could have molested Tori. "Not that I know of," Steve answered. Randy asked Steve if he remembered saying to Sgt. Davis at the time of his arrest that it was his own son, Luke, who was the person who was having sex with Victoria. Steve answered, "I never made that statement." "So if Detective Davis would come forward and testify that he heard that statement, then he, too, would be lying," Randy asked. "He would be," Steve countered. Randy asked why Detective Davis would lie about that. "I'm not sure about Detective Davis. The first time I met him he was not very nice. He did go with me when I was incarcerated in Jefferson County and was very, very happy to see me contained…He's a very vindictive person, though…" Steve replied. Randy asked, "So he would make all that up to also get you in the penitentiary." Steve answered, "It would support his case and give him a good reason for the indictment, wouldn't it? Isn't that called job security?" With that answer, Randy finished his questioning. Stewart had no further questions and Steve stepped down from the witness stand and returned to his seat next to Stewart.

Randy re-called Bill to the witness stand. As Bill sat back in the witness chair, Randy asked if Steve had been given his Miranda Warning. "Twice," Bill said. He told of one Beaumont officer who had accompanied him to Lumberton to make the arrest and by the judge in Lumberton prior to Steve being brought back across the county line. Randy asked Bill if he struck up the conversation with Steve while waiting for Judge Dollinger to enter the courtroom to again read Steve his rights and to set bond on him. Bill corrected Randy saying, "He began the conversation." Randy asked what was said and Bill testified that Steve told him he had the wrong person. Bill said he responded to Steve's statement by saying, "I don't want to have the wrong man arrested. So, if you know the person who has, in fact, molested Victoria Carpenter, please tell me because I don't want to have the wrong person in custody." Randy asked if Steve told him who had molested Tori. "He told me it was his son, Luke," Bill stated. "Tori's older brother?" Randy asked. "Yes, sir," Bill answered. Continuing, Bill said, "I asked him how he knew this, did he walk in on them in a compromising situation where they were in the middle of a sex act or partially clothed or something like that, and his answer was no." Randy asked Bill if he asked Steve how he knew it. Bill answered that Steve told him, "He said he thought it." As Stewart cross-examined Bill, he asked, "And did Mr. Carpenter plead not guilty?" Bill answered, "To the best of my knowledge." Stewart then asked, evidently grasping at straws, "And that's saying he didn't do it; is that correct?" Bill answered, "Yes, sir." Stewart's questions to Bill were very weak. Randy's questions were very substantive. Randy had established more probable cause for the jurors to ponder when making their verdict at the end of testimony.

Randy now called a new witness in his rebuttal testimony, June Green. June told the court that Steve was her older brother and she had some difficulties with her brother. Randy asked June if she ever told Tori what to say. "Absolutely not," June declared. "Did you coerce her or offer to reward her in any way?" Randy asked. Again June profoundly stated, "Absolutely not." Randy passed the witness and Stewart had no questions. June was stepping down from the witness chair as Randy declared that the state rested their case. Stewart did the same. Randy felt there had been enough testimony for the jury to find Steve guilty. Stewart either thought there wasn't enough testimony for the jury to find Steve guilty, or, enough damage had been done. Either way, he rested also. A legal matter of Judge Barnes writing the charge against Steve was the next order of business. This was the document the jury would have with them when they went to the jury room to decide Steve's guilt or innocence. It was close to the end of the day, so the Judge recessed court and released the jurors until 9:00 a.m. the next morning. He and the two attorneys then retired to his chambers to write the document.

Court resumed the next morning with everyone in their respective places, the Judge began reading the charge for the jury:

"The defendant stands charged by indictment with the offense of aggravated sexual assault on a child, alleged to have been committed in Jefferson County, Texas, on or about November 2, 1993. The defendant has entered a plea of not guilty to this indictment. Our law requires that I submit the following charge to you in this case. This charge contains all the law necessary to enable you to reach a verdict. If any evidence was presented to raise an issue, the law on that issue must be provided.

Sexual assault of a child. A person commits an offense if the person intentionally or knowingly causes the sexual organ of a child to contact the sexual organ of another person, including the actor.

Aggravated sexual assault of a child. A person commits an offense if the person commits sexual assault and the victim is younger than fourteen-years-of-age.

Definitions. So that you can better understand some of the words and terms used in the charge, the law provides the following definitions:

Intentionally. A person acts intentionally, or with intent, with respect to the nature of his conduct or to a result of his conduct when it is his conscious objective or desire to engage in the conduct or cause the result.

Knowingly. A person acts knowingly, or with knowledge, with respect to the nature of his conduct or to circumstances surrounding his conduct when he is aware of the nature of his conduct or that the circumstances exist. A person acts knowingly, or with knowledge, with respect to a result of his conduct when he is aware that his conduct is reasonably certain to cause the result.

Child means a person younger than seventeen-years-of-age who is not the spouse of the actor.

Sexual contact. Sexual contact means any touching of the anus, breast or any part of the genitals of another person with intent to arouse or gratify the sexual desires of any person.

Extraneous offenses. Evidence may have been introduced in this case regarding the defendant having committed offenses other than the offense now alleged against him. You cannot consider this testimony for any purpose unless you believe beyond a reasonable doubt that the defendant committed such other offenses, if any. Even then, you may only consider the same in determining the identity of the defendant or the issues of intent, motive, system, scheme or design in connection with this offense and for no other purpose.

The charge itself. Now, if you believe from the evidence beyond a reasonable doubt that in Jefferson County, Texas, on or about November 2, 1993, the defendant, Steve Elton Carpenter, did then and there sexually assault Victoria J. Carpenter, hereafter styled the complainant, a person then younger than seventeen years of age and not the spouse of the defendant, by intentionally or knowingly causing the male sex organ of the defendant to contact the female sex organ of the complainant and the complainant was then and there younger than fourteen years of age, you shall find the defendant guilty of the offense of aggravated sexual assault on a child as alleged in count number two. Unless you so find, or if you have a reasonable doubt thereof, you shall find the defendant not guilty. General instructions:

Number one: you have a right to consider all the facts that are shown by the evidence and to draw natural and reasonable inferences from such facts. You alone have the authority and duty to determine what the facts are in this case. In evaluating the evidence, you must totally disregard what you believe is my opinion about any factual matter.

Number two: all persons are presumed to be innocent, and no person may be convicted of an offense unless each element to the offense is proved beyond a reasonable doubt. The fact that a person has been arrested, confined or indicted for or otherwise charged with the offense gives rise to no inference of guilt at his trial. The law does not require a defendant to prove his innocence or produce any evidence at all. The presumption of innocence alone is sufficient to acquit the defendant unless the jurors are satisfied beyond a reasonable doubt of the defendant's guilt after careful and impartial consideration of all the evidence in the case. The prosecution has the burden of proving the defendant guilty, and it must do so by proving each and every element of the offense charged beyond a reasonable doubt. And if it fails to do so, you must acquit the defendant. It is not required that the prosecution prove beyond all possible doubt. It is required that the prosecution's proof excludes all reasonable doubt concerning the defendant's guilt.

Number three: a reasonable doubt is a doubt based on reason and common sense after a careful and impartial consideration of all the evidence in the case. It is the kind of doubt that would make a reasonable person hesitate to act in the most important of his affairs. Proof beyond a reasonable doubt, therefore, must be proof of such a convincing character that you would be willing to rely and act upon it without hesitation in the most important of your own affairs. In the event you have a reasonable doubt as to the defendant's guilt after considering all the evidence before you, and these instructions, you will acquit him and say by your verdict.

Number four: you cannot question the bailiff concerning the testimony or the law, nor should you discuss this case in his presence. If any question about the law develops during your deliberations, it must be reduced to writing, signed by your foreperson and given to the bailiff. The question will then be answered by the Court as soon as possible, to the extent allowed by the law.

Number five: questions and comments of the attorneys do not constitute testimony and must not be considered as evidence. You must also disregard any statement of the attorneys that is inconsistent with the law contained in this charge.

Number six: any physical exhibits admitted into evidence will be furnished to you by the bailiff upon your request.

Number seven: you must not consider facts that have not been introduced into evidence or legal principles not contained in this charge. It is improper for any juror to discuss or consider anything which they know or have learned outside of the testimony presented to you and the law contained in this charge. If a juror should discover that they have any outside information, they must not mention this information to any other juror, nor consider it themselves in arriving at a verdict.

Number eight: you are the exclusive judges of the facts proven, the believability of the witnesses and the weight to be given their testimony. However, you must be bound by and strictly follow the law contained in this charge. Your failure to follow the law could result in a mistrial being declared, and your deliberate violation of this charge could subject you to being held in contempt of court.

Number nine: after the attorneys present their arguments to you, you will retire, select a foreperson and consider your verdict. The arguments are not evidence, and you should give the arguments only the consideration you feel they deserve during your evaluation of the evidence. It is the duty of your foreperson to make certain that your deliberations are conducted in accordance with this charge. After you have reached a unanimous decision, your foreperson should sign the appropriate verdict attached to the charge. In returning your verdict, it is your responsibility to make certain that justice is done in this case. Verdict forms are as follows:

First one, "We the jury, find the defendant not guilty," and a place for the foreperson to sign.

Second form, "We the jury, find the defendant guilty of aggravated sexual assault on a child as alleged in count number two of the indictment," and a place for the foreperson to sign.

Judge Barnes completed reading the charge. It was lengthy and full of legalities, yet in layperson's terms so each of the jurors could understand not only the law, but also the legal responsibility each of them had in weighing all of the evidence presented to them to render a verdict. The judge said their decision must be individual. To find Steve guilty, all twelve individuals had to vote "guilty." This guilty verdict would be a victory for justice on the part of Tori, Martha, Luke, and the prosecution. To find Steve not guilty, all twelve individuals had to vote "not guilty." A not guilty verdict would be a victory for justice on the part of Steve and the defense. However, if a unanimous verdict could not be reached, it would be a victory for the defense. It would mean that if a guilty verdict was to be attempted again, the entire case would have to be retried. Tori would have to get on the witness stand again and testify again about the sexual abuse she endured at the hands of her father. For a victim, it is hard to build up the courage to testify one time.

To do it again is nearly impossible. Therefore, without a unanimous verdict of guilty, Steve would more than likely go free. It was time for the closing arguments from Randy and Stewart.

"Ladies and gentlemen, as I have to keep track of my own time, the only thing I will talk to you about here in my very brief opening statement is a little bit about the law," Randy began. "That's because the law makes it clear that the State of Texas, having the burden of proof, gets to go first and gets to go last because he who has the burden is given that opportunity. The law is also clear that The State is allowed to present evidence on more than one method of committing the same offense but prior to presenting the case to the jury, as we are doing now, having to elect which of the two methods of commission will actually be presented to the jury. The law is clear on that, the law allows and we do not wish to believe that there is anything odd or unusual about that set of circumstances. It is a common everyday occurrence in the criminal courts. What we say is argument. It is not fact. It is not evidence. If we even try and express our personal opinions to you, that is incorrect. All we can do is attempt to lead you to what we believe the facts in the case show because it is your decision. It is your job. It is your responsibility to decide what the facts are in this case. So, as you listen to the arguments, always compare the arguments to the facts. You know them. You heard them. You listened to every painful, excruciating minute of testimony. So, always in the center of yourself, as you listen to the arguments, always remember what you heard from that witness stand – what you believe, what you didn't believe, what had the ring of truth and what had the hollow sound of falsehood. Remember that. Thank you."

Stewart followed Randy with his argument. "Ladies and gentlemen of the jury, in voir dire I asked why do we have jury trials; and the answer was for you to follow the law and decide the facts. You've come to that part now. The Judge is going to give you the charge which carries in it the law, and the law says The State of Texas must prove their case and must prove each and every element beyond a reasonable doubt. In the charge you're given the definition of reasonable doubt, and it is blown up here. Reasonable doubt is a doubt based on reason and common sense after a careful and impartial consideration of all the evidence in the case. It is the kind of doubt that would make a reasonable person hesitate to act in the most important of his own affairs. Proof beyond a reasonable doubt, therefore, must be proof of such a convincing character that you would be willing to rely and act upon it without hesitation in the most important of your own affairs. Remember in voir dire I went over the different burdens of proof we have in our legal system, and proof beyond a reasonable doubt is the highest burden. And I submit to you that being that highest burden of beyond a reasonable doubt, it's not guilt perhaps or suspected or possibly or probably or likely or even strongly believed. Guilt beyond a reasonable doubt is the highest burden. Reason and common sense. Use that in your decisions. The facts, deciding the facts. It's an awesome responsibility to sit in judgment of another citizen, especially one in this kind of case. What evidence have you heard? What evidence have you seen? Well, Detective Bill Davis. "I spent some time with Mr. Carpenter, and he said someone else did it." "I didn't do it." If you were wrongly and falsely accused, wouldn't you profess your innocence? He didn't record it. Teresa Franz – she said, "I didn't want to get involved"; but in her actions she's all involved. She says, "I was shocked when he said, 'I never forced her.'" Mr. Carpenter said, "That's not what I said. What I said was, I would never, I would never." Again, any recordings? You are the judges of the credibility of the witnesses and their believability. Barbara Harrison, the sexual assault nurse expert told you, "Well, I'm here, you know, with this forensic evidence." However, there's no forensic evidence to tie Mr. Carpenter to anything. Was there trauma? No. Was this thinning of the hymen recently caused, caused over long-term? No testimony on that. She went to school to learn how to testify. To learn how to tell the truth? What did she tell you? Victoria Carpenter did not want to move to West Texas, did not like home-schooling. She's living in a construction area, her whole home. She's working long hours. And the story she tells you fits exactly with what her mother tells, exactly. Reason and common sense. An exact story? Martha Carpenter, again, the exact story. She didn't stay at church that night because she was uncomfortable at church. She caught her own son, Ronnie, molesting

Victoria. She was molested herself and put her stepfather in jail. She didn't like living in construction. She didn't want to move to West Texas. Do you think the Mercedes would fit into West Texas? She got everything in the divorce – the land, the rents, everything. Mr. Carpenter took the stand and absolutely denied this happened. He maintained his innocence. He wrote over one-hundred-fifty letters, and you've got some blowups and the rest of the letters here. Read those letters. Read what they say. He talked about believers and nonbelievers, forces of light and dark, deliverance from a demonic spirit. If you were falsely accused, ladies and gentlemen, for a horrendous crime, would you not profess your innocence? Would you not try and save the ones that you love? The State at all times carries the burden of proof to prove to you beyond a reasonable doubt each and every element of the offense charged. I submit to you The State has failed in that. Twelve individual jurors holding The State to its burden, the discussions and deliberations seeking justice, that's an awesome responsibility you have. I submit to you The State has failed in its burden. Thank you very much."

Stewart's argument was over. He had done his best to articulate for his client that the jury find him not guilty. In doing so, he had gone above and beyond explaining 'reasonable doubt.' He had explained 'beyond any possible doubt,' which is not in the law. He had tried to make the jury believe that Tori got on the witness stand, was questioned about very personal and embarrassing events in her life that spanned a total of seven years, just to keep from moving again and to please her mother. Hopefully the jury saw beyond this meager persuasion. Bill Davis, a veteran sex crimes detective would have seen through a charade like this when he began the investigation, had it been true. The investigation would have gone no further. Such was not the case. Stewart had tried to 'browbeat' the jury into believing their job to find Steve Carpenter guilty was so overwhelming, that a guilty verdict would be impossible. It was now Randy's turn to have the final argument.

"Sometimes people say when I do my final argument that I don't argue so much as I preach," Randy began. "If I do that, I'm sorry. If that offends anyone, also I'm sorry. Maybe that's just because, well, I get worked up sometimes. What are our themes for this trial today?

Courage versus cowardness, faith versus hypocrisy, and the truth versus outright lies. That's what we're talking about today. That's what we've been talking about for the last two days. Remember, I talked to you about the ring of truth versus the hollow sound of outright lies. And did you notice when the defendant testified, no matter what happens to the defendant, it's always someone else's fault, isn't it? "My business went down the tubes. That's because of my brother. He's part of the forces of darkness. And that was in conjunction with my sister. She's part of the forces of darkness as well. And that's why my sister, together with my wife – "I assume his wife must be part of the forces of darkness – conspired to get my daughter," who is now, of course, part of the forces of darkness, "to lie against me," and of course, easily mixed up since this evil paranoia empire is out to get you. Of course, this woman of faith, Teresa Franz, has, of course, also become part of the forces of darkness. And Bill Davis, or, he just wants to build up his case. He just wants to send someone to the joint. He, of course, too, is also part of the forces of darkness. And through this whole thing, who's the only claimed beacon of light? The man who stands accused, the man who doesn't want to go to the penitentiary. Truth versus outright lies and faith versus hypocrisy. You can use your reason and your common sense. If you're asking someone to tell the truth, do you ask them to recant what they said? Do you ask them to take back the story? Or do you tell them, "Just tell the truth?" I know people sometimes don't like to make a lot of difference between the way you use words, but that's what lawyers do every day. So, we have to look carefully at a word that is used. Did he once say in these letters, "Tell the truth." "Recant what you said. Take it back. Drop the charges. Even a lie, if for a righteous person, will be rewarded by God." See what I mean by faith versus hypocrisy, and manipulation using the hypocrisy to try and overcome the true faith? "I beg you, please, to recant your story to Hardin County and Beaumont. Do whatever it takes to convince them that you made it up and rehearsed Tori," not, "Go and tell them the truth," not "Be truthful with yourself," no. "Go and convince them you made it up." And then he calls on religion. "Abraham was rewarded when he lied. Rahab, the harlot, lied. I don't approve of lying, but this will save our marriage." Even he knows, even he knows, he's asking them to go back and lie and say they made it up. He's asking them to take back the truth and replace it with outright lies because what's the one thing that will save him? Not faith, not truth. Only hypocrisy and lies will save him. Courage versus cowardness, along with truth versus outright lies. Courage. You saw that little girl get on that witness stand. You saw what she had to go through. You saw a field trip of a high school come in while she's having to tell twelve, now maybe sixty-five, strangers about her first sexual experience at the hands of her own father. Did she continue? Did she go on and tell you what had happened to her? Did she show courage? Of course, she did. Is any child going to put herself through that because she didn't want to move, to get away from her dad who's already, before she comes in to testify in this courtroom, already divorced from her mother? She's not going to have to move to West Texas. She's not going to have to go back and live with dad. They're divorced. So, she comes in here and subjects herself to that just to continue the lie, to continue the fantasy? No. She came in here to tell you the truth of what happened to her. "He told me that not all fathers and daughters can do things like this. He told me it was a secret." It's an absolute total destruction of the trust that a child should be able to have in a parent, the person you can count on to protect you from that kind of thing. And he uses that to prey on you, to gratify himself at the expense of your youth, at the expense of your childhood, because it's all about him. It's all about what he wants, what makes him feel good, what will get him out of trouble and set him free. That's what it's all about. You ask Martha Carpenter, "Did you ever suspect that anything like that this was going on?" "No, I never did." You ask Teresa Franz, "When you found out about this, would you have looked at this family and sensed something like this?" "No, of course not," she said. That's why it was so shocking to both of them when they found out. And put yourself in Martha Carpenter's place, especially – no disrespect intended. You've been in what you think is a loving, caring marriage for twenty-one years; and you find out that your husband is having sex with your daughter. Are you going to stick around the house? Are you going to pack up the kids and get out? Are you going to do anything you can to get away? Of course, you are. Are you going to go down and try and get yourself shed of that fool as soon as you can? Of course, you are. Are you going to go down and tell the police what happened as soon as you can? Of course, you are. Are you going to hold it against Martha Carpenter for doing what any mother would do, what any mother should do, to protect the children of her flesh and blood? No, you can't. I'm always surprised because, one way or another, a defense final argument is always the same. If the stories of The State's witnesses differ at all, they start talking about these wildly diverse stories; and if people can't say the same story, well, then, of course, it must not be true. Well, then, on the flip side, if the stories are the same, oh, my God, how could they come up with the same story? They must have rehearsed it. It's kind of like damned if you do, damned if you don't situation. No matter what The State's witnesses testify to, there's always something wrong with it. No one ever talked about the second possibility when the stories are the same except me. Because they're true. It's because it happened exactly the way it was described, and it was experienced by more than one person. Yeah, maybe they will tell the same story. Maybe they have a shared experience, even though the situation of a mother and a daughter, having to share the same sexual experience with the same man, boy, we don't like that, do we? That makes us sick to our stomachs, doesn't it? Makes us wonder why things like this happen, doesn't it? And again, that's because of the difference between courage and cowardness, the courage to come forward and the cowardness to lie. If nothing happened, if all this was made up, then why did you try and blame someone else? Do you realize why we brought that evidence before you? When first brought to book, when first taken into custody, he tries to blame his own son for doing this. And here in front of you, "Well, no, it just didn't happen. It's not true. All these evil forces of darkness have conspired to bring this up against me." Well, if you want to believe someone who gives you two radically different stories at two different times and there's no way to reconcile those two stories one with the other, there's something wrong in believing that person. I'm sorry. Either someone did it, or it didn't happen. And if someone did it, then isn't it strange that you happen to admit it to the lady who didn't have a dog in the fight? And you asked her, "Well, on the one hand, yeah, would you pray for me? I've had the demons cast out of me." But what's every other word? "And can you get Martha to drop the charges? Oh, by the way, can you call Martha and ask Martha to drop the charges?" And when you call back the next day, "Well, is she going to drop the charges?" "No, she's not. But, you know, I'll pray with you, Steve. I'll pray for you if you want to." Has he ever called, written her, tried to contact her in any way to pray for deliverance, to pray for salvation? No. Why? Because that won't get him out from under it. So, it's not convenient for him; and since it's not a question of faith, it's a question of hypocrisy, why even try? Barbara Harrison is very truthful in telling you that she cannot, except under those circumstances that were described, be able to get certain kinds of physical evidence, have any hope of identifying who the perpetrator is. She told you the absolute truth. But what she did tell you, gee, how coincidental happens to physically corroborate exactly what that child said about her father sexually abusing her. "Sometimes he'd stick his finger in me. That would hurt." "Where is the hymen absent?" "In the upper quadrant." "Ms. Harrison, why is that consistent?" "Well because with digital penetration, that is the usual angle of penetration, upwards. The damage will be in the upper quadrant of the hymenal rim." "Ms. Harrison, where is the hymenal rim reduced in size, that would be consistent with the other history presented, the contact of sexual organ to sexual organ with some penetration of the lips or the labia?" "Yes, that would be." "Why is that, Ms. Harrison?" "It's because of the angle of that type of penetration of the male sexual organ into the female sexual organ." Is it totally gone? No. It's been diminished. It's been reduced. Did she ever testify that her father fully penetrated her with his sexual organ? No, she did not. If there is not full penetration, there will, of course, only be partial reduction of the hymenal rim in the lower quadrant. So, everything that Ms. Harrison saw and commented upon, duck-tailed with the history provided by the victim. If you read through some of those letters, the entire ones, if you want, I want you to look for the hypocrisy in those letters because you will note that every quotation of scripture, every mention of God, every mention of the

Bible, talks about the necessity of keeping the family together under any circumstances, of the subservience of a wife, the obedience of a wife to a husband. They don't talk about, ladies and gentlemen, control because that's what this is all about, control. From a nice house in the West End of Beaumont to an isolated location out in the woods in Hardin County, with a future move to a mountaintop in far West Texas in Jeff Davis County, why do you isolate? Why do you convince people that it's necessary to home-school? Because you can hang onto them right there. They're in your clutches. You're controlling them. You've got them under your thumb where you can do anything you want to them, and that's exactly what he did. He did anything he wanted to his own baby girl from the time she was four or five until he finally got caught, and you need to tell him that's wrong, that you don't do that, that you're not just legally but you are morally reprehensible, that you will be found guilty and you will be punished for what you have done to that family, the family you're supposed to cherish, the family you're supposed to protect and you're the one that's torn it apart for your own sexual pleasure. Ladies and gentlemen, I beg of you, return a verdict of guilty as charged in the indictment. Thank you."

Randy was done. He'd come within a few seconds of using all of his time allotted by the court to state his final argument. But he did it. He had used Steve's own words, spoken from the witness stand and from letters, against him. The irony that few people notice, Stewart never objected to one word Randy had said in his closing argument. He couldn't. Randy rolled seven years of sexual abuse that Tori endured into his closing argument. He rolled an extensive investigation conducted by Major Ben Moore and Sgt. Bill Davis into his closing summary. He rolled years of control that Steve subjected Tori, Martha, and Luke to into his closing words. Was it enough?

"Members of the jury, if you'll go with the bailiff, please, he'll place you in the jury room for your deliberations," Judge Barnes stated. The twelve jury members stood and exited the courtroom in single file. Court was adjourned for deliberations at 9:40 a.m. Martha, Tori, Luke, Teresa, June, and Bill prayed.

It was 1:38 p.m. The jury deliberated for three hours and eight minutes. They notified the Judge through the bailiff that a verdict had been reached. As everyone took their seats in the courtroom, Judge Barnes instructed the bailiff to bring the jury into the courtroom. The twelve jurors walked single-file into the courtroom and took their seats in the jury box. "Ms. Forelady, would you hand your verdict to the bailiff so I can check it first, please," Judge Barnes said. The lady that had been selected as the foreperson, handed a sheet of paper to the bailiff. He immediately took it and walked to the Judge's bench. The Judge took a few seconds to scan the document. Everything appeared to be in order. The silence in the courtroom was deafening. Judge Barnes handed the document back to the bailiff who walked to the jury foreperson and handed it to her. The Judge turned to Steve and stated, "Mr. Carpenter, if you'll stand please." Steve did as the Judge ordered. "Ms. Forelady, if you'll stand, please, Ma'am, and read your verdict for me." She stood and looked down at the document. "We, the jury, find the defendant guilty of aggravated sexual assault on a child, as alleged in count two of the indictment," she read aloud. Steve had been instructed by Stewart that no matter what verdict was rendered, he was to remain motionless, expressionless. The people in the courtroom had also been instructed by Randy to revere the court and not let their emotions become overwhelming. Yet, as the word "guilty" was heard, tears flowed. Everyone had been holding hands so tightly, they were hurting each other. It didn't matter. Steve had been found guilty. The judge advised the jury that if found guilty, the defendant wanted the jury to assess his punishment. He gave the jurors a short recess. Legal matters had to be dealt with before phase two, the punishment phase of a trial, could begin.

    As Judge Barnes reconvened court and as the jury took their seats in the jury box once again, Randy called Sgt. Bill Davis as his first witness of the punishment phase. As the detective took the stand, Judge Barnes stated, "You're still under oath, Bill." Bill nodded in acknowledgement, and grinned. He and Judge Barnes were good friends. The Judge didn't call him, Sgt. Davis, or Detective Davis, or Mr. Davis. It was "Bill." Maybe it was a slip of the tongue, but Bill noted it. Yet, the courtroom was always, all business. Randy asked Bill if he and other officers had the occasion to respond to a call for help at June's residence. Stewart quickly objected, but was overruled by the Judge. Bill responded, "Yes." Randy continued, asking if there had been temporary restraining orders issued by a family court in Hardin County. Bill again answered, "Yes." Randy asked Bill if he responded to June's call to him for help because Steve had shown up at her residence. Bill explained he had been unable to leave his office due to another case. But, he stated, he immediately called dispatch and patrol cars were dispatched immediately. Bill said he arrived a short time later. He was advised that Steve had left the area by the time officers arrived. Randy then directed Bill's attention to August 11, 1997, and asked him if that was an easy date for him to remember. Bill grinned and looked at the jury. "Yes, sir, it's my birthday." Several of the jurors grinned back. Randy asked Bill if he received a call from Hardin County authorities, and he responded, "Yes, sir, I did." Why did you end up having to go to Hardin County? What was the nature of the call you received?" Randy asked. "The call stated that Mr. Steve Carpenter had just shot himself attempting to commit suicide." Bill stated that Steve shot himself in the upper left-hand shoulder with a .22 short caliber bullet. Randy had Bill acknowledge that he had dealt with guns and bullets most of his life and carried a weapon every day. The prosecutor then used the cover tip of an ink pen and had Bill indicate to the jury just how small a .22 caliber short bullet was. "Little bitty bullet?" Randy asked. Yes, sir, it is." Randy then turned to when Bill arrested Steve. "Now, in an earlier phase of the trial, the defendant testified that he voluntarily surrendered himself at the time that he was taken into custody. Is that exactly how it happened, Detective Davis?" "No, sir…he did not fight or put up any kind of resistance; but he did not voluntarily bring himself into my office at the Beaumont police station where he knew the warrant was going to ultimately wind up and go ahead and surrender himself," Bill explained. Randy passed the witness. Stewart asked if he was saying a .22 bullet could not kill a person? "Not at all, sir," Bill replied. "How fast does a .22 short round travel?" Stewart asked. Bill thought for a second what a ridiculous question he had just been asked. So, he answered with a smile, "Well, faster than some bullets and slower than others."

As questioning ended for Bill and he stepped down from the witness chair, Stewart informed the Judge that his witness had arrived. In Phase Two of a trial, it is similar to Phase One in that the prosecution has all of their witnesses testify and they rest their case. Then, the defense attorney has all of their witnesses testify and they rest their case. However, this witness needed to testify and leave and Judge Barnes was allowing the change in the rule of order so the jurors could hear all testimony before deliberating Steve's punishment. Stewart called John Morrison to the stand. He was an attorney for a local law firm. He testified that he had known Steve for about nine years through several construction projects Steve did for him. He stated that Steve always handled himself in a professional manner. Stewart passed the witness. Randy had the attorney acknowledge that his relationship was not one of friendship but merely an acquaintance. He stated there was one occasion when he and his family visited Steve and his family after church one Sunday when they lived on Rosewood Street. Morrison had to admit that he could not speak of Steve's moral character. He was not much of a character witness to keep Steve from going to prison. After Stewart's witness stepped down from the witness chair, Randy called his next witness, Martha. After some introductory questions, Randy asked, "How has what has happened over the past few years affected your daughter?" "She's very suspective of people. She's emotional. She bounces off the walls. She goes from very happy where she's giggling all the time to crying, and you can't get her to stop." Randy asked about her being suspicious. "People's attention," Martha explained. "If any male comes up to her and hugs her, like, "Hi, Tori, how are you doing," she just gets that scared look on her face. There are only a few people I know that she doesn't give that look to, but she admitted that – she has an uneasy feeling, even for people she's known for a long time, when they hug her." Martha described her daughter now as "emotional." Randy had Martha talk about her restraining order from Hardin County. She testified that she was at Bill's office when Bill received a call from June stating that Steve was there. Martha said Bill got off the phone with June and immediately called the police dispatcher to send a patrol car to June's house. "When you heard that he was there at the house, what was your reaction?" Randy asked. "I was scared," Martha replied. Randy then turned his questions dealing with Steve's letters. "How often did you receive a letter from Steve?" he asked. "Almost every day," she replied. "What kind of letters would he send you in the last couple of weeks?" Randy asked. "Very pleading," Martha said, "making me feel sorry for him, using the Bible, just begging me not to testify, don't show up, stuff like that." "And your reaction to that?" Randy asked. "Disgusted. I was tired of it because he had been asked not to do it anymore," Martha said. Randy turned questioning over to Stewart, who had no questions. Randy now called Steve's sister, June. His questioning began with June's relationship with her niece. June stated that Tori was a very good child and June adored being with her. June said she had a very close relationship with Tori when she was very little. But, when she was about four to five years old, Steve made it more difficult for her to see Tori and have her for overnight visits. She stated that Steve became more reluctant to let Tori visit and put greater restrictions on when she could come and under what circumstances. Prior to this age, June said that Steve would let Tori stay a week to ten days at a time with her. June continued to explain prior to Tori turning four years old, she was allowed to go on vacations, including out-of-state trips. Then, suddenly, she was four years old and couldn't spend the night. Randy continued, having June elaborate on Steve being more controlling with Tori and then isolating her and the family with the move to Hardin County. Randy asked June how she felt the day she found out about Steve molesting Tori. "I was devastated," June stated. "Why?" Randy asked. "Well," June answered, "I was devastated for her and what had been going on; and I was even more devastated because Steve did the same thing to me when I was a small child." "How old were you when Steve used to do this to you?" Randy asked. "Three to five," June answered. June continued her testimony, telling how she received an injury at age six and she had to be with one of her parents 24/7 for several weeks. With one parent or the other constantly present, Steve did not have any opportunities to molest June. As her injury healed and Steve tried to molest her again, she told him he wasn't going to do those things to her again. She testified that he got very angry and in front of the whole family, shot himself in the chest. June also stated that she purposely did not tell Martha, Tori, or Sgt. Davis that Steve molested her as a child until after Bill completed his investigation. She said she had only told her husband and a therapist up to that point about her molestation. She said she did not want what had happened to her as a child to influence anyone involved with Tori's investigation. After Bill completed Tori's investigation, she revealed her childhood to him. June stated she, her husband, Tori, and Luke were at her house on a Saturday morning when Tori heard the sound of a diesel truck motor. When she looked out the window, she screamed and said, "It's my dad," and ran into the bathroom and locked herself in there. June also testified that Steve was constantly sending letters to her house and even sent flowers on one occasion. Randy asked her, "On the date that he sent the flowers, did that connect with any other event?' "Yes," June answered. "The day he had flowers delivered to your house, what else happened that day?" he asked. "He shot himself again," June replied. With that answer, Randy turned the witness over to Stewart. He had no questions. Randy rested his case for punishment. Stewart called Steve back to the witness chair. The Judge allowed Steve to ramble as he told the jury how he'd been a model prisoner for fifteen months. He told them how he'd not had one violation while incarcerated and that he was a deacon, a minister, and how he was conducting Bible classes with inmates while in jail. "I would ask this Court to consider me for a short probation. I have been a productive pillar in the community," Steve told the jury. After a few more questions and answers, Steve stepped down from the witness chair and returned to his seat beside Stewart. Randy called June one more time to the witness chair. Steve had testified that he never threatened anyone in reference to this case. "… he's always had a fascination with guns, and we were very afraid that there would be some violence. I am very concerned to this date," June emphatically stated to the jury. Her questioning was over. Makin had no further witnesses. It was time for Judge Barnes to issue the punishment charge to the jury. He let them have a short recess.

As the jurors took their seats after their break, Judge Barnes began reading the punishment charge to them.

"Members of the jury, the punishment charge is as follows:

You have found the defendant guilty of the offense of aggravated sexual assault on a child. It becomes your responsibility to assess the proper punishment. This offense under our law is a first degree felony.

First degree felony punishment. Our law provides that an individual adjudged guilty of a first degree felony shall be punished by confinement in the Institutional Division of the Texas Department of Criminal Justice for life or any term of years not more than ninety nine years or less than five years. In addition to imprisonment, an individual adjudged guilty of a felony of the first degree may be punished by a fine not to exceed $10,000.00.

Instruction on community supervision. The defendant has filed an application for community supervision. Community supervision means the release of a convicted defendant under conditions imposed by a court for a specified period during which the imposition of sentence is suspended. Our law provides that after punishment is assessed, the jury may recommend community supervision of that punishment if, number one, the prison term assessed does not exceed ten years confinement in the Institutional Division of the Texas Department of Criminal Justice, and number two, the jury finds that the defendant has never before been convicted of a felony in this or any other state and recommends community supervision. Our law further provides that if a jury recommends community supervision, it must be granted by the Court. Your first responsibility is to assess what you believe is a proper punishment for the defendant in this case. Then, if, and only if, the prison term you assess does not exceed ten years confinement, you may consider granting the defendant community supervision of that punishment should you find the defendant is legally qualified to be considered for community supervision. If you grant community supervision, you place upon the Court the responsibility to supervise the defendant. In discharging this responsibility, the Court may impose any reasonable terms and conditions necessary to protect or restore the community, protect or restore the victim or punish, rehabilitate or reform the defendant. You are allowed to assess a punishment of ten years or less and not recommend community supervision. You are further allowed to grant the defendant community supervision of the penitentiary term, a fine, if one is assessed, or both. If you grant the defendant community supervision and the Court subsequently finds that the defendant violated one or more of the conditions imposed, the Court may either continue, modify, or revoke the community supervision.

Good time credit and parole. Under the law in this case, the defendant, if sentenced to a term of imprisonment, may earn time off the period of incarceration imposed through the award of good conduct time. Prison authorities may award good conduct time to a prisoner who exhibits good behavior, diligence in carrying out prison work assignments, and attempts at rehabilitation. If a prisoner engages in misconduct, prison authorities may also take away all or part of any good conduct time earned by the prisoner. It is also possible that the length of time for which the defendant will be imprisoned might be reduced by the award of parole. Under the law in this case, if the defendant is sentenced to a term of imprisonment, he will not become eligible for parole until the actual time served equals one-half of the sentence imposed or thirty years, whichever is less, without consideration of any good conduct time he may earn. If the defendant is sentenced to a term of less than four years, he must serve at least two years before he is eligible for parole. Eligibility for parole does not guarantee that parole will be granted. It cannot accurately be predicted how the parole law and good conduct time might be applied to this defendant if he is sentenced to a term of imprisonment because the application of these laws will depend on decisions made by prison and parole authorities. You may consider the existence of the parole law and good conduct time. However, you're not to consider the extent to which good conduct time may be awarded to or forfeited this particular defendant. You are not to consider the manner in which the parole law may be applied to this particular defendant.

Extraneous transaction or acts. You are instructed that there is evidence before you in this case regarding the defendant having committed or participated in other acts or transactions other than the offense alleged against him in the indictment in this case, that you cannot consider such other acts of transaction, if any, unless you first find and believe beyond a reasonable doubt that the defendant committed or participated in such acts or transactions, if any. But if you do not so believe, or if you have a reasonable doubt thereof, you will not consider such evidence for any purpose.

General instructions. The attached verdict forms are supplied for your use. When you have reached your verdict, your forelady should fill in the appropriate form and sign their name as foreman. In arriving at your verdict, it is not proper to fix the punishment you assess by any system of averaging. Your verdict must be determined only by a full, fair, and free exercise of opinions of each juror based upon the evidence presented. Your verdict must be unanimous. Your failure to follow the law contained in this charge could result in a mistrial being declared, and your deliberate violation of these instructions could result in your being held in contempt of court.

Verdict forms are as follows:

The first one, "We, the jury, assess the defendant's punishment at confinement in the Institutional Division of the Texas Department of Criminal Justice for a term of blank years. We further find that the defendant has never been convicted of a felony in this or any other state and recommend that this punishment be probated."

Next form, "We, the jury, assess the defendant's punishment at confinement in the Institutional Division of the Texas Department of Criminal Justice for a term of blank years. We further assess a fine of blank. We further find the defendant has never before been convicted of a felony in this or any other state and recommend that this punishment be probated."

Next one, "We, the jury, assess the defendant's punishment at confinement in the Institutional Division of the Texas Department of Criminal Justice for a term of blank years. We further find the defendant has never before been convicted of a felony in this or any other state and recommend that this punishment be probated. We further assess a fine of blank."

The next form, "We, the jury, assess the defendant's punishment at confinement in the Institutional Division of the Texas Department of Criminal Justice for a term of blank years."

Next one, "We, the jury, assess the defendant's punishment at confinement in the Institutional Division of the Texas Department of Criminal Justice for a term of blank years. We further assess a fine of blank."

Next form, "We, the jury assess the defendant's punishment at confinement in the Institutional Division of the Texas Department of Criminal Justice for life."

And the last one, "We, the jury, assess the defendant's punishment at confinement in the Institutional Division of the Texas Department of Criminal Justice for life. We further assess a fine of blank."

Whew!~~~~

Everyone in the jury box seemed to take a deep breath of air. For now, the charge for punishment seemed to be more complex than the charge that was given to them to find Steve guilty as charged. It was obvious they would have to take all of these different forms, lay them on the desk in the jury deliberation room, and vote on each one until they reached a unanimous verdict as to Steve's punishment.

It was now time for closing arguments in Phase Two, the punishment phase. Randy strategically waived his opening argument and let Stewart go first. "Ladies and gentlemen of the jury, it's often said that after a guilty verdict is returned wherein you have pled not guilty and put on a defense, one of the most difficult jobs in the world is to address a jury on punishment. I disagree with that. You have heard the evidence. You weighed it. You took your time. You did your job. Now you come to the next part of your job. We told you in earlier voir dire that the job of the jury was to hear and take the law and apply the facts to it, and that is what you have to do in this phase also. The charge tells you what the law is. It sets out a broad scheme of punishment – and that's what we are here about, punishment. And the legislature said that for a first degree felony, those offenses that are first degree felonies, there's a range of punishment, five to ninety-nine years or life and ever and everything in-between and in some circumstances when the jury feels it appropriate and correct, probation. That's what you have to do. You take all the facts you've heard from the first phase of the trial and the second phase and decide wherein does that lie. Does every aggravated sexual assault on a child case warrant life imprisonment or ninety-nine or fifty? Who knows? That's why we have juries. That's your job to weigh all that and determine. That's the law. You've heard the first part. You've gotten a picture of outwardly a happy family but something seriously wrong inside. The outcry, the destruction in the family. Was it a suicide or a suicide attempt? Was it an expression of forgiveness? You've heard the evidence. You have to decide. Ms. Carpenter says they still have the black couch. Reason and common sense – why would they still have that black couch? Ms. Green, "Something horrible happened when I was young." But yet later she lived with Mr. Carpenter. Mr. Carpenter's been incarcerated. And has he wasted that time? Has he involved himself in the changing of his life? Has he worked with the church in the jail, trying to help others? Maybe all that means nothing. Your job – and it's an awesome responsibility, once again – is to take all that, look at the law and decide what the appropriate punishment is, twelve individual jurors agreeing on what the proper punishment is. It's an awesome responsibility. Thank you."

Stewart used his quiet demeanor to plead in an unusual way for the jurors to feel the weight of their awesome responsibility to make their decision. Maybe his underlying hope was that the job of taking away someone's freedom for a long time was such an awesome responsibility, someone would succumb to the pressure and give Steve a light sentence in prison.

"One of the powers that a jury has is to always make reasonable inferences from the facts that have been laid before them, to use your common sense," Randy began. "Right? We told you that from the word "go." Reason with me here. Reason someday a young woman twenty or twenty-two years old falls in love, decides she wants to make a life with a young man, build a family, build a future and she thinks she can do it. She wants to do it. And everything seems to be going along just wonderfully well. But her young husband can't understand why it seems she's standoffish sometimes when he can't seem to get close to her, why when he tries to express love to her in the way men and women have expressed love to each other within a marriage since the dawn of time, why she can't be intimate with her own husband. Do you see how that could happen to a victim of this kind of abuse? Is that a reasonable inference? Is that the victim's fault? Is that the fault of the young man who's fallen in love with her and wants to make a life with her; or is it the fault of the man who did it to her, if it comes to that point? Do you think that happens to some victims? Of course, it does. Do you think that happens to all victims? No, of course not. But we know that Tori Carpenter is not the same girl she was. Her mother tells you that. Her aunt tells you that. You have seen what this can do to someone, an adult woman, educated, a trained professional, a lawyer, partner in her own firm. And what is she reduced to on the stand? Pure emotion, pain. Even now, years after the fact, the pain is there. It flows from her. Again, is that her fault that she feels pain? Is it her fault that she tried to tell the man that she loved why she acted the way she did? It's not her fault. It's his fault. Do you notice that, when confronted with reality, when confronted with no longer being able to control circumstances around him, when confronted with having to face the music the two times that this has happened, what does the defendant do? He tries to divert attention onto himself in the exact same way both times. He puts his signature on these offenses. "No, don't pay attention to the victim. Pay attention to me. Look at who I am. Look at my face. Look at what I believe, what I profess. Look at what happened to me." And that's all he does; and it's his fault, no one else's. He put himself there; and it is up to you to judge him, as you already have by finding him guilty. How do you punish a man, any man, for taking away his own daughter's childhood? Do you have memories of Barbie dolls, or do you have memories of your dad sticking his finger up inside you until it hurts? Do you have memories of birthday parties and pretty little party dresses, or do you have memories of your dad moving you back and forth on his penis until he ejaculates? Do you have memories of sleepovers with your friends and going to school and hanging out with the other girls in the neighborhood, or do you have memories of being isolated so that dad can have funzies with you whenever he wants? What kind of childhood is that? It's not. And it's his fault that that happened, no one else's. What memories do you have of twenty-one years of marriage destroyed in a single moment of realization, "My God, what is he doing to our child?" Twenty-one years of faith, trust, and partnership destroyed. Is that Martha Carpenter's fault? No, it's his fault, the man sitting there at counsel table, the man whom you convicted of sexually assaulting his own daughter, no one else's fault. He's not the victim, no matter how much he may try and paint himself as the victim in this case. And I will repeat this because I think it needs repeating. Once again, what do we see – and yes, I will tell you it is faith versus hypocrisy because, once again, when given an opportunity to apologize, does he take it? No. When given an opportunity to atone, to beg for forgiveness, does he take it? No. What does he do? He tries to cover himself with the Lord. And can you see right through that? I know you can. Because in truth and in fact, that man doesn't believe in anything but what he wants, what he wants to get, what will gratify him, what will save him, not for eternity, but what will save him from going to the penitentiary for a long time. That's all he believes in. What is the purpose of this part of the trial? Well, you have to decide what gets done. Now, I may not be a very religious man but I know one thing and I think we all know the same thing because I think we all learned at some point in our lives the same thing. If you want to be saved, if you want to be redeemed, you've got to accept responsibility for what you did; and then you've got to atone for it. You've got to do penance for it because until you do that, until you accept what you have done, you will not, whether in this world or in any other world, be saved. So, you can't save that man, can you? He's the only one who can. Do you believe him when he tells you that he is saved? No, ladies and gentlemen, I submit to you, you should not. We don't call this the forgiveness phase of the trial. We don't call it the salvation phase, redemption phase. It's the punishment phase of the trial. That's what we're here to decide. And as you think about punishment, what are the things that you can validly consider? Well, all the things I've talked about — what this man has done to his daughter, what he's done to his sister, what he's done to his family.

What else can you consider? Well, you can consider what message your verdict will send. What do you tell the other people of Jefferson County happens when someone comes into this court and is convicted of sexually assaulting his very own child and you are shown a history of that kind of abuse, unto even his own sister? And do you think it's valid for you to consider what other people will think of your verdict? It's a message to the community. It is our plea that you use that as a message to the community and as a tool of enforcement of the law because you're enforcing the law today. You're not the cop out on the street. You're not the detective working through mounds of photographs. You're not the sexual assault nurse examiner trying to – but you are the law today, you twelve good men and women. Does someone who did that truly deserve to walk free in the community? Because when we talk about community supervision, talk about probation, however you want to talk about it, I'm going to break it down to one thing. Three days from now if you're sitting in the Golden Corral, do you want to see him sitting two tables over from you? Because that's community supervision. Does he deserve to be able to do that in your minds? I can't tell you that. You have to decide that. I will never say that your job is easy because it's not. Can your job be clear to you? Yes, it can. Can what you have to do be clear to you, be apparent to you, be right out there in front of you? Yes, it can be. Can you always remember who is the man who did everything that you've convicted him of, who did everything that you heard about, who you have found guilty and whom still will not accept responsibility for what he's done? Punish him, ladies and gentlemen, punish him severely, knowing full well that that is the only thing – if anything will ever teach him a lesson – and frankly, I don't think anything ever will – but at least we can maybe teach somebody else a lesson at the same time. Thank you very much."

    Randy was done. Throughout his closing argument that lasted almost fifteen minutes, the jury had focused on his every word. They intermittently looked at him as he spoke, but also gazed into the courtroom audience and watched Tori, Martha, and June crying silently and wiping their tears. Randy had emotionally and legally brought all of Steve's transgressions to light. He summarized not only what Tori had gone through with her victimization, but also sought justice for June, who had lived with her molestation at the hands of her brother for decades. He also summarized the victimization of many young girls who had their innocence stolen because of a pervert they had to live with while growing up. He brought it all to the forefront for the jurors to consider. It was 4:00 p.m. Judge Barnes retired the jury to the deliberation room.

No one left the courtroom except the Judge. The bailiff placed Steve in a holding cell behind the courtroom. No one knew how long the jury would deliberate Steve's punishment. Would he get probation? Would he get a short prison sentence? Would he spend the rest of his life in prison? How long would it take? The tension, the anxiety, was almost overbearing for Tori, Luke, Martha, and June. Teresa had not left. She was still there. Bill was also there for them. He had been the one who had given them assurance that justice, in some form, would be served.

Judge Barnes entered the courtroom and sat on his bench. He announced the jury had reached a verdict. It was 4:38 p.m. They had deliberated only thirty-eight minutes. Judge Barnes instructed the bailiff to bring the jury in. They filed into the courtroom, single file as they had done several times before. As they took their seats, Tori, Martha, Luke, Teresa, June, and Bill held hands so tightly their fingers were numb. Everyone was scared to breathe. "Ma'am, would you hand your verdict to the bailiff so I can check it first, please," Judge Barnes instructed. The bailiff handed the document from the forelady to the Judge. He studied it for only a few seconds. Everything was in order. He handed the document back to the bailiff who delivered it back to the forelady. "The defendant will stand, please," Judge Barnes ordered. "Ms. Forelady, would you stand, please, and read your verdict," he instructed. She stood. All eyes were glued on her. "We, the jury, assess the defendant's punishment at confinement in the Institutional Division of the Texas Department of Criminal Justice for a term of seventy-five years," she stated. As the forelady sat down, Judge Barnes declared, "Being no legal reason why sentence should not be imposed, the defendant's hereby sentenced, in accordance with the jury verdict, to confinement in the penitentiary for a term of seventy-five years. He'll be given credit for any previous jail time served. No bond will be allowed. He'll be transferred immediately to the penitentiary. Mr. Carpenter, if you'll go with the bailiff, he'll place you back in custody; and your lawyer will be back there to visit with you in just a second."

Judge Barnes thanked the jury for their service and dismissed them. He then declared court adjourned. It was over.

Yet, was it? Yes, the trial was over. Tori had faced the overwhelming pressure of testifying not only in front of her father, but also in front of a classroom full of teenagers who listened as she described the horrible atrocities she had been subjected to by her father, and she courageously succeeded. However, this was only the end of one chapter in her life. There would be many more chapters to come. Tori mustered an amount of courage that few people have testifying in court. She would have to find the strength and faith to overcome even more obstacles as she grew older.

Martha had gone to work for Tim Landry, the attorney for the divorce, prior to the trial. Her position at the law office was filled by her daughter-in-law, Sheila, while the trial took place. The verdict and punishment occurred on Sheila's birthday. She proclaimed that the court's decisions were the best birthday presents ever because of her past, and for Tori's sake as well. Now, Martha would have to continue being a single mother and providing for her two children. It would be a challenge, but her faith in God was strong.

The media reports on the outcome of trials. They tell the public of a court's verdict and punishment, and often states that the innocent family members now have closure. But, do they? Steve's perverted love to his family was strictly self serving. There is only one perfect love, which comes from God. Steve's love was so imperfect it damaged everything and everyone in its path. His victims will have to endure his imperfect love for decades. The imperfection from him continues as a daily challenge for each person he negatively affected. There was also imperfect justice. No matter how stiff Steve's prison sentence may be, it can never undo the atrocities he committed. Tori later said she was glad her father would never breathe another breath of free air. Steve's long prison sentence gave her that reality of freedom. Tori's fight to overcome the damage committed by her father is a daily one. It is a fight, and a challenge, that is faced and shared by far too many other Toris in our world.

    Bill had more investigations to work on. He walked to his office from the courthouse with one goal in mind – to save one more child.

Imperfect Love ~ Imperfect Justice

EPILOGUE

Steve will spend up to seventy-five years in prison or until he dies. Under current law, he must serve at least thirty-seven-and-one-half years in prison before he is eligible for parole. Parole is not usually granted to a convict on their first, or even second, time up for parole. Considering Steve's age when he entered prison, it is very possible that Tori's wish – "that he die in prison" – may come true. Steve has stated he believes he is in prison to carry on missionary work for God. Steve committed an unconscionable sin against God, humanity, and the law.

One is reminded of the Bible's scripture, "Vengeance is mine, I will repay, thus sayeth the Lord." (NKJV: Romans 12:19)

Martha, a wonderful Christian woman, tried to be a good Biblical wife. Looking back, Steve used his position as head of the house in a Christian home for his own deviant, selfish goals. The moment she walked into her home on July 16, 1994, and discovered that her daughter had been sexually molested by her husband, Martha became a 'mama bear.' She protected her daughter at all costs. Martha said God protected her and Tori through the horror of that night. She said as she got Tori out of the house and away from Steve, they passed his gun safe containing several loaded guns that he could have easily reached and used on them. Martha had no idea where or how they would live. She had helped Steve with their business. She didn't really have a job other than being a full time wife and mother. She knew that somehow, some way, she and her children would survive. She also knew her first priority was to protect Tori and Luke, and she did. Tori once told her mom when they had no money and no income, "I wish I'd never agreed to testify." Martha quickly replied, "No, baby. We'd be dead. We'll make it." Martha got help from her son, her sister-in-law, June, and June's husband, Frank, from her friend, Teresa, and from Bill. God protected Martha and her children while Steve stalked them, and Steve never found them to hurt them. Martha got a job with Tim Landry, her attorney for the divorce. She was able to sell the house and land in Hardin County and move to a smaller location in Beaumont. She suffered several severe physical illnesses and setbacks – being in a diabetic coma for two weeks, suffering a stroke, and having heart bypass surgery. Yet, her faith in God never faltered. It strengthened. Tori quit college and stayed by her mom's side 24/7 until she regained consciousness from the coma. The doctors told Tori her mom would be a 'vegetable' for the rest of her life. Martha regained consciousness and made a full recovery. One year later, Martha suffered a stroke. Luke took her to the hospital within forty-five minutes. She received the reversal medicines and made a full recovery. She also made a full recovery from a heart attack and quadruple heart bypass surgery. Martha said, "God sent a hand here and a hand there to help us along the way." She realized one day that to survive within herself, she had to forgive Steve. She remembered the Biblical scripture from Jesus's sermon-on-the-mount,

> "For if you forgive men their trespasses, your heavenly Father will also forgive you. But if you do not forgive men their trespasses, neither will your Father forgive your trespasses." (NKJV: Matthew 6: 14-15).

Martha also told Bill one day, "I knew if I was ever to be free from Steve, I had to forgive him. That was my way of setting myself free. Otherwise, he would still be controlling us with our anger every day. Then anger would cause us to go down wrong paths in life and we would hurt ourselves by making bad choices because of his actions."

Greg struggles with what Steve did to his little sister. Even though several years have passed, Greg told his mother that he could not find it within himself to forgive Steve and he hates him with a passion.

Luke was able to have surgery on his knee. Teresa knew a sports medicine orthopedic surgeon through her church contacts. The doctor examined Luke's kneecap, found the problem, and performed surgery. The medical bill was covered through the Texas Attorney General's Crime Victims Compensation Fund because Luke was also considered a crime victim through Steve's actions. Luke continues to experience knee pain and a limited range of motion due to his injury. Luke took his mom to their property in Hardin County. At the end of the entry to their driveway, he showed her where Steve and he used to shoot their guns for target practice. He also showed her some pine trees just beyond the area where the targets would be posted. Martha could see chest-high bullet holes that were still in the tree. Luke explained the bullet holes were made by his father. Steve would shoot at Luke, barely missing him, when he would be checking the targets. Luke told Bill in an interview for this book that he never hated his dad. He was a Christian. After Steve was in prison, Luke went with one of his aunts to visit his dad. Luke wanted his dad to know he wasn't afraid of him. He also told his father that he forgave him for what he'd done. Luke was able to release his spirit from the bonds his father had held on him.

From the beginning of her outcry, Tori ran the gauntlet of emotions. At first, she was relieved the ordeal of being sexually abused by her father was finally over and he could never molest her again. She was relieved and thankful that her mother believed her. She understood then, and understands now, that many young girls are not believed. At the time of her outcry, Tori had, and still has, support from her brothers, Luke and Greg. Most of the people she thought were her friends at the time of her outcry weren't truly her friends. They did not support her as she underwent her ordeal or when it became public. On many occasions after the investigation and while waiting for the trial, Tori told Martha she was mad at God and even hated God for Him letting her go through years of sexual molestation. Martha advised Tori, "Don't be afraid of what man can do to your body, but what man can do to your soul." Martha also quoted,

> "And do not fear those who kill the body but cannot kill the soul. But rather fear him who is able to destroy both soul and body in hell." NKJV Matthew 10:28,

Martha said that one of Tori's many blessings was God sending her a Christian man, who is also a Marine veteran, to fall in love with her and marry her. Tori and her husband have also been blessed with two beautiful children, a boy and a girl, and Tori has been able to be a stay-at-home mom. Martha said one of the greatest obstacles Tori she has yet to overcome is trust. She is fearful about making friends with someone and suspects they will want to know her life story, which she does not want to share. Martha said that when Tori goes somewhere, such as the grocery store, and sees a dad with his daughter, she always wonders if he is sexually molesting his daughter like her father did to her. Tori and her family lived in another state for years. They recently moved back to Texas and closer to family. Her husband mentioned to Martha that they were looking for a church home for themselves and their children.

To think of the sexual molestation Steve subjected upon Tori is almost unthinkable. It is understandable for Tori to wonder why God allowed her to go through so many years of abuse. Martha reminded Tori many times that even Jesus's disciples were subjected to abuse and torture. The saying is so true, 'If He leads you to it, He will lead you through it.' Surely God will reveal to Tori His reasons for allowing her to go through the victimization by her father. One of those reasons may be to help someone else who is going through a similar situation. Perhaps this book will reach a victim/survivor, and as they read Tori's story they will see they are not alone in their ordeal. Through Tori and her story, others may receive the helping hand of God and strength to survive and overcome the tragic trials and tribulations of their own story.

The Mother's Advice To Her Daughter:

The mother in this story gave the following advice to help her daughter cope with what her father did to her: "Don't be afraid of what man can do to your body, but what man can do to your soul."

Matthew 10:28   "And do not fear those who kill the body but cannot kill the soul. But rather fear him who is able to destroy both soul and body in hell."

The Mother's Message to Victims/Survivors:

There is a lot of hindsight as the years go by. At first there is anger, hurt, tears, and questions that will never be answered. There are lots of ways to hurt yourself because of feeling bad, hurt, lonely, feeling not worthy, etc. – from comfort eating to depression, sex to drugs, alcohol, nicotine, bad lifestyle, bad constant thoughts – but that is letting the "bad" win. The ultimate worst is becoming like the person you hate. This lets the "bad" win. The point comes when you have to forgive (sometimes multiple times per day), not the actions, but the person who hurt you. It's a healing for you, not them. Never let them back into your life so you can be free to go on.

You must also forgive yourself. What happened IS NOT your fault. You were manipulated. You cannot change the events in your life that are in the past, but you can make choices in your present and your future. Everything you've gone through molds who you are and who you become. You can use your past to help others, or to hurt others, or to hurt yourself. Don't let the past hurt you any more, otherwise, the "bad" wins. You are a victim, but let it make you strong. Make good choices and YOU become the Survivor – thus, You are the Winner, and You are Free.

Sgt. Bill Davis is a thirty-six-year veteran of the Beaumont, Texas Police Department. He honorably retired from active duty with the police department on January 31, 2008. Even though retired from BPD, Sgt. Davis is still a law enforcement officer, commissioned through another local law enforcement agency. Sgt. Davis holds an active Master Peace Officer license with the Texas Commission on Law Enforcement. During his thirty-year tenure as a sergeant, he spent over twenty years with the Juvenile Division and the Sex Crimes Unit, specializing in child abuse and sex crime investigations. Sgt. Davis has investigated over 7,000 child abuse and/or sex crime incidents. From 1991 to retirement, Sgt. Davis was the most decorated officer with the Beaumont Police Department. He is an internationally recognized motivational speaker and consultant, and since July 1983, Sgt. Davis has conducted lectures, workshops, and programs on the awareness, prevention, and intervention of child abuse, sex crimes, and safety throughout the United States and abroad to over 300,000 people. He has had articles on child abuse published in state and national publications. Sgt. Davis received numerous awards for his work. Some of these awards include two Honorary Life Membership awards from the Texas Congress of PTAs, the 1991 Governors Award in Law Enforcement, and the 1994 Child Advocate of the Year award from the Court Appointed Special Advocate (C.A.S.A.) program in Beaumont. In 1995, two attorneys donated $50,000.00 to a local children's advocacy center in

Sgt. Davis's honor for his work with child abuse victims. In 1996, Sgt. Davis was awarded the Layperson Exemplary Service Award from the Texas (school) Counseling Association. On February 22, 2001, Sgt. Davis received the Kinder Award for Art and Literature from Memorial Hermann Hospital, Houston and Univ. Texas Medical Branch for his child abuse programs and his first true-crime novel. Houston's Kinder Clinic treats alcohol and drug-born infants. On January 23, 2002, Sgt. Davis received the Outstanding Leadership Award from Prevent Child Abuse Texas for his leadership role in working to curtail child abuse throughout Texas. In 2012, a local attorney made a $10,000.00 contribution to the local women and children's shelter in Sgt. Davis's honor for his work with family violence and child abuse victims. On December 12, 1998, Sgt. Davis's nationally acclaimed first true-crime novel, *So Innocent, Yet So Dead*, was published. His book has sold over 35,000 copies and continues to sell throughout Texas and the U.S. Sgt. Davis's second true-crime novel, *Imperfect Love~Imperfect Justice*, was published on April 1, 2016, by Coastal Winds Publishing House, Port Arthur, Texas.

Both of Sgt. Davis's books are available through Kindle at Amazon.com.

CPSIA information can be obtained
at www.ICGtesting.com
Printed in the USA
FSOW03n0117290316
18550FS